The Pig in the Barber Shop

Books by H. Allen Smith

MR. KLEIN'S KAMPF

LOW MAN ON A TOTEM POLE

LIFE IN A PUTTY KNIFE FACTORY

LOST IN THE HORSE LATITUDES

RHUBARB

LO, THE FORMER EGYPTIAN!

LARKS IN THE POPCORN

WE WENT THATAWAY

PEOPLE NAMED SMITH

MISTER ZIP

SMITH'S LONDON JOURNAL

THE COMPLEAT PRACTICAL JOKER

THE REBEL YELL

THE AGE OF THE TAIL

WRITE ME A POEM, BABY

THE PIG IN THE BARBER SHOP

Selected by H. Allen Smith

DESERT ISLAND DECAMERON

With Ira L. Smith

LOW AND INSIDE

THREE MEN ON THIRD

The Pig

in the Barber Shop

by H. Allen Smith

LITTLE, BROWN AND COMPANY

Boston   Toronto

The author thanks the following for permission to reprint copy-
righted material:

Carleton Beals for brief excerpts from his writing; Harper &
Brothers for an excerpt from MEXICO TODAY by John Crow; Mrs.
A. Hyatt Verrill for a brief quotation from THE AMERICAN IN-
DIAN by A. Hyatt Verrill.

Published simultaneously in Canada
by Little, Brown & Company (Canada) Limited

PRINTED IN THE UNITED STATES OF AMERICA

"The Mexican situation . . . seems fraught with interest."

— From a caption for a drawing
by Peter Arno in *The New Yorker*

Principal Characters

CARLOS CAMPO, *a sit-down comic*

MAXINE SMITH, *a small ball of fire*

CHARLIE BOWERS, *enemy of a duck*

PEPE ROMERO, *a leaping legume*

SANTIAGO REACHI, *a judge of mountains*

MAMA REACHI, *his mother*

RODERIC, *a Spanish skirt-lifter*

DIEGO RIVERA, *who painted nice*

LÁZARO CÁRDENAS, *a violent controversy*

BILL O'DWYER, *a conquistador*

ABEL GREEN, *proprietor of a lingo*

HENRY FINK, *who has a Shangri-La*

PAPA BULL, *who yearns for heaven*

BOY BULL, *who yearns otherwise*

MME. CALDERÓN DE LA BARCA, *a wise woman*

JOSÉ CLEMENTE OROZCO, *a painter of magueys*

MICKEY FINN, *a native of Jalapa*

GENERAL MOLINAR, *usurper of beds*

BISHOP OF ALVARADO, *who utters a curse*

MR. STOTEWELLER, *a henpecked Oklahoman*

JOSEPH SCHUTZ, *a consul*

RED-WHISKERS, *a nuts-sayer*

SEÑOR ROMERO, *who uses holy punctuation*

GENERAL BARRAGRAN, *who willied his gots*

GENERAL JOSEPH SHELBY, *a Southern ham*

HERNANDO CORTEZ, *a sinner*

MALINCHE, *reverse of an Indian maiden*

QUETZALCOATL, *good god*

ALMA REED, *La Peregrina*

FELIPE CARRILLO PUERTO, *a great man*

DON QUIXOTE, *a garrulous Aztec*

MAXIMILIAN, *who had two coaches*

JUÁREZ, *who had one*

CARLOTA, *who had tea*

DON PORFIRIO DÍAZ, *who draped some breasts*

CHOLLY LIMBURG, *a park*

SEÑOR DUCK, *patron of the Hotel Reforma*

DENISE DARCEL, *who is properly shaped*

CUAUHTÉMOC, *called "Mister Mexico"*

FRED VOSBERG, *friend of the frankfurter*

LARRY BROOKWELL, *semi-retired*

ANGEL BOCANEGRA, *a hero*

Señora Milpa, *who saw a pregnant sow*

Tepoztecatl, *an oddball deity*

Meester Johns, *a place to go*

Mario Moreno, *a Cantinflas*

Carpface Al Capone, *late of Chicago*

Emiliano Zapata, *a continuing enigma*

Leslie Figueroa, *First Lady of Taxco*

Vicenta, *who worked for Obregón*

John Steinbeck, *known as "Shinnerick"*

Rosa King, *who joined a death march*

William Spratling, *a lover of strawberries*

Dorothy MacDonald, *of Casa del Corazón*

Natalie Scott, *who rode a horse*

Mrs. Hapless, *whose limes vanished*

The Fireworks Man, *of Casa Boom-Boom*

La Acrobata, *who wears high heels*

Mike, *an Aztec hot-rodder*

D. H. Lawrence, *the perfect dinner guest*

Bob Prescott, *a Crosby man*

Margaret A. Honey, *who loved Veracruz*

Paul Kennedy, *critic of toad-worshipers*

Bob Peck, *seller of dead fleas*

Dick Oulahan, *a lifer, doing time*

Rafael Delgado Lozano, *no friend of Lola*

Agustín Lara, *who is for prosterity*

María Felix, *one of his Moo-hairs*

Rosa, *a whirr in a whirrhouse*

Bill Shelburne, *a September singer*

The Golden Girl, *whose house is my house*

Anita Brenner, *a picknicker*

Martha Davis, *who speaks folklorically*

Father Hidalgo, *whose grito is bollixed up*

Miguel Alemán, *a duffer*

Andy Leone, *who reads pure Castilian*

Margaret Cousins, *a gardenia-lover*

Guadalupe Posada, *a nine-fisted tequila drinker*

Juan O'Gorman, *a huevo-head*

Señor Tourist Trot, *an Aztec god*

Pepito, *a licentious adolescent*

Ruiz Cortines, *who saw 100 bow-ties*

Horse Mariles, *once known as General*

Christopher Columbus, *who pleads for women*

Carranza, *an ad for safety razors*

Pedro Armendariz, *victim of the altitude*

La Corrigadora, *who hollered through a keyhole*

El Presidente, *who smiled at two Gringos*

Herb-Hernando, *who spoke The Awful Obscenity*

Eduardo Cárdenas, *a mistaken identity*

Norman Cousins, *host at a luncheon*

White Sombrero, *a ferocious villain*

MELCHOR OCAMPO, *whose heart is in a jar*

WILL ROGERS, *who didn't say it*

JUAN ZUMÁRRAGA, *who redeemed himself*

HUDSON STRODE, *who met a music-lover*

PYTHAGORAS, *a dirty hypocrite*

JOSEPHINE LITTLEJOHN, *hostess with the* mole

VAN HEFLIN, *who saw the water dance*

FRANCES HEFLIN, *loser of many gloves*

FRED DAVIS, *who is met only at breakfast*

HILDEGARDE, *a lover of Mexico*

FUNGO P. NUBB, *a distance friction man*

HOWARD PHILLIPS, *a many-splendored editor*

SANTA ANNA, *Father of Chewing Gum*

Contents

Principal Characters	ix
Prólogo	3
Peppers to Mexico	6
The Ever Heroic	45
Peregrina and Don Quixote	86
The Road to Taxco	115
Noches de Mexico City	174
West to Pátzcuaro	237
Señor Duck and Some Burros	271
Epílogo	315

The Pig in the Barber Shop

Prólogo

DURING that first memorable expedition we were in the colonial town of Taxco when I decided it was time for me to get my first Mexican haircut. I went wandering through the cobblestone streets, looking for a barber shop. The name for a barber shop in Spanish is *peluquería* while the name for the lowest type of Mexican saloon is *pulquería* and I have trouble distinguishing between the two. On this particular morning I wandered around for a while, peering into *peluquerías* only to have them turn out to be *pulquerías* and then finally I came upon a genuine *peluquería* called La Rosita — the Little Rose.

The barber was an elderly man considerably in need of his own ministrations. His shop contained two chairs but one was untended. The chairs were of a squarish, wooden construction and had the general appearance of the instrument used to extinguish human beings at Sing Sing prison. The shop had no electricity and no running water, as is true in most small town *peluquerías*. (Some of them keep their water supply in old restaurant-size coffee urns.)

Just as in the small towns at home there were three or four village loafers sitting in the chairs along one of the walls. Also present was the wife of the barber, who served as his helper, handing him his tools after the fashion of a nurse handing instruments to a surgeon.

It soon became apparent that no one in the shop spoke a word of English, and I spoke no more than a dozen words of shredded

Spanish, so I climbed into one of the chairs and pointed to the back of my neck and then made scissoring motions with two fingers. Thus we got under way.

The barber stepped back and gave me a long look straight in the face and then he said, *"Cerveza, Señor?"* This being Spanish I understood, I nodded vigorously and said, *"Sí, sí, por favor."* He spoke sharply to his wife and she went trotting out of the shop and in a few minutes came back with a cold bottle of Carta Blanca beer. I sipped at this beer all during my haircut and I have often wondered if that barber provides a beer every time he works on a Gringo or if he simply decided from my looks that I was a man who would enjoy *cerveza.*

We were about halfway through when the drove of pigs came down the street. I could hear them approaching and then in a moment I could see them as they went past the open door. The air was filled with gruntings and squealings and the shouts of the pig-herders and then all of a sudden one pig made a wrong turn and came into the barber shop.

He should have looked around and recognized the fact that he was out of his element and then gone on his way. Instead, he made straight for a dark corner of the room. The barber let out a yell and charged after him, closely followed by his wife, who was closely followed by the town loafers. The barber was shouting what must have been horrible things in Spanish and trying to stab the pig with his scissors. The wife had grabbed up a large bottle and was swinging it wildly and one of the loafers was holding a chair above his head, ready to brain the animal. And the pig itself was shrieking and screaming and scrabbling madly around the floor, now and then trying to climb up a wall, blindly staying away from the direction where freedom lay. It was all over in a minute or two. The pig finally found the door and went through it like a gray cannonball. Then quiet was restored and the old barber began speaking to me in Spanish, showing great emotion. He was, quite clearly, apologizing for this unhappy incident. He and his wife and even the town loafers had all been deeply embarrassed at having a pig come into the barber shop at a time when they had a Gringo in the chair. I'm sure that the barber was trying to tell me that this sort of thing didn't happen often. In any event, he resumed his work and after a while finished with me. He pointed to a square five-gallon can standing on the floor near the chair. It was two-thirds full of a dark green grease, and had a homemade wooden paddle stuck in it. By gesture he explained that it was for greasing the hair. I said no. I paid him and stepped out of the shop and stood on the cobblestones, in the warm sunshine, and then I said to myself: *Por Dios,* I think I'll come back and see a lot more of this country!

1

Peppers to Mexico

January 8

IT SEEMS a bit ridiculous, but we always approach these projects in the same frame of mind; we have planned this journey to Mexico as if we were pioneering into virgin territory, as if we were the original conquistadors, as if nobody else from north of the border had ever looked upon the wonders of Tenochtitlán, or eaten an enchilada.

So it has been disheartening in recent days to find that almost everyone we know has already been to Mexico or is getting ready to go. My neighbor Avery came up to the house today, slipping and sliding on the snow-covered driveway, to warn me about certain hazards that lay ahead. Don't drink any of their poisonous water, says Avery, unless you boil it or load it with chlorine pills. Don't eat their lettuce or any other vegetables that haven't been cooked, or you'll get the forty-mile trots.

"When were you in Mexico?" I asked him.

"Well," he said, "to be accurate about it, I've never been there, but I had a partner was down there fifteen years ago and he was sick all the time."

Other friends and neighbors have given freely of their advice. Be careful of the altitude. Go to this town. Don't go to that town. Stay away from other Americans. You won't see the *real* Mexico unless you see Oaxaca. Don't miss Guadalajara whatever you do. Stay away from Veracruz — nothing there worth seeing. Don't go near that Dago Rivvy-era, he's a goddam commie. The food'll kill ya. Watch out for the Mexico City taxi drivers — the government gives them a medal for every American they bring down.

I heard about a travel writer who has been lecturing around the country recently. Subject: Mexico. At one point in his recitation he says:

"Now, we hear a lot about tourist sickness, and we hear all kinds of rules about eating and drinking. Well, my friends, let me tell you something. Just recently I spent six solid months traveling up and down and back and forth across Mexico. I was in cities and I was in tiny villages. I went everywhere. I drank the water wherever I went and I ate everything that was put before me — all the raw vegetables and all the fruits. I did all this and I want to tell you folks something — I was sick as a dog all the time!"

Among all the people who have given us advice, the principal concern is with diarrhea. Nobody calls it diarrhea or even *turista*. It is always known by clever and witty names, such as the Aztec Two-Step, or Montezuma's Revenge. As a sickness it is a real serious proposition among tourists, yet most people treat it as a rousing joke and when it is discussed they smile and snicker and guffaw. Most of all, however, they recite preventatives and remedies. This medical advice usually comes from the women and it is my impression that they are more susceptible to the gallops than the men. One lady told us that there is only one positive remedy for Montezuma's Revenge — an American drug which she wrote down, and I have the memorandum in front of me now. The drug, she says, is Sulfasuckadyne. Honest to God — Sulfasuckadyne. Another woman told us that if we get the sickness we should cook a pot of rice, throw the rice away and drink the broth.

Among other suggestions: drink quarts and quarts of tea and stay in bed; eat nothing but applesauce; drink large quantities of guava juice. My favorite remedy, however, was given to us by a lady who has been to Mexico three times. "Mix up a drink," she instructed, "with equal quantities of Chilean red wine, gin, tomato juice. Sprinkle celery seed in it. Drink a tall glass of it every two hours. You'll soon be over the Two-Step." I should think so. And have the Four-Step.

I have been able to hold my peace, to refrain from reminding all these helpful people that last year we spent a month roaming around Central Mexico, casing the joint, and that we came away loving it all, including even the tap water and the raw lettuce. We decided, in fact, that in many respects it's a better place to visit than Europe, and we fair worship Europe.

January 9

ABOARD Air France nonstop from Idlewild to Mexico City. We are traveling first class. There is a difference of about fifty dollars between first class and tourist class tickets. The flight we are on, I've just learned, is called "dual configuration." Who in the name of God, shown that phrase, would ever be able to figure out that it means what it means? I had to ask for a translation and found that it means the tourist class people are right here on the same plane with us aristocrats. All that separates the sheep from the goats, the plebs from the quality, is a door which stands open most of the time.

The difference between the two classes is clearly demonstrated by airborne behavior. We in first class drank champagne and Burgundy and ate like pigs. After that the door leading into the tourist section was closed, the lights were turned off, the chairs tilted back, the blankets brought out, and everybody was asleep and snoring in half an hour. Everybody but me. I watched the stewards going up and down the aisle, opening the door of the tourist section frequently as they carried in food and booze. Judging from the glimpses I got, the tourists were not asleep. They seemed to be mixing around, drinking with one another, telling rowdy stories, and I heard fragments of a song "Down by the Old Mill Stream." There were also noises which suggested that either a crap game or a poker game was in progress. For a few moments a crazy notion brushed my mind — a wish that I were in tourist class — but then my good breeding prevailed and I settled down and tried to review some of the things I've learned about Mexico.

A scant two years ago I knew almost nothing about the country and shared the attitude of many Americans who have judged Mexico on the basis of border towns such as Tijuana and Nogales and Juárez. A newspaperman of my acquaintance, hearing of my plans, wrote me a note saying: "Why Mexico? There's nothing down there but a lot of goddam Mexicans." I made inquiry and found that his estimate of Mexico is based on two sprees in Tijuana. I've been in the border towns and I'd like to suggest that their honky-tonk character is actually no fault of the Mexicans. The responsibility rests mainly with us. If it were not for the steady influx of Gringo dollars, those towns would not be the way they are. And the evil works in both directions. There are quiet, respectable Mexicans in all of those border towns but they stay within their walled homes. They get a bad impression of the Gringo from the fact that he's usually interested only in drinking and whoring and gambling. The Gringo, on the other hand, seeing nothing but battalions of pimps and peddlers and sombreroed drunks, acquires an equally bad impression of Mexicans. An enormous number of Americans think that all of Mexico is like that, and hold it in contempt. Their prejudice grows so strong that they would never even consider a trip to the interior of the country.

Come to think of it, it's surprising that I've grown somewhat ardent on the subject of Mexico. Charles Flandrau said that a well-regulated, systematic, and precise person always detests Mexico and can rarely bring himself to say a kind word about anything in it, including the scenery. My wife will tell you in ringing accents that I am the kind of person Flandrau described, and yet I have many kind words to say about Mexico. It is not a place to please the eye and mind of a man with strong prejudices, and I am also that kind of man.

Depending on who you are, there is something for you to hate in Mexico. With me it's bullfighting and graft. An antiseptical person who admires good plumbing could very well grow to despise the whole Raypooblico. The old cleavage between liberal and conservative was never more pronounced than it is in Mexico — we have never had anything to equal it, even in the time of Franklin D. Roosevelt. There is the businessman-mind versus the "damned wantlessness" of the Mexican masses — a condition that would drive a supersalesman into a Trappist monastery. There are the believers in siesta versus the one-hour-for-lunch advocates. There are the Catholics versus the anti-Catholics, and the Indian worshipers against the Cortez worshipers. On and on, endlessly, neighbor against neighbor — just as it is everywhere else.

Approaching the broad subject of Mexico, I have no fear of making any statement of fact or opinion that might be disputed by the experts. The experts are mostly idiots. Mexico has frequently been described feelingly as the land of astonishing contrasts; more important, it is a land of astonishing contradictions. No two people in Mexico agree on anything. No two writers can agree on a single fact. During the last year I have read upwards of forty books on Mexico and I have never seen anything that would equal the contradictions to be found among all those truth-seekers. "Mexico," says Ernest Gruening, "is an extraordinarily difficult country in which to reach the rock bottom of fact. Far more than in any other country with which the writer is familiar, things are not what they seem." My facts, then, are just as good as anybody else's facts — maybe even better.

Several days ago I wrote to Carlos, suggesting that if he were not playing dominoes tonight, he might drive out and meet us at the airport. It was around midnight when we landed and I didn't expect him to be there, but when we arrived at the immigration-customs barrier and looked through the big plate-glass window, there he was, white teeth flashing in a big smile of welcome.

During our previous visit to Mexico we spent about a month with Carlos, traveling around the country. Ever since then I have been getting occasional letters from him, all in the same vein. Here is one of the most recent:

SEÑOR GOBERNADOR:

I write with my deepest regrets as I have to report that things are worst than ever before. Nothing seems to be the same since you left. Do you remember good old Carta Blanca? Well, she became ill because your mellodious voice ceased to calling her. Her constant cry is, "Allen, Allen, where are you? Have you so soon forgotten the good times you spent in my company specially in the night?" But I promise her your quick return and she does not believe me so you will have to do something about this real quick.

I have another bit of bad news for you. Taxco is an awful town now. I can't go there anymore. The people there discovered that a crazy Gringo several months ago protected a *puerco* that was being kicked and stabbed in one of the town's barber shops while he was getting a hair cut and at the same time drinking a beer. Well, the people of Taxco have elected a committee to raise some funds to erect a monument to the memory of their beloved Gringo. It is to have the inscription: "To Allen, the Gringo husband of Nelle, Great Benefactor of the Puercos."

This idea was so great and naturally you know how human beings are so jealousy crep into the minds and hearts of ranchers, farmers, peasants, and specially Bar-tenders. The farmers stated that the magueys along the highway from Querétaro to Mexico City were generously watered by that extraordinary Gringo H. Allen Smith, but since he went away no one else has watered them ever since. But the Bar-tenders say if it was not for them and their *cerveza* the magnificent Gringo would never have watered the magueys so much and the farmers say they don't care what caused it, just so long as it happened.

In San Miguel the people all say, where is the Gobernador, who was the great movie actor in our town? My poor half-starve family will thank heaven for your coming. They have not seen a chilli bean in ages. All except my dog Queenie, who will try to take a bite of one of you hairless spaguetti legs. *Salud, mi amigo, cabrón!*

CARLOS

People who travel in foreign lands almost always boast about the guides they hire; usually they insist that they had the best and most wonderful guide in the whole history of tourism. I know one couple who engaged a guide in Paris to drive them around the southern part of France for ten days. At the end of that time they had fallen so thoroughly in love with the man that they invited him to go with them, as their guest, on a month's expedition into Africa.

Carlos Campo is easily the most wonderful guide in the whole history of tourism. After I had known him for two days I handed him all my money, without counting it, and told him to take care of all expenditures, and at the end of the month to give me back whatever was left. He always traveled with us as a companion rather than a hired hand, eating with us, going along when we called on important people; and all over Mexico people were constantly asking us, "Where on earth did you ever get hold of Carlos?" This was Nelle's achievement, and she always told about it in the same efflorescent detail that is used in the story of Juan Diego's first meeting with the Virgin of Guadalupe. She was sitting in the American Express office in Mexico City when a young Spanish woman sat down beside her. They fell into conversation and Nelle asked her if she knew a good Mexican guide. The Spanish girl said indeed she did, that she knew a marvelous man named Carlos Campo who had been most helpful to her American husband, and she gave Nelle the phone number of this Carlos Campo.

Carlos is a stocky, powerfully built man in his forties. He was once a star soccer player in a land where soccer is almost the national sport. Later he was a coach of a championship team and became quite famous. Traveling with him is somewhat the same as it would be to travel around the United States with Red Grange.

The two really important qualities possessed by Carlos are his efficiency and his sense of humor. His jokes, which he calls yokes, are told in halting English with little speech mannerisms that give them character, and his spontaneous humor and wit sometimes border on the classic style of japery. I remember once when we were in a store in Cuernavaca where he was buying a new pair of sun glasses. He tried on a pair and then turned to me and said, "Look, Allen, how smart is God, to put the ears in just exactly the right place to hold on the glasses." On another occasion I read to him, from a news magazine, an account of a soccer game in El Salvador. In this game the two *capitanos* appeared on the field wearing pistols. Midway in the contest there was a disputed decision, out came the pistols, the crowd swept onto the field swinging machetes, and in the end six were dead and many gravely wounded. When I had finished reading the item, Carlos gave me a solemn glance and then commented: "The Salvadoreans, they play soft." And once when I was making some harsh remarks about Mexican political dishonesty, he said, "You better shut your big mouth, or I will Alamo you."

In our earlier ramblings around Mexico there were periods in which we would reverse positions; I would be the guide and Carlos would be the Gringo tourist. We took hold of history by the neck and shook it to pieces, and we made up our own as we went along. Carlos, impersonating a Gringo, was always fun. "Bonus Notches, Seeeenore," he would say in a high, whiny voice, "and what is the altitude in this place, Seeeenore?"

And so during the long ride in from the airport we reminisced and laughed and reminisced some more. "Remember that day in San Miguel, when we made the movie?" I would say: "*Sí, Gobernador, sí!* And the day on the beach at Acapulco when you tried to pet the *puerco!*"

It was quite late when we checked in at the brand-new Continental

Hilton Hotel. Carlos went on home, carrying the Eight Chiles of Kisco.

January 10

HAVING been open but a few weeks, the Hilton is somewhat disorganized. Each time I get in the elevator on the ground floor I say to the boy, *"Cuatro."* And every time I say it he turns to me and in solemn manner declares, "You speak a-very good Espanish." It is obvious that he's been told to say it every time he hears a Gringo struggling with his language.

There's a large group of American financiers staying in the hotel and I've encountered several of them in the corridors upstairs. They walk along, eyes down, preoccupied, and I hear them muttering words in Spanish over and over. They are practicing, and the words they are all muttering are the same: *"Uno, dos, tres, cuatro, cinco . . ."*

It will become apparent before long that I am not indifferent to Mexican food. I probably violated international bug regulations but I brought with me eight chiles, or hot peppers, which I grew in my own garden in the northern part of Westchester County, New York. I harvested and dried the peppers and eight of them came with me in a small plastic bag. I am probably the only traveler who ever carried chiles to Mexico.

This morning I went to the hotel desk and asked the clerk which of the restaurants in the place served Mexican food. "How do you mean, Mexican food?" he asked. I told him, and he seemed bewildered, and spotted a man standing in the lobby, the very man who was in charge of the hotel's dining rooms. He took me over and introduced me to this fellow, who had on striped pants. "Which dining room serves Mexican food, *por favor?*" I asked. "How do you mean, Mexican food?" he said. "Enchiladas," I told him, "and frijoles — stuff like that." And he said, "Oh, we don't serve any of that." He said it as if hc considered Mexican food to be so foul that it cost him effort to even talk about it. So I thanked him and turned and walked out of the place. Glancing down the Paseo I saw, two or three blocks distant, the Hotel Reforma.

I was familiar with the Reforma, having called on friends there several times, and I knew of its colorful history. Among the major hotels of Mexico City, it is the one with the most glamour and atmosphere. So I walked over and asked the Reforma desk clerk if the dining room served Mexican food. Certainly. Enchiladas and frijoles and *carne asada* and things of that nature. "But," he said, "if you really like Mexican food, there is a fine place in walking distance of the hotel, Fonda Santa Anita, and I'd recommend you try that." He gave me directions to Fonda Santa Anita and for some reason I decided that I liked the Hotel Reforma.

I crossed the lobby to the Bar Jardín, ordered a beer and gave the bartender a one-peso tip. He picked it up and started toward the far end of the bar, and as he walked I noticed that he made the sign of the cross. Then he put the peso in a box beneath the bar. I thought about this for a while and concluded that the man makes the sign of the cross for each peso tip he receives. I thought it would be fun, if I could afford it, to walk in some morning and hit him with a tip of one hundred pesos — and cripple his right arm. On the way out I made reservations to move into the Reforma tomorrow.

Tonight we walked to Fonda Santa Anita. There are two of them, one in the center of town, and one far out on Insurgentes. The one we visited is on Humboldt and has the cruddiest decorations of any restaurant in the world — strings of dirty-looking Spanish moss, the remains of Christmas *posadas*, dime-store Japanese lanterns, unattractive furniture — and simply beautiful food. There was another Gringo couple at a table near ours and I heard the lady say to the waiter, "Pore fay-ver," with the accent on the fay. This reminded me of the effort I made back home to learn a little Spanish. Years ago, when people first started putting language courses on records, I fell for one of the ads and bought a Spanish course. There were twenty records, forty sides, and a couple of books. I played one or two records and then put the whole thing in the attic and forgot about it. Recently, however, I dug it out and spent hours getting the forty sides transferred to tape. Then I sat down with the tape recorder, ready to learn some Spanish. Within an hour I had given it up. One of the early records in the set was devoted altogether to phrases such as, "I don't speak Spanish," and "I only know a few words of Spanish," and "Where can I find an interpreter?" and "Please speak very slowly." I refused to have anything to do with those records, and turned to a book of phrases.

Every book of foreign phrases I've ever looked at is a compendium of tragedy and disaster and gloom. This one was no exception. Here are just some of the things its authors proposed that I learn:

I am cold. I am hot. I am hungry. I am tired. I am ill. Help! Fire! Thief! Be careful! Can you help me? It is not my fault. I cannot find my hotel. I have lost my friends. I forgot my money. I forgot my key. I have missed the train. I have missed the plane. They are bothering me. Go away. I will call a policeman. I have been robbed. Where is the police station? Where is the Lost and Found desk? I cannot find my baggage. I am a little seasick. I want some air. My tire has a slow leak. My car has broken down. Can you tow me? It is in the ditch. My car is stuck in the mud. Please drive more carefully. Where is the bathroom? Have you something better? I should like to speak to the manager. Please spray for mosquitoes. This is not clean. This is overcooked. This is not cooked enough. This is too tough. This is too sweet. This is too sour. Take it away. There is a mistake in the bill. I do not like this. I have lost a filling. I want adhesive tape. I want castor oil. I want to send a telegram for money.

There was much more of the same, but I was already thinking of canceling my plane reservations, so I read no more. At length I concluded that if a tourist can learn about six or eight simple expressions, he can go anywhere and get away with anything. They are the phrases of courtesy. *Buenos días,* of course, and its companions, *Buenas tardes* and *Buenas noches.* The two really important phrases, however, are *Por favor* and *muchas gracias,* plus the common response to the latter, *De nada.* And *Con su permiso* . . . , which you always say when you go to the bathroom. Mexicans, being the most polite people on earth, appreciate politeness in others — especially in Gringos — and they will bust an *intestino* to help a tourist who shows even rudimentary signs of mannerliness. Here in Fonda Santa Anita I lectured Nelle on this subject, drilling her in the phrases of courtesy while we consumed gorgeous *Chiles rellenos.* Later we wandered up and down the Paseo, feeling good to be in Mexico, loving the street, loving the city, loving the whole country.

January 11

THIS morning we checked in at the Reforma and soon were in the hands of a ninety-pound ball of fire named Maxine Smith. I had met her once in Hollywood years ago, but she has been in Mexico for ten or twelve years, knows everybody, speaks perfect Spanish, and heads up both the public relations and sales departments of the hotel. It turned out that she and I lived within blocks of each other when we were children in Decatur, Illinois. She has been a newspaperwoman, a championship golfer who once beat Babe Didrikson, a wartime pilot and a Hollywood columnist. I am her *tocayo,* while she is my *tocaya.* These expressions are widely used between people who have the same names, whether last names or first names. Maxine says that there is a sort of special affection existing between *tocayos* in Mexico, which seems a strange thing to me, for I have known several people named Smith for whom I have openly advocated euthanasia, with a hammer.

Maxine introduced us to Charlie Bowers, the Reforma manager, a suave gentleman who speaks with a slight accent. We visited briefly with him and then went down to lunch with Paul Kennedy of the New York *Times.* Paul brought with him a character about whom I have been hearing for years — Pepe Romero. Pepe writes a daily column in the local English-language newspaper, the *News*, and every English-speaking person in Mexico reads it. Pepe is a painter, and the author of a book, *Mexican Jumping Bean*. He is pure Mexican but he spent his formative years in New York and other parts of the United States and speaks flawless English. He, too, knows everybody, and has offered to introduce us to anyone we want to meet.

Tonight Pepe took us to the Hotel Lincoln for dinner. This is a small downtown hotel that is famous for its food. We were introduced to mescal from Oaxaca — the kind that has a maguey worm floating inside the bottle. Mescal is supposed to be one of the strongest libations on earth and the presence of the dead worm somehow makes it look even more powerful. The liquor itself is a product of the maguey plant, and so is the worm. It is the same worm that is fried and eaten in Mexico and regarded as a great delicacy.

In the last few years worm-type foods have been growing popular in the United States. I have seen the ads for them in New York — fried worms, fried grasshoppers, octopus, rattlesnake, chocolate-covered ants. Some people will eat anything, out of curiosity or out of a desire to tell other people about it, to brag about it the rest of their lives, as was the case with William Seabrook, who claimed that he once dined with a tribe of cannibals and sampled human flesh. I'm not that kind of adventurer. I do not plan to eat any maguey worms in Mexico. Furthermore, I don't intend to drink a certain Mexican wine — I have read that the vats at this winery are first given a good scrubbing and then rubbed thoroughly with turkey dung, which imparts a special piquancy and verve to the wine. I don't want any of it, at room temperature or otherwise. Tonight I even balked at drinking the mescal because of the worm.

"Why is the worm in it?" I demanded.

"Oh," said Pepe with a large shrug, "it is not important. *Es la costumbre*, as we say. It is just a custom. The worm has no meaning."

"It has meaning to me," I said, looking again at the little bastard floating on top of the mescal.

"The little worm," he said, "was born and grew to manhood inside a maguey plant and has never known anything but sweet juices and clean, lovely fibres. There can't be anything really wrong about that little worm. Now, go on and take a drink and quit being critical of Mexico."

I poured out a jigger of the mescal — a special spout prevents the worm from leaving the bottle — and after looking at it for a few moments, tossed it off. It didn't taste wormy, although it caused my toes to curl up inside my shoes.

Pepe's jocular reference to my being critical of Mexico reminded me of a thing I heard somewhere today. I was told that it is not wise to be hypercritical of Mexicans in the presence of Mexicans. A few years ago there was a Gringo playboy-creep, a cadger of drinks, operating around the plush hotels and bars of Mexico City. It was his custom wherever he happened to be to make slurring remarks about Mexicans in a loud voice. One night he was seized, beaten unconscious; his head was shaved and painted red, white and blue, and he was deposited on the steps of the American Embassy, where he was found at dawning. I want to make it clear that I have no intention of criticizing Mexicans but I do reserve the right to speak harshly of a worm.

It may have been noted by this time that I have been referring to citizens of the United States of America as Gringos. In Mexico we of the United States are customarily called Americans or *americanos* or *norteamericanos*. Yet every sensible Mexican resents such designations, sometimes with bitterness and certainly with justification. A Mexican is as much an American as I am; so is a Guatemalan, a Peruvian, and an Aleut. In many cases a Mexican has a greater moral right to the title "American" than most of us. Nor is the term *norteamericano* correct. Mexico is as much a part of North America as the United States or Canada. It would be nearer correct to refer to us as *mittelnorteamericanos*, although I'd just as soon nobody did. The fact remains that we permit ourselves to be called Americans, glorying in the title and wagging the flag real hard when we hear it, and we

refuse to think of a Mexican as an American. And the fact also stands
that we are sadly lacking in a proper appellation for ourselves. We
can't very gracefully be Unitedstatesers, or U-essers. I have heard
suggestions that we all be called Yankees, but those suggestions have
come from small minds, unaware of the domestic situation at home.
The South sends thousands of tourists into Mexico each year, and I
have it on unimpeachable authority that they might object to being
called Yankees.* In the past, relations between the United States and
Mexico have not always been pleasant, and for a long time the word
Gringo was a fighting word, just as was the word Greaser. That isn't
true any longer. Gringo has become almost a term of affection.

For years I have been hearing how, during our war with Mexico,
our soldiers were almost constantly singing "Green Grow the Rushes,
Oh!" even when going into battle (if it's true I'm surprised they ever
won). The Mexicans, hearing this song so often, began calling the
enemy "Green Grows" or "Gringos." I have read this story, put forth
as God's own truth, in at least a dozen books. I have had people sit
down and tell it to me as an indication that they are exceptionally
well informed on the subject of Mexico. Even such a prominent historian as Hudson Strode falls for it. The truth is, the story is impure
mythology. It has been disproved time and again, yet people go on
reciting it, the same way they go on about how Mark Twain said
that about the weather which he didn't say at all.

Dr. Frank H. Vizetelly, one of our greatest etymologists, made a
special study of "gringo" and traced it back to 1787. Other investigations have been made by H. L. Mencken and by Elliott Arnold. The
story on which all three seem to be agreed is put this way by Dr.
Vizetelly:

> Gringo dates back to 1787. It is explained in . . . Dic-
> cionario Castellano . . . published in Madrid in that
> year: "Gringos — the name given in Malaga to those for-

* In certain sections of Latin America they do have a name for us:
Yankee-blofero.

eigners who have a certain accent which prevents them from speaking Spanish fluently and naturally; and in Madrid the same term is used for the same reason, especially with reference to the Irish.

Elliott Arnold, in a prefatory note to his historical novel, *The Time of the Gringo,* quotes still another definition, as follows:

Gringo (green-go): (coll.) Unintelligible, gibberish: applied to a language. (vulg.) A nickname given to one who speaks a foreign language.
—VELÁSQUES: *A New Pronouncing Dictionary of the Spanish and English Languages.*

H. L. Mencken's researches also brought forth the information that "*gringo* is applied in Mexico and Honduras to Americans, in Chile and Peru to Englishmen, in Guatemala to Englishmen and Germans, and in Venezuela to anyone who speaks Spanish badly or not at all." And just to brighten matters all around, John Gunther has written that *gringo* originated in Argentina where the natives heard British visitors singing, "Green Grow the Rushes Round." I have heard and read even daffier versions. One says the word came from Mexican misunderstanding of the phrase "green coat" — the American soldiers were supposed to have worn jackets of a greenish tone. And I heard a man on a Sunday afternoon television program say something to the effect that *gringo* came from misunderstanding on the part of Mexicans gazing across the border into California and hearing talk about "green grow the crops in Southern Cal." Intelligence is said to prevail in television on Sunday afternoons.

We arrive, then, at the conclusion that *gringo* is fundamentally not an opprobrious word, that it merely designates a person who is not adept at speaking the language of the country in which he is visiting. He doesn't *have* to be an Irishman.

Thus far I have found no evidence that any *mittelnorteamericano* has, in recent years, taken offense at being called a Gringo, and so

I intend to use the word whenever I feel like it. Carlos and I, being inclined to insult each other from morning till night, use both Gringo and Greaser constantly. Carlos will sometimes say to a comparative stranger: "I want you to meet my friend Señor Smith. He is not really as funny-looking as he looks, but on the other hand he is not to be trosted because he is a Jonkee Gringo Greaser Puerco Cochino and a Chip Baster."

January 12

A BEAUTIFUL Mercedes-Benz, driven by Tomás, picked us up this morning at the hotel. Tomás is a handsome young man who speaks not a word of English; apparently he speaks not a word of anything, for, in response to all questions, he simply shakes his head from side to side. We drove down the splendid highway to Cuernavaca, a journey with which we were already familiar. We were in Cuernavaca three or four times during our previous Mexican trip, and each time we liked it less. But today a wooden gate in a wall swung open and Tomás drove us into the estate of Santiago Reachi and we soon understood why Cuernavaca has a reputation for both luxury and beauty. It is this way all over Mexico — the beautiful homes and gardens are hidden from sight. The street outside the Reachi place is an ordinary street full of bumps and burro droppings, and if you looked at the wall you might conclude that it concealed a factory, or a slaughterhouse, or a junk yard.

I should now like to present an important piece of original historic interpretation. The reason that Mexicans live as they do, hidden behind walls, is that a man named Roderic lifted the skirts of a lovely young lady named Florinda in the city of Toledo in Spain some time during the year 711. Roderic was the last of the Gothic kings and is one of Spain's legendary heroes. His palace was in Toledo and one day he glanced out the window and saw, in a neighboring patio, the beautiful Florinda taking a sun bath. Florinda was the daughter of an important governor named Count Julian. That didn't stop Roderic. The urge surged, and he went right down and laid siege to Florinda and in no time at all he worked his will with her. (What a way to say it!) Apparently Roderic wasn't too discreet because Count Julian found out about it. The Count was real sore. He was so sore, in fact, that he decided to chastise Roderic. He conspired with the sons of a former king and together they invited the Moors of North Africa to come over and conquer Spain. Seven thousand Moorish troops landed at Gibraltar. Roderic was heroic, and came dashing down the peninsula with a force of sixty thousand. It should have been an easy matter for sixty thousand to lick seven thousand, but Count Julian, still sore about his daughter, threw in with the Moors, and Roderic was beaten. And so the Moors took over Spain and remained in control of the Iberian peninsula for something like eight hundred years. They brought many of their customs and traditions with them from Africa, including the custom of living behind walls. After they had been expelled from the peninsula, the Spaniards continued to live behind walls; and when the Spaniards conquered Mexico and built cities and towns, they put their houses behind walls, and so it is, you see, that if Roderic had kept his hands off Florinda, the Mexicans would today be living right out in the open, just like the rest of us. Let this serve as a warning to one and all — a little sex can go a long, long way.

Inside the doorway of Santiago Reachi's house is a wall which separates the foyer from the living room. This wall is covered on both sides by Diego Rivera murals. On the foyer side the scene is of a Christmas *posada* procession, with the life-size Mexican children carrying the images of Joseph and Mary. On the living room side the scene depicts the same children engaged in the Chirstmas custom of breaking the *piñata*. The whole effect is almost staggering in its brilliance and Reachi told me that one important art critic called it Rivera's best work. Reachi is a friend of Rivera and when he engaged him for the project, outlined precisely what he wanted on the two walls. Rivera produced some sketches which showed the Mexican children to be dirty, ragged, half-starved urchins while Joseph and Mary were depicted as drooling imbeciles. Reachi is not a timid man, and he gave Rivera a substantial dressing down. "This is my house," he said. "This is where I live. I want them to be nice children, and a nice Joseph and Mary." Rivera protested. He didn't want to paint any nice people, and most particularly he didn't want to show Joseph and Mary as nice people. Reachi leveled an index finger at the artist and roared, "Paint them nice!" And Rivera painted them nice. Real nice.

Santiago Reachi is that kind of a man. He is a movie producer, born in Mexico of Lebanese parents. He is said to be the only Mexican movie producer cut to the pattern of the dynamic Hollywood article. He is the partner and mentor of the great Mexican comedian, Mario Moreno, known the world over as Cantinflas. He is of medium build with swarthy skin and a hawklike face and he speaks faultless English.

We had lunch on an enormous terrace, situated so that the snow-capped volcanic peaks, Popocatépetl and Ixtaccíhuatl, stand out in the very center of the vista as if they were painted on a postcard. Santiago's mother, who is in her eighties, presided at the table and also present were two attractive young women from Lebanon named Natasha and Colette.

There was no Mexican food on the table. We had chicken with rice and piñon nuts, also boiled chicken, roast beef and vegetables. It was all excellent, but when Reachi asked me what I thought about Mexican food I said that I loved it. He then said that it is a cardinal rule all over Mexico that when Americans are being entertained they should never be served Mexican food, because so few of them like it and many of them cannot eat it at all.

Mama Reachi speaks a marvelous brand of broken English which she acquired during a period of residence in Hollywood. She was embarrassed about the Mexican food and ordered a dish of *salsa mexicana* for me to slosh onto my chicken. She is a great character with a fine sense of humor and an infectious laugh. She usually gets a special serving of boiled meat and vegetables. Her son once had her fitted with a fine set of false teeth and she tried them for a few days. Then one evening at dinner she uttered a stout epithet in Arabic, took out the teeth, placed them in front of her plate, shook a finger at them and said, "Now, you stay there and mind your own business. I will take care of the eating." And she has been taking care of it ever since.

Santiago was born in the Cuernavaca area. He told me that when he was a boy he knew Emiliano Zapata and that during the revolution he went north and fought with Villa and was wounded three times. He said Zapata was not really a visionary or an idealist, but simply a rough man. "His intelligence," said Santiago, "didn't extend beyond the basic idea that he would kill every Spaniard he could find and burn every hacienda and take over the land."

I asked Santiago and his mother to pose for a picture, standing against the terrace rail with the volcanoes in the background. "Everybody tries it," said Santiago, "but I can promise you, the volcanoes won't show in the picture." I didn't believe him. Who was he to make such a statement? He's nothing but a big movie producer — what does he know about cameras? I took the picture.*

Afterward Santiago and I withdrew to a corner of the terrace and talked about Cantinflas. Someone had told me that Santiago was the "discoverer" of the famous comedian. "That's nonsense," he said. "This whole business of one person 'discovering' another person is ridiculous." He said that within a few days he would arrange a meeting with Cantinflas and that he would get me together with the man who was Zapata's "brain trust" — an old intellectual named Soto y Gama now living in Mexico City. I was beginning to think that it was indeed a lucky break for me to make the acquaintance of this man Santiago Reachi.

Tomás drove us back to Mexico City and then Carlos picked us up and took us to his home in Colonia Irrigación. His house is not to

---

* When the film was finally developed the two volcanoes could be seen quite distinctly.

be compared with Reachi's mansion, but it's comfortable enough, and filled with the warmth that goes with a genuinely affectionate family. His wife, Isobel, is the assistant principal of a big school and she herself was educated in the United States. They have a son, Alfredo, who is at present attending school in Detroit, and a daughter, Luisa — a shy and beautiful teen-ager. Present also were Isobel's mother, and the dog Queenie, and the cook Josefa. We knew all these people from previous visits and tonight Josefa had cooked up a Mexican feast. Once before, after another such dinner, I had summoned her from the kitchen, exclaimed *"Muy, muy bien!"* and kissed her hand in tribute. Nothing like that had ever happened to her before, and she remembered, and tonight she went all out with turkey and green *mole*. It was superb, but the real feature of the dinner — borne aloft by Josefa as if it were a tribute to the great Aztec god, Quetzalcóatl — was the *salsa* which she had prepared from my eight chiles. It was fiery, but we all doused it on, and it rattled the fillings in my teeth but I loved it.*

After dinner we sat around and told "yokes" and I asked Carlos to repeat the story of his family and Zapata because I had forgotten some of the details.

"My father," he said, "was an officer in the federal army and he was shot by Zapata's shooting squad. My uncle was hung by the neck by Zapata. My other uncle was hung by the toes till he was dead, and Zapata did it. My grandmother was shot and killed by Zapata. Sometimes I do not think I like Zapata very much."

January 13

AT LUNCH today the people at the next table, tourists from the Midwest, were talking about their visit this morning to the Shrine

---

* *Salsa* is sauce, and *salsa mexicana* is hot sauce. I make it back home and served some once to Ginny Street, and she loved it but could never remember the word for it. She ended up calling it *alka salsa*.

of Guadalupe. "I tell ya," said one man, "I ain't a Cath'lic but I'm tellin' ya, a strange feelin' come over me — almost like as if somebody had come up behind me and hit me on the head with a club."

A copy of the English-language magazine, *Mexico This Month,* arrived by messenger with the compliments of its editor, Anita Brenner. Miss Brenner wrote a famous book, *Idols Behind Altars,* back in the 1920's, and ever since she has been a prominent figure in Mexico. There is an article in the current issue of her magazine on the *abrazo.* This is the Mexican embrace, which attracts the attention of Gringos for the reason that it is most commonly practiced among men. Anyone who has looked at Mexican television for more than fifteen minutes has seen the *abrazo.* Mexican television seems to consist largely of newsreels, and Mexican newsreels seem to consist largely of meetings and luncheons and dinners attended solely by men featuring one vigorous *abrazo* after another. The speaker speaks, and finishes, and then the man on his left gets up and gives him an *abrazo,* and the man on his right gets up and gives him another, and then somebody comes up from the audience and they indulge in an *abrazo,* and it goes on and on.

The *abrazo,* as I have observed it, consists of two men embracing with their left arms. Then they pound each other on the back with their right hands, usually from three to five wallops. The harder the blows, the greater the love. I learned from the article that there is such a thing as a formal *abrazo.* It is nothing more than a reversible double *abrazo,* performed as just stated and then performed again in reverse, using the other hand for pounding, and after that a handshake. This is the kind of *abrazo* you would likely receive if you were elected president, or if you assassinated a president, or if you killed a bull with a butter knife.

The magazine article points out that the *abrazo* is employed in Mexico in all situations which are handled Stateside by telegrams, greeting cards, congratulations on your salary raise, good wishes for your graduation, and so on. The essay continues: "How, when, and how much to embrace (as well as who!) is very necessary knowledge for anyone who wishes to live in Mexico successfully — or even stay a longish while. The proper moment, the number of clinches, when to pound on the back, and the degree of pressure, are all delicate decisions which, when made correctly, may assure you of a lifelong friend."

Early this evening in the Reforma bar we were trying to decide about dinner when along came Pepe Romero with a scheme. He said that Bill O'Dwyer was having dinner with the Abel Greens at the Normandia and that we would go down and wander in "by accident" and of course we would be invited to join the party.

In the car Pepe talked about O'Dwyer. "In the first place," he said, "we couldn't understand why the American newspapers set up such a howl when Truman appointed him Ambassador to Mexico. It made us a little suspicious and we didn't know what to expect. I remember when he and Sloan arrived. I was at the airport, along with an army of newspapermen and photographers and a crowd from the Embassy. They got off the plane and someone led Bill over to a mike that had been hooked in to a couple of Mexican radio stations. He started speaking and he addressed the Mexican people in excellent Spanish. From that moment on he was in. Almost everything he did while he was Ambassador made the Mexicans love and respect him. He was informal, and he had a hearty friendliness for the Mexican in the street — so much so that he shocked other members of the diplomatic corps — you know yourself that most of them are horrible stuffed shirts. Another thing — Bill didn't sit in his fancy office waiting for people to come to him. He was on the go all the time, traveling to every part of the country, getting acquainted with the people and letting them get acquainted with him. I don't care what the people in your country think about him. I've talked to many prominent Mexicans about him, and most of them agree that for friendliness and warmth and good will, you have never had his equal as an Ambassador to this country, and that includes Dwight Morrow."

And so we arrived at the Normandia, a French restaurant much favored by the former Ambassador. We strolled in and in a moment Bill O'Dwyer hailed Pepe and we went over to his table. Abel and Grace Green were there, and Marjorie Farnsworth from New York.

"Sit!" said Bill O'Dwyer, and it turned into a pleasant dinner party with lots of good talk. I had little opportunity to question O'Dwyer. When he asked me what things in Mexico interested me most, I couldn't think of anything better to say than, "Well, I'm interested in finding out whether Zapata was a hero or a beast." He considered the matter for a moment, then said, "Zapata was a good man, a genuine hero of the people. In the state of Morelos he ranks almost as a saint."

We might have gone on from there but I overheard Pepe telling Marjorie Farnsworth about a woman from South Carolina who was always saying, "Poh favoh" — and then the usual remarkable flow of language from the lips of Abel Green. Abel is editor of the theatrical trade paper *Variety* and has been my friend for twenty-five years. The argot of *Variety* is one of the wonders of the modern world and it has always fascinated me that Abel *talks* the way *Variety* reads. He is a world traveler, once lived in Europe, and yet this is his first trip to Mexico and I asked what he thought of it. Among other things he said:

"The Tourist Bureau doesn't put the right accent on the fundamentals — that drinking and dining in the better *boîtes* is not flirting with galloping tummyache, yclept the *turista* bends. I think Mexico is a revelation as an ultramodern, highly civilized country loaded with fancy grocery spots and de luxe accommodations. But that pink-toothbrush scare has so inhibited most Americans that the basic creature comforts — such as being free to do the molars in anything this side of bottled water, or not having to worry whether the ice in the Scotch-*and* won't give 'em the hoof-and-mouth disease — well, those migraine matters prevent full enjoyment of this land of *mariachis* and tequila. Yes, we did the Acapulco bit — a Western Hemisphere road company of St. Tropez and Juan-les-Pins, a seaside fishing village with ideal weather and all its leading citizens waltzing around on water skis. Also some of the poorest food this side of Max's (now Manuel's) Busy Bee. The only real beef I've got is a one-worldish observation anent traffic with the petty larcenous customs kiddies and their quick hint that everything can be smoothed over with a few pesos. This country is a better country than that. Hey, Bill, remember that night we were crawling the pubs with Jolie and . . ."

Abel said later that Henry Fink expects us to call on him in Cuernavaca. "You'll find him," he said, "at his own hostelry right in the middle of town — just ask for Henry Fink's Shangri-La."

January 14

PEPE has sent over a copy of his book and I spent a couple of pleasant and profitable hours with it today. It's real good stuff for anyone interested in Mexico and it supports one of my arguments. Almost all the Americans who come down here to write a book go out looking for primitive villages and mountains and jungles and they all but ignore one of the most fascinating cities on the face of the earth. So do many tourists, who look upon Mexico City as nothing more than a transfer point, a brief stopover before proceeding to "the real Mexico." Pepe's book is almost altogether concerned with Mexico City and it's a better book than many of those volumes treating of quaint customs amongst the more primitive Indian tribes. The customs amongst the Gringos of the capital are a hell of a sight quainter. The generality of American authors stay away from the cities and head into the wilderness where their shoes wear thin, permitting the entrance of a bug which bores through the soles of the feet and climbs around inside the body, until the owner of the body starts doing back-flips inside his sleeping bag. Strange things happen to authors after they are turned loose in Mexico. Most of them take down with mountain-describing. Even Carleton Beals, who goes along for quite a while with real interesting stuff, and then looks up and sees a mountain, and is off in a torrent of purple and amethyst prose. For myself, I think it is sufficient to say that they are as beautiful as any mountains in the world and let it go at that.

There are many informative items in Pepe's book that I'd like to quote, but they belong to him and I intend to stay within the legal bounds known as "fair usage" and restrict myself to only a few. Such as this:

"And when an *hombre* is over-pleased as a well-stacked girl goes by, he says, '*piocha*' — which means a little beard like a Vandyke — and then he strokes a make-believe beard in mimicry, with a downward motion."

I have given some thought to this custom, and arrived at some interesting theories, but they all vanished when I looked in my English-Spanish dictionary, which mentions no beards, but says a *piocha* is an aigrette on a woman's hat.

January 15

IT IS my custom to carry a small notebook in my pocket and today, glancing through it, I came upon a single word in a strange handwriting. The word: *Parangaricutirimicuaro*. I didn't recognize the handwriting and I didn't come anywhere near recognizing the word. But after studying it awhile it came back to me — it's the village near Paricutín, the volcano that came busting up through a cornfield some years ago, attracting more worldwide publicity than any other eruption in history, with the possible exception of the eruption of Mrs. Oliva Dionne. Somebody told me that I should not miss *Parangaricutirimicuaro* and the volcano, but I have decided to skip them both. I have been reading about Paricutín. When the farmer saw the ground open up just ahead of his plow, he raced to the village to get the padre. He might as well have run for a fly-swatter. By the time he and the padre got back they found a hump as big as a house and it was spitting red-hot boulders. The padre made a few vague gestures at it, but it didn't pay him any heed, and went on spouting and growing and covering up the village until it was a full-sized mountain. My information is that in order to get to the volcano it is necessary to have traffic with saddle horses and mules and burros and a lot of dirt and ashes and general all-around hardship and as for that sort of thing, I'm in the same mood as yesterday. And I still don't know who it was that wrote *Parangaricutirimicuaro* in my notebook.*

This afternoon we went to Bill O'Dwyer's penthouse on top of the Hotel Prince. The Abel Greens were there, and Henry Fink of Henry Fink's Shangri-La, and Marjorie Farnsworth. The former Ambassador lives in style, and has a Hungarian cook who can shovel it out beautifully. We sat around on the terrace, soaking up sun and discussing Mexico. O'Dwyer began talking about Cortez and the route he took when he brought his forces up from Veracruz to conquer the Aztec capital, Tenochtitlán. There is a thing about O'Dwyer that is not generally known in New York where he was Mayor. His family in Ireland wanted him to become a priest, and when he was eighteen he was sent to the University of Salamanca in Spain. It was there that he learned his Spanish and that he became interested in the *conquistadores*. He was so taken with the story of Cortez and Pizarro and the others that he resolved that some day he would retrace their routes. When he was twenty he left the university and traveled to New York by steerage. He became a coal passer, a hod-carrier (during construction of the Woolworth building), a bartender at the Plaza Hotel, a cop, a lawyer, a district attorney and Mayor of New York. During all those years he kept up his study of Spanish and when he reached the point where he could afford it, he began taking his vacations in Latin America, pursuing his hobby — following the tracks of the *conquistadores*. Few people knew all this at the time Truman appointed him to be Ambassador to Mexico.

O'Dwyer wanted to know if I planned on visiting Veracruz and I told him what had happened back in New York: In spite of dis-

* The correct spelling is *Parangaricutiro*. The mystery deepens. Or, at least, it lengthens.

couraging reports, I had decided that we would go to Veracruz. Various people said there was nothing there worth seeing. And then, one day, I was in the New York office of the Mexican Tourist Bureau. The head of the bureau is a personable young man named Carlos Hernandez and I had had several discussions with him about our expedition. He knew I was planning a book about Mexico and that afternoon I told him that I was going to visit a city not greatly favored by tourists.

"Which city is that?" he asked, quite casually.

"Veracruz."

He let out a cry, jumped clear over his desk, seized me in a warm *abrazo* and shouted, "Is my home town!" Before we were finished I thought he was going to *give* me Veracruz. His conduct proved the truth of a statement I had read — that in spite of all their tribulations and sorrow, the citizens of Veracruz are the most patriotic people on earth, so far as their city is concerned. I told Bill O'Dwyer that within a few days we would be heading east. And I told Henry Fink that I'd see him later, either at his Shangri-La or in Mexico City.

January 16

I'M CONVINCED that if I were ever so foolish as to get myself lost in the remote jungles of Chiapas, I wouldn't have to wait long before a Lacandon Indian maiden arrived on the scene selling lottery tickets. Anywhere you go in Mexico you'll find the ticket-sellers roaming the streets and highways. Mexico City swarms with them. There are three drawings a week and in each of these drawings the top prizes are a million pesos, a half million and a quarter million. (A million pesos is eighty thousand dollars.) Several times a year there are special drawings, held on big holidays, in which the top prize is around fifteen million pesos.

More than a million Mexicans buy lottery tickets every week and there are more "systems" for choosing numbers than there are for beating the horses. Toss Olsen of *Mexico This Month* has made a study of these "systems" and finds that the ordinary Mexican has great contempt for a person who just walks up and buys a ticket — any ticket. Such a person is looked upon in the same light as a hunter who shoots a bird on the ground, and Mexicans feel he should be denied the privilege of playing the lottery. My favorite system player is known as the casual-number man. As described by Toss Olsen, he adds casual numbers all day long; he begins, say, with his own age, and then adds on the license number of a car that almost clips him, and then the first telephone number he calls, plus the given age of his girl friend. Eventually he arrives at a total, which is too large, so he divides by the number of asparagus stalks he is served at lunch, and thus he gets the number he loses on.

In his book Pepe Romero tells of a man who played the same number every day religiously for twenty-five years, buying it always from the same vendor, and on the day when it finally won, he dropped dead.

Almost every day we go for a walk, even though walking is difficult in Mexico City. The streets were not planned for pedestrians, especially along the Paseo de la Reforma. All along this splendid boulevard there are frequent points where the traffic comes at you from unexpected directions, and when the traffic comes at you in this town it comes at you briskly. The gay insanity of automobile drivers in Mexico is legendary, and not exaggerated. Stan Delaplane says that the taxi drivers, if they hit a pedestrian cleanly, expertly, with grace and finesse, are awarded both the ears and the tail of the victim, as at the bullfights.

Before we left home I considered driving my own car to Mexico City. I hadn't made up my mind about it when a news dispatch out of Mexico settled the matter. It told of two Mexican trucks, each loaded with dynamite. The drivers were playfully jockeying each other around on the highway and then they began racing, roaring along side by side, yelling and jeering back and forth. Neither driver seemed to notice that a train was coming and both trucks rammed into the train. The explosion killed more than a hundred persons including, of course, the two fun-loving truckers. This is not my idea of careful driving.

Some people say that the Mexican driver is a frustrated bullfighter at heart, and that the fenders of other cars are the horns of the bull. And years ago Stuart Chase made an interesting observation touching on Mexican driving habits. He said that Mexicans are the world's worst mechanics — that they have no real understanding of the functions of an automobile. When driving a car, he said, they are still in spirit on horseback and the Mexican horseman always was a great one for coming to a stop with an abrupt, skidding flourish.

Los Angeles drivers were once described as coming up to a stop light like a baseball player sliding into second, surely the Angeleno's heritage from Old Mexico. It is just as bad here, or probably worse. At intervals along the Reforma are traffic circles, called *glorietas*. They usually feature a large central monument, plus a fountain and many flowers. In the United States we have signs which say, TRAFFIC CIRCLE — SLOW. I feel certain that there are signs here saying, GLORIETA GIVE 'ER THE GUN. It is a fact that Mexican drivers, especially taxicab jockeys, put on steam as they come into a traffic circle. They do this because the traffic circle, or *glorieta*, is a sort of battlefield in which all the cars are clawing and clamoring for position. The Mexican driver figures that if he comes charging into the melee at high, roaring speed, he'll frighten hell out of the people already in the whirlpool and they'll hold back and let him have his way. It never works out that way.

Ensayo on the Bulls

Thus far we have had three invitations to go with people to the bullfights on Sundays. In each instance we have declined, saying simply, "We have seen the bullfights." We sat patiently through the killing of six bulls and then departed with the rest of the crowd, and we had little enthusiasm for what we had witnessed. In fact we had none.

I am eternally perplexed and mystified by this bullfight business, and the lunatic fervor of its apologists, especially such Gringo apologists as Hemingway, Barnaby Conrad, Tom Lea, Bob Ruark, Rex Smith, and assorted literary critics and movie reviewers. I read their stuff and I actually don't know what they are talking about and I suspect that *they* don't know what they're talking about. Especially when they're talking about the Moment of Truth. This is the moment when the matador (a word which means, literally, a killer) raises his sword and confronts the heaving, bloody mess that a few minutes ago was a respectable animal. The killer makes the sign of the cross with the point of his sword — a little gesture in the direction of Jesus (what would HE have thought of this business?). That is the Moment of Truth.

Tom Lea describes the process of stabbing a bull to death as "a combat without adornment, all tragedy, all truth." Truth again! What are these people mumbling about when they mumble about Truth? Is there some definition of Truth that I don't know about — meaning maybe blood and agony and torture and death? Here it is again, a guy reviewing a bullfight book: "The black and powerful truth that fills the book is the truth of death that marines learned on Pelelius' Bloody Nose Ridge." So, was that pretty? Was the Bloody Nose Ridge affair worth paying money to see and to cheer? Truth of death? Who needs to be told the Truth of death? Anybody who doesn't know it has had too large a dose of Billy Graham.

A movie reviewer for a news magazine speaks of bullfighting as "an art, a code of honor, a yardstick and symbol of courage." Doesn't he know that a bullfighter — that most honorable, artistic and courageous hero — believes that if he encounters a cross-eyed person before a fight he will be very unlucky and may likely die in the arena? This is true, and the matador who does encounter such a cross-eyed person will usually back out of his engagement for that day. (I have resolved that if I ever meet up with a bullfighter on bullfight day, I'm going to look cross-eyed at him and perhaps save the life of a worthy bull.)

It is written that the qualities summed up in the word *bravo* as applied to bulls are comprised "not of treacherous blood lust, nor of fear, but chiefly of noble anger." That's the kind of anger I've got about the whole thing — noble anger. And I have also read about Don Pepe Madrazo, who breeds bulls for the ring and who describes his sensations when he sees one of his own animals dragged dead from the ring, minus tail and ears, after an especially fine fight. "You feel," said Don Pepe, "that you've helped to create something noble, something brave, which knows how to die with greatness."

Listen to the California author, Max Miller: "Yet one must remember that the bull itself has taken the initiative in starting the killing . . . the fresh and uninjured bull has sighted somebody out there apparently alone and apparently helpless." Alone? The pigtailed bastard has half-a-dozen helpers running around with sharp instruments to jab into the bull. Please, Mr. Miller, kindly do not tell me what goes on in a bull's mind. And kindly don't ever try to tell me that *the bull started it*. What kind of Mongoloid reasoning is that? I can be just as silly and tell you that the killing of bulls is wrong because there is at least one bull in Heaven. The Mohammedans are positive that the ox of Moses has a special place in Paradise, and an ox is a bull in every way except one (or, rather, two). And if Mohammedans believe that there is one bull in Heaven, I can believe that there may be nothing else in Heaven *but* bulls.

I'm growing more than a little weary with the *aficionados* who insist that "Americans just don't *understand* the bullfights." I understand them well enough. I sometimes think that I'd much rather see a Mexican president assassinated than a bull killed by a matador. The bull has done nothing to deserve his bloody and ignominious end — I say ignominious and I mean it, for there is nothing noble and heroic and glorious in it from the bull's point of view. In the light of all we know about politics, the president very probably has performed a series of evil deeds and may deserve death — at least his assassin thinks so.

The boys who write the glowing prose about bullfighting are almost comical in their search for justification of the "art." They remind me of the early days of cockfighting in the United States, when the promoters were trying to counteract the constant attacks against their "sport." They issued statements claiming that cockfighting was a good thing because it developed a ruggeder breed of fowl, resulting in eggs that had better flavor and greater nutritive value.

The great majority of American tourists in Mexico, as well as in Spain, are opposed to bullfighting. Many of them are sickened by it. The sale of the bull-books indicates that there are many Americans who are fascinated by bullfighting, but they are a minority. Those who dislike it, even hate it, are in need of an eloquent spokesman — a man with the ability to compose a prose poem *against* it.

I have read in the books, with special reference to the bullfights, that we should not deign to criticize our neighbor nation on this score — that, in fact, we should never criticize the customs and traditions of other peoples simply because they are alien to our way of life. Okay. I'll go along. Let us by all means cease complaining against the customs and traditions of the Soviets under which they enslave and torture their people. If in Rome they should suddenly revive the custom of feeding Christians to the lions, it is none of our damn business. If in Spain they should suddenly renew the Inquisition, let us refrain from even commenting on it.

You insist that we should respect the culture and institutions of other lands? Okay. Let us turn to the head-hunters of Ecuador and extend the hand of good neighborliness. These are the Jibaro Indians and the purpose of their head-hunting is to get heads to shrink. The basic motive for this art-form seems to be that the Jibaro thinks the head has some soul-matter in it; if he captures a head and brings it in to camp and shrinks it, he forces the soul-matter out, and it is added to the general stock of soul-matter belonging to the community, and this helps toward the fertility of the human population as well as the cattle and the crops. Makes sense.

Now. The Jibaro goes out and finds a loose human being and takes his spear and makes the sign of the cross, for the Moment of Truth has come, and kills the brave man. He cuts off the head and takes it home, where he has two different procedures for shrinking it. He can remove the skull and then pack the skin with hot sand and it will shrink down to the size of a small monkey's head. Or he can use the more classical method, as described by A. Hyatt Verrill in *The American Indian:*

> The bones are first broken by pounding with a wooden club and are then removed through the opening in the neck. The head is then steeped in a tanning solution and is dried in smoke until thoroughly cured. As the skin shrinks and hardens the cartilaginous portions of nose and other features retain their form to some extent and the result is a hard, almost black, miniature head. But in nearly every case the features are distorted and bear little resemblance to those of life. Heads prepared as trophies always have the lips sewed together, the Indians believing that if this is not done the spirit will curse the head-taker.

Oh, how I do wish I were able to write beautiful, pellucid, singing prose — the way Hemingway and Barnaby Conrad and Bob Ruark do it! Then I would write in stirring salute to the head-shrinkers in Ecuador. The bullfight boys insist that it's not a sport, but an art. So, I say, is head-shrinking. If there ever was an art on this planet, it is the art of the Jibaro Indians. The American people are highly susceptible to eloquent writing and the Hemingways and Conrads and Leas and Ruarks have convinced them that there is something spiritually beautiful about bull-killing. So I would dearly love to sell the American people on the art of the head-hunters. I would like to be able to describe head-shrinking in such soul-stirring terms that my readers would exclaim: "By god, I'm gonna shrink me a head if it's the last thing I do on earth!"

One of the finest books ever written in English about Mexico is the work of Madame Calderón de la Barca. Her *Life in Mexico,* written over a hundred years ago, has been saluted time and again as the work of a wise and perceptive woman. In the time when Madame Calderón was living in Mexico City, the bullfighters had at least one extra divertissement. Before the kill the matador would throw a net of firecrackers, "adorned with streaming ribbons, which stuck on his horns and enveloped him in a blaze of fire." While this was going on the mounted picador would grab the bull's tail, wheel his horse and throw the animal on his face — all this, of course, to stir sensations of pride and nobility in the soul of the bull. Listen to Madame Calderón:

> Maddened with pain, streaming with blood, stuck full of darts, and covered with fireworks, the unfortunate beast went galloping round and round, plunging blindly at man and horse, and frequently trying to leap the barrier, but driven back by the waving hats and shouting of the crowd. At last, as he stood at bay, and nearly exhausted, the matador ran up and gave him the mortal blow, considered a peculiar proof of skill. . . . One has more sympathy with him [the bull] than with his human adversaries. It cannot be good to accustom a people to such bloody sights.

Perhaps the bull-writing boys of today didn't know about the firecracker bit; now they'll complain that the game has grown soft, and they'll ask for a return to the firecrackers. And why not? There's always room for one more Moment of Truth.

The pro arguments of the *aficionado* go beyond the ridiculous to the point where they become sublimely comical. He says that the bullfight illuminates human character during its finest moment — when man faces death unflinchingly. I would remind him that a bullfighter won't ever tackle a cow, because he's afraid of a cow; a cow is never fooled by the cape, even the one called a Veronica after the woman who washed Christ's face; a cow refuses to go for the cape, and goes for the man instead.

The *aficionado* says: "You eat meat, don't you? And the meat comes from animals that are killed in the slaughterhouse. The killing of a bull in the ring is not as brutal as the killing of a cow in one of your slaughterhouses." Answer: Probably so, but we don't sell tickets to the killing of the cows and we don't converge on the slaughterhouses in vast numbers, to jump up and down and play band music and throw seat cushions and holler "*Ole!*"

The *aficionado* says: "Your big complaint used to be about the horses. Now that they are padded, I don't see what objection you have to the fights." Answer: Don't give me that grap. I know all about the horses, and so do you. You would much prefer to have it the old way, with the horses unpadded so the bulls can rip open their bellies and strew the arena with their guts. You deplore the padding as a sissification of the game, an unreasonable concession to those who have weak stomachs. You say, and I have heard you say it, that the horses are old and weak and worthless; that the tremendous blows they get through those pads scramble their insides and they usually die soon afterwards, but it's a slow death — not a quick death as when their entrails descend and get tangled up in their feet. So, you insist, it would be far, far better if the pads were taken off. It would be humane to let the horses be split open and die quickly. The most celebrated American apologist for bullfighting is Hemingway. He contends that the spectacle of a horse galloping around with his innards spilling out is true comedy, a very funny sight, "a complete burlesque of tragedy." This is the same Hemingway who is one of our bonded Thinkers of Great Thoughts.

The *aficionado* says: "The bullfight is not a sport, but an art, one of the most beautiful of all the arts. It is, in reality, a ballet, and its purpose is to demonstrate the aesthetic poise and grace of the *torero*." Answer: So why the need for all that blood-spilling? Why put a big, handsome bull into a ballet and jab him and stab him until he is dead? It could be done another way; if the aim is to show off the gracefulness of the man, then he needs no real bull. IBM or Remington Rand could today turn out a mechanical bull that would charge a cape, snort, paw the ground, bleed three-in-one oil when jabbed with sharp poles and pointed sticks, and even try to climb over the barrier.

The *aficionado* says: "You speak of the bullfight as being a cruel spectacle. Is it any more cruel than the boxing matches which are so popular in your country?" Answer: There's a difference. The boxer has a slight amount of intelligence — not much, but a little more than a bull. He knows what he is doing. Nobody tricked him into going into the ring, and he gets paid for doing it.

The bull doesn't know what he's up against. If he did, he wouldn't have anything to do with it. The *aficionado* seems to think otherwise. He always speaks of the "brave bulls" and tries to make it appear that the bull has the mentality and the character of Young Lochinvar and spends his life yearning for the hour when he is allowed to enter the ring and get a sword rammed through his heart. I just choke up with admiring sentiment when I think of it.

I can visualize a scene on the ranch, with Papa Bull having a heart-to-heart talk with his son:

"My boy," says Papa, "it is time that I told you the facts of life. You didn't know it, but you are not an ordinary bull. You are one of the special bulls, one of the *brave* bulls."

"I knew it already, Papa," says the son. "We kids talk about it out back of the barn. But I don't feel very brave."

"Of course not," says Papa. "You've got to be told about it, and then you'll feel real brave."

"What have I got to be brave about?" asks the boy bull.

"Oh, not much," says Papa. "Someday they'll come and get you and haul you down to Mexico City and put you in a place that is pitch-dark and keep you there in darkness quite a while. Then, all of a sudden a door will open and you will go through it into the light. The light will blind you, and there will be several thousand wild Two-Leggeds all around you, making terrible noises. And you will blink your eyes and slowly adjust them to the light, and then you will see these Two-Leggeds with the pointed sticks. This will be your finest hour. You will be a hero among heroes. You will rise to greatness as you set yourself and then drive down upon these creatures with the pointed sticks. Oh, you will make them hop and skip and jump! If only I could be there to see it, to see my own flesh and blood scattering the Two-Leggeds! But I must caution you about one thing. Don't worry when they're sticking all those things into your back and shoulders. It won't hurt very long. Everything will turn out fine and in just a few minutes you'll be hearing beautiful harp music and eating grass with honey smeared on it. Oh, I do wish they'd let me go down to Mexico City and enter the ring, instead of making me stay up here all the time and do nothing from morning to night but breed. I yearn for greatness and beauty and art and grass with honey smeared on it."

"Papa," says the boy bull, "you can go in my place if you want to. I'll be glad to stay here and take care of the breeding."

"No," says Papa, "I'll stay here and do the tiresome work. Matter of fact, I think I'll do some of it right now."

By this time I think it may be clear to the reader that I am somewhat prejudiced in the matter of bullfighting. Life is life; a bull is vibrantly alive; and from the look of him, he must enjoy living — at least some phases of it. And so I offer a final recommendation:

If there must be bullfights, then the bulls should be given their Moment of Truth. Let several matadors be loaded into a truck and transported to one of the famous bull-breeding ranches. Let the matadors be placed in a dark room at the edge of the corral, and kept there for about forty-eight hours. Then throw open the door and thrust one of the men out into the sunlight — where eight or ten eager bulls are waiting for him. Not with lances and *banderillas* and swords — just with their sharp horns. Thus would simple justice be served.

2

The Ever Heroic

January 18

OFF with Carlos this morning on our first expedition, covering the route of Cortez, Maximilian, and most of the presidents who have had to flee for their lives. We headed east for Tlaxcala. I had read a lot about this town in one of Carleton Beals's books. We parked in the plaza, alongside the church of San Francisco where the first Christian services were held on this continent. The site of the church also is associated with the name of Camaxtli, the great war god of the Tlaxcallans. The books say that his *maxtli* hung clear down to his knees. A *maxtli* is a loincloth; it is not explained why Camaxtli's *maxtli* was such a poor fit, but in thinking about it I was reminded of the time Dick Bradford, Roark's son, was in Mexico and wrote home to Mary Rose that he was having a terrible time keeping the laundress from putting starch in his jock straps, because he didn't know the Spanish words for either starch or jock strap.

Our primary interest on arrival was not in Camaxtli, but in finding a rest room. We circled the plaza and finally came to a small restaurant that looked tolerably clean and respectable. We took a table and ordered some drinks and Carlos asked the girl about rest rooms. She said Oh *sí*, señor, we have one, and *Sí*, it is *muy* clean. Nelle tried it first, heading back through the kitchen, and she was gone quite a long time, and when she returned she said, "Well, you won't believe it till you see it." So I made my way through the kitchen and another rear room and arrived in a tiny unroofed enclosure. A couple of inches of dirty water stood on the concrete floor and I sloshed through it to the dilapidated cubicle where stood the Juan. I will not describe it, beyond saying that it was dirty, and that the tiny enclosure was inhabited by one tethered turkey, two loose chickens (loose in the sense that they were not tied up), one caged parrot and one smaller bird in a cage. These witnesses gobbled and clucked and awked all through my performance and when I returned to the table I said, "Let's get the hell out of this town." Carlos, however, insisted that we must see the beautiful Sanctuary of Ocotlán which stands on a hill above the town. It was beautiful all right, and had a miracle in its past. The Virgin appeared here to a lowly peon named Juan Diego, just the same as the Virgin appearing to a lowly peon named Juan Diego up at Guadalupe. Somebody was lacking in originality.

Cortez spent many months here in Tlaxcala, preparing for his second invasion of Tenochtitlán. I would suggest that if he ever had to go to the toilet, he wouldn't have been here ten minutes.

We headed south for Puebla, along the same route taken by Cortez, and I remembered, too late, that I had wanted to see one of the herb sellers in Tlaxcala. They sell a kind of seed which you put in a girl's ear and she will go crazy for you. I wanted a packet.

We rode through maguey country — vast fields and hillsides covered with the fabulous growth, called properly *agave Americana* and known in the United States as the century plant. I had been doing some research on the maguey, so we stopped on the highway and Carlos cut off the tip of one of the leaves. Back in the car he separated it, part by part, demonstrating how the Indians used one part to make paper, another part to make soap, and so on.

Most tourists think of the maguey plant (if they think of it at all) merely as the source for pulque, tequila and mescal, plus Pepe Romero's wretched little worm. It is so much more than that; I doubt if there is another plant anywhere in the world so useful as the maguey.

It has been such an important factor in the history of Mexico that it

is, or should be, the national symbol. When the Aztecs were wandering down from the north, seeking a place to settle, their gods had
instructed them to keep going until they saw an eagle perched on a
cactus, devouring a snake, and this would be the spot to found their
city. (Personally, if I saw an eagle sitting on a cactus, devouring a
snake, I'd consider it the worst spot on earth to settle.) The Aztecs
did see the eagle and the cactus and the snake, and that's how they
came to start up their city of Tenochtitlán. I should imagine that the
cactus was actually a maguey, for the maguey was even more important to the Aztecs than to later arrivals. It has been painted over
and over again by Mexico's greatest artist, José Clemente Orozco,
who recognized its paternal character — not alone as a phallic symbol, but as Mexico's "good provider."

Prescott called the maguey "a miracle of nature." He says that the
Aztecs took one part of the leaves and made a paste, from which they
created paper more soft and more beautiful than parchment. The
roots were once considered edible, and from the rest of the plant came
a black honey, and a vinegar, in addition to the intoxicants. The
fibers produced a strong thread called *pita* which was used to make
a sturdy cloth, and which also was twisted to make cords as strong as
rope. (The sisal hemp of Yucatán comes from an agave plant related
to the maguey.) The thorn at the tip of each leaf is extremely strong
and sharp and was used as a pin, as a needle or as a nail. The ancient
Aztec priests used the thorns to tear their arms and rip their breasts.
A gummy, soapy juice from the leaves will lather, and was used
as soap by the Aztecs; in more modern times it has been discovered
that this juice may be used as a detergent where alkali would be
injurious.

The thick, strong leaves of the maguey supplied an impenetrable
thatch for humble dwellings. Sometimes the middle shoot (the male
principal of the maguey) was permitted to grow, and served as a
beam supporting a roof. The pulpy leaves, when dried, made excellent firewood. Stripped in a certain way, they were also used to make
shoes. And those same leaves, with their curved conformation, prob-

ably served as the world's first gutters, fitted together at the eaves of adobe huts and houses.

In more recent times it has been found that the sap of the maguey contains agavose, one of the rare sugars. Also that the firm, white, pithy interior of the flowering stem can be dried and sliced and used in several ways, for example as a natural razor strop, and as insulating material.

The reason the maguey has been cultivated extensively in modern days is, of course, for the production of pulque — that stinking tipple of the people. Madame Calderón wrote that in her time many of the richest families in the capital owed their fortunes to pulque. From the looks of the landscape throughout the central plateau, I should say that the same thing is probably true today. We have driven through fields of maguey, set in orderly rows, for mile after mile after mile. These plants are grown solely for pulque and its fiery offspring, tequila and mescal.

On the road where I live in New York State tobacco has been grown on a small scale. I myself have grown hot peppers. Why not a few maguey plants? I wouldn't want them for pulque or tequila or mescal — just for the thorns, to tear my arms and pierce my breast each day after reading the newspapers.

January 19

HERE in Puebla this morning Carlos, who is a proper Catholic, said: "If you don't mind we will not visit the Hidden Convent. Nobody believes it anyway and sometimes I think I don't believe it also."

The Hidden Convent is not far from the center of town. When Juárez closed the convents in 1857 a group of nuns established themselves in this hidden retreat and stayed there for seventy-seven years until their secret was discovered in 1935. The place is a congeries of cells and cloisters with secret passageways and trap doors, and the entrance is through an ordinary-looking residence. The reason Carlos has lost interest in it I think may lie in the fact that it has been a politico-ecclesiastical football in recent times. The Church says: "Look what cruel and inhuman things the Government compelled these pious sisters to undergo." And the Government says: "Look how sneaky, how treacherous, these people are in their defiance of the law of the land."

I was willing to pass up the convent, for there were other things I wanted to see. We proceeded to the main plaza, and I began searching for a sign, stooping and crouching so I could examine the base of each of the tiled benches. "Why are you estooping like that?" Carlos wanted to know. "I'm trying," I said, "to get the viewpoint of a dog." To which he replied, "You do not need to estoop to get that." I explained to him that I had once read about a sign in this plaza, a sign done in beautiful tile, saying, *Todo Perro Que Pasa Suelto por los Jardines Sera Sacrificado.*" This translates: "Any Dog Who Passes Unaccompanied through These Gardens Will Be Killed." The wording of that sign indicates that the dogs themselves should read it. Its message is directed at dogs who are unaccompanied; it warns them to get out of the plaza or suffer execution; since the dogs for whom it was intended would have nobody with them, they would have to read it for themselves. Therefore my shrewd logic told me the sign would be placed at dog level, near the ground. I searched and searched but couldn't find it. Carlos said he didn't believe there ever was a sign made for dogs to read — that Mexicans are not that dumb. He recognized my disappointment, however, and told about some other famous Mexican signs. He said that in the state of Jalisco there is a village with a new footbridge over a *barranca,* and a sign informing the people: This is called a bridge — it is to walk across only on top of. He told about another town in Chiapas. A few miles out from the town is a fork in the road. One fork leads to a jungle, the other leads into the town. One day the mayor had a sign made with the intention of placing it at the fork and bringing in some business. The sign said: The road to the right goes to the terrible jungle, full of bandits. The road to the left goes to

A NICE TOWN. Then the assistant mayor looked at the sign and said, "But what of the many poor people like me, who cannot read?" The Mayor pondered this question for a few moments, then added a line at the bottom of the sign: TO THOSE WHO CANNOT READ: BETTER TAKE THE ROAD TO THE LEFT.

Our hotel, the Lastra, is up on a hillside within sight of four famous volcanoes — Popo, Issty, Malinche and Orizaba. A few steps up the street is Fort Loreto, where the Mexicans defeated the French on the 5th of May in 1862, thereby giving every sizeable town in Mexico a street name: Cinco de Mayo. Unhappily, Mexico has very little to brag about when it comes to military triumphs. There has been plenty of fighting down through the centuries, but it has been mostly intra-mural. When it has been with other countries, Mexico has usually lost. So the victory of the Cinco de Mayo is important to the Mexi-cans, and is memorialized in all those streets that are named for it. Never mind the fact that, although the Mexicans won that particular battle, the French soon afterward won the war.

I should like to observe at this point that Mexicans apparently know very little about the art of electrical wiring. Even in some of the newer hotels the wires are exposed, stapled across the walls and ceilings and around the wainscoting. If you ask the hotel people why they do it this way, they say they want to keep the wires where they can get at them handily. In one hotel I remember that when we turned the floor lamp on or off in our room, the telephone rang — the two had been hooked somehow into the same circuit. In another place we stayed a Mexican gentleman guest was making a great fuss with the management about having received a terrible shock. He had been trying to repair some faulty wiring in his room. He fastened the loose end of a wire to his belt buckle and then thrust the tongue of the buckle into the socket. Knocked him right on his *trasero*.

We were in two famous churches today at the insistence of Carlos, and I find that I am getting church-drunk, so tonight I told him firmly that in the future I don't intend to enter more than one church per week. I don't want my readers to think that I am lacking in sanctity. By religion I am a Knipperdollinck, a follower of Bernt Knipperdollinck of Münster. We don't care for baptism but we believe in polygamy, plus the right to behead any wives we don't like. (I say "we," although, to be strictly truthful, I don't know any other Knipperdollincks.) Also we believe that nobody should ever run for public office — if that doesn't solve the problem of government, nothing ever will.

January 20

WE RETURNED today to the Zócalo and wandered through the *portales*, and Nelle discovered an interesting item, which we bought — a tiny wooden pig, the body made from the shell of a pecan, with movable wooden ears, tail, and eyes. The girl at the booth showed us how to remove the snout and said we should catch a *mosca*, or fly, and put him inside the pig's body. The snout is then replaced, the fly starts crawling around inside, and the ears and the tail and the eyes jiggle.

One form of wildlife not lacking in Mexico is the *mosca*. We returned to the hotel and decided to try out our little pig in the lobby. There was a television set in one corner and about eight guests were watching the bullfights on it. Nelle and Carlos and I began trying to catch a fly. Our wild grabbings attracted the attention of the desk clerk and the bellboy and they came over and Carlos explained the pig to them. They were quite enthusiastic and joined us in the fly hunt. Here were five of us at one end of the lobby, swinging wildly with cupped hands, and the bullfight people began glancing back at us, wondering what we were trying to do. At last one of the boys caught a fly that looked big and athletic enough, and Carlos put him inside the little pig, and then put the pig down on a coffee table. Immediately things started happening. The tail wiggled, then the tiny ears began to jerk back and forth, and the little red eyes vibrated, and then the tail again. We were all laughing but I thought the bellboy would rupture himself with his howls. In half a minute two of the *aficionados* left the television set and came over to see what was happening, then one by one the others arrived and there we were in a large huddle, all staring at the little pig and laughing and shouting. The little pig had defeated both the bull and the matador and stolen their audience, and the Mexicans in the group were now crying, *"Ah, sí!* Moves the tail!" And, *"Arriba!"* And even, when the tiny ears began to jump, *"Ole!"*

January 21

I WAS awakened around 5 o'clock this morning by a concatenation of noises that continued for an hour or so. The bells in the Puebla cathedral and in a lot of other churches began bong-whonging; factory whistles were sounding; there were noises indicating that a herd of Mexican locomotives were mating; there were sounds of either gunfire or firecrackers; five thousand dogs were howling, screeching and barking — and all this *before daylight.* They did everything but shoot off the four volcanoes. I was told at the desk that this happens every morning, but that the people of Puebla are accustomed to it and sleep right through it. In that case, I wonder why they go to all the bother.

The hotel bills down here are, of course, rendered in pesos. I try to hide them away but quite often I'll come into the room and find that Nelle has gone into my bags and got one out and is sitting with a pencil, figuring over it. She doesn't know a peso from a posse, but she's an incorrigible bill-checker (she's convinced that every bank statement is chockful of errors but she has no notion of how to go about proving it). As she sweats over the hieroglyphics, achieving nothing, she keeps muttering, "There's something wrong here, I just *know* it!"

We left Puebla and rode for several hours within sight of that symmetrically beautiful peak, Orizaba, and we talked about mountain climbing, which I consider to be the pursuit of half-wits. Carlos said he has a cousin who is a hypochondriac and is always saying, "I shouldn't go out to the movies tonight because I'll catch cold," or, "I shouldn't go to this picnic because I'll surely catch a cold." Yet, said Carlos, this same man's hobby is mountain climbing, which takes him into snowdrifts a mile deep. And this reminds Carlos of another cousin, or rather, a cousin-in-law, "who got very fat from itting sotch big mills." This cousin-in-law went to a doctor who wrote out a diet and said, "From now on, this is what you must eat." The cousin-in-law looked at the list of foods and sighed and said, "Well, all right if you say so." So he went home and gave the list to his wife and told her what the doctor said and thereafter he ate all the diet foods between his regular meals, even though he found it pretty difficult getting that additional provender down.

We arrived at the village of Banderilla, named for the barbed sticks that are jabbed into the bulls, and went through some famous gardens maintained by the Lecuona family. There were acres and acres of flowering jungle, with more than two hundred varieties of orchids and plenty of azaleas and gardenias. At one point we came upon a shrub with two old cotton gloves draped over its limbs. "Pay close attention to this," said Carlos, "for it is the famous glove bush, known only to Mexico." Later he pointed out a small plant growing in a quart oil can. He called our attention to the label on the can and said, "This is a very rare Mexican flower, the Veedol."

We checked in at the best hotel in Jalapa, capital of the state of Veracruz. The most famous brand of chiles in Mexico is the Jalapeño, supposedly grown and canned here in Jalapa. Carlos and I walked over to the State Capitol and finally located Señor Juan Sanchez Miguel, local representative of Turismo. He spoke no English and Carlos had some difficulty explaining that we wanted to visit the chile-canning factory; he couldn't understand why a tourist would want to see such a thing. He didn't know where it was but he knew about a store where the canned chiles were sold, so the four of us walked up a steep hill and found the store and a beautiful *señorita* explained at great length just how to get to the cannery. Now we walked a half mile or so, and arrived at the address — a big door in the customary wall. After much knocking on the door it was finally opened by a young man and we were admitted into a big, dark room. There were only two men in the whole establishment and they were greatly confused, and acted as if we were a raiding party of bandits; apparently nobody else had ever come to look at the birthplace of the famous Jalapeño chile. Finally one of the young men explained that the business had been founded by his great-grandfather. The chiles were then grown exclusively in this section and canned in this very room, but the product had become so popular and so famous that other people in distant parts of Mexico began growing and canning "Jalapeño chiles." I tried to find out if there wasn't some Mexican law to protect against such piracy, but nobody seemed to understand what I was talking about. The next question was: Where could we go to see a chile plantation? There was a long four-way discussion between the two chile men, Señor Sanchez Miguel and Carlos, after which I was informed that this was not the season for growing chiles and, therefore, not the season for canning chiles. If we could hang around Jalapa for a few days . . . I asked how many days. Well, say a matter of a month, or two months. I said no. The great-grandson of the founder then presented me with three cans of the original, genuine Jalapeño chiles. On the way back to the hotel, Señor Sanchez Miguel was most apologetic, as if he were personally responsible for chiles being out of season. At his office I showed him a wonderful letter of introduction to the Governor of Veracruz, and he said it was very nice but that the man wasn't the Governor any more. His name was Marco Antonio Muñoz and Carlos said, "Why, I know him personally — he is a wonderful man, one of the best Ping-pong players in Mexico."

I asked Señor Sanchez Miguel if he knew of any jalap farms near

Jalapa. He said he thought there ought to be some, but he didn't know where they might be. Jalap is a drug made from the roots of a convolvulaceous plant, and it takes its name from Jalapa because it was grown here more than anywhere else. It is a powerful purgative used on cows and bothersome drunks. I have always been interested in it because it is the chief ingredient of the Mickey Finn. A Mickey Finn is not to be confused with knockout drops. A Mickey, properly confected, is a hydragogue, a powerful cholagogue, and has scammony in it (and so have I). It is designed to get a troublesome customer out of the saloon where he is making trouble. It generally sends him away with the speed of light. So I am happy to be here in the ancestral home of the Mickey Finn, and in my romantic imagination I have often pictured the inscrutable Indians tenderly cultivating their jalap patches on the mountain slopes, preparing the roots which, perhaps, someday will send a belligerent drunk high-tailing out of a bar-and-grill in Omaha, Nebraska. Thus is the world knit together.

In our hotel this evening I phoned down for a bottle opener and a boy came up and showed me how to use the catch on the snap-lock at the door. Beer doesn't come in cans in Mexico, and bellboys seldom come with bottle-openers, so this lock trick is a good thing to know. After the boy had gone I noticed that the metal catch was loose and was, in fact, about to fall off. I called down to ask for a screwdriver but couldn't make myself understood. So I called Carlos in his room and asked him the word for screwdriver. He spelled it out for me over the phone: DESTORNILLADOR. I hung up and looked at the word a long time and tried to say it, and then decided that I'd leave the damn door rot and fall to pieces.

All in all, our brief visit to the town known as the Athens of Mexico has not been an unqualified success: no Jalapeño chile plantation, no jalap patches, no *destornillador,* and the Governor isn't Governor any more.

January 22

FROM Jalapa to Veracruz is downhill, the road descending with constantly changing scenery until we were in the tropics, passing great belts of land devoted to coffee, then bananas, and then papayas. Carlos said that in Cuba a papaya is not called a papaya, but some other name, because in Cuba a papaya is part of a woman.

A while later I remarked that I hadn't seen any men carrying machetes in this section, and I asked if the peons used them here. "Only," said Carlos, "to cut the truts of each other." In the past the machete has served the rural Mexican as an all-purpose tool. With it he cultivated his milpa and bean patch, cut material for his hut, spanked his babies, walloped his wife, mixed and moulded adobe, killed game (sometimes by throwing it), cooked on its broad blade, and cut the trut of his enemy. Legend says that the word machete is a corruption of Massachusetts, where the first of them were made; today, according to some writers, most of the machetes are manufactured in Connecticut, where some of the "typically Mexican" mottoes are engraved on the blades, such as, IF THIS REPTILE BITES YOU, THERE IS NO CURE IN THE DRUGSTORE." When I told this to Carlos he exploded in Spanish, using words which I'm happy I didn't understand.

Arriving in Veracruz, we drove south eight miles to the Hotel Mocambo, a big resort on the beach. We had reserved Room 95, which was supposed to be one of the nicer rooms. Moment of Truth! That room had been usurped by a Mexican General. The desk clerk was apologetic but he explained that when a general calls for a room he must be given the best there is lest he declare war on the hotel. Up to this moment I had thought all Mexican generals were comic characters. Now I felt like yelling *"El paredón!"* This is the cry used by old Mexican women when they get furiously angry with somebody, usually around the markets, and it means, "The wall!" — with special reference to the spot where people are executed by firing squads. And so we were installed in a lesser room at the Mocambo. Tonight I found out that the name of the usurper is Gral. (not Gen.) Molinar, and that he is the chief of police of Mexico City. I'm not even mollified by the fact that in our present room I sleep beneath the Rivera portrait of Zapata and his big white horse.

The Mocambo is a place with great sweeping semicircular decks and tiled terraces and swimming pools. It could be one of the most splendid hotels in Mexico, but apparently capital is wanting. The paint is peeling, the woodwork is collapsing in some places, and the formal gardens have been taken over by the weeds. In spite of all this deterioration, however, it is a spectacular establishment, especially in the evening when the warts and blemishes are not showing.

We were sitting on the main terrace early this evening when I noticed an elderly, white-haired man in a nearby deck chair. He was slumped in the chair, and had his right hand against his head, and I thought for a few moments that he had suffered a stroke. But he raised his head, caught me staring at him, and called out, "Texas!" I said, "You from Texas?" He said, "Oh, no — I got Texas." He came over with a transistor radio on which he had been getting a Texas station. He said that sometimes he can get Oklahoma and New Orleans and once he got St. Louis. He is eighty-one years old, spends every winter in Mexico, and devotes most of his time to "getting" Texas and the other places. He said he eats nothing but eggs, bread and tomato juice, three meals a day, all winter, every winter. He made me think of a man we met in Acapulco, on a terrace high above the lovely bay. He too had a small radio plastered against his ear and he complained, "This is the noisiest no-good god-damn country on earth!" He had been trying to listen to a football game in the United States and the typical Mexican sounds drifting up from the town — dogs and chickens and burros and pigs and speedboats and people and automobiles — had him thoroughly frustrated. I offered him no sympathy.

We drove downtown tonight and walked around the streets, even though we were very tired. I simply couldn't wait to have a look at this fabulous city.

When I told the man at American Express in New York that I planned on visiting Veracruz he seemed surprised and said, "We rarely get anyone for Veracruz — just an occasional fishing party."

In 1944 Sydney Clark, a veteran writer of guidebooks, dismissed the city with a line: "No one lingers needlessly in Veracruz."

In 1936 Max Miller found Veracruz distasteful and fled from the place, mainly because he couldn't stomach the steady procession of beggars and street peddlers.

Veracruz is Mexico's busiest port and has a population of around 100,000. It got its name from Cortez, who may or may not have been its founder. Some writers say the present Veracruz — *La Villa Rica de la Veracruz* — is not to be confused with the colony of the same name founded by Cortez soon after he landed on Mexican soil. Other writers say the present city is the one Cortez laid out and named. Disagreement is the staff of life in Mexico.

While the place bears the official name of The Rich Town of the True Cross, it is known elsewhere in Mexico by another name: *La Siempre Heroica* — The Ever Heroic. It is so known because other Mexicans can't understand why the people of Veracruz are so foolhardy as to continue living there. The city has a history of recurrent misfortune and adversity the like of which would be hard to equal anywhere else in this hemisphere. If ever the Four Horsemen of the Apocalypse had a home stable, it is in Veracruz.

It has been invaded and bombarded and sacked and burned again and again and yet again. It is a town that was invaded before it even existed, for Cortez was an invader and he was responsible for its founding, whether he founded it or not. All during the Colonial centuries it was subjected to periodic assault by pirates; whenever a pirate couldn't think of anything else interesting to do, he sacked Veracruz. They looted and burned and raped and raped and raped. The worst of these assaults was led by a scoundrel of unsurpassed cruelty, Lorencillo. He locked fifteen hundred men, women and children inside a church without food or water and kept them there for four days; many of them suffocated, or died of thirst, while Lorencillo and his boys were loading up their loot. Even today when a Veracruz citizen loses some money, no matter how, he remarks, "*Lorencillo lo ha tomado.*" (Lorencillo has taken it.) Another pirate gang slaughtered the citizens in the streets and in their homes and then hauled three hundred of the survivors out to the Isle of Sacrifices and left them there to starve to death.

The fleeing Spaniards razed Veracruz in 1821 before they surrendered to the Revolutionary forces so, as someone has remarked, the Conquest of Mexico began and ended in this city. By the time it had been rebuilt, in 1838, French ships moved in and blew it to bits. Eight years later the United States landed troops here. From 1861 to 1867 the French came back and occupied the town. In 1914 the American marines landed and took over.

In between these invasions the town could depend on having either destructive storms or devastating epidemics of cholera, typhoid, malaria and assorted other miseries. Pandora kept her famous box in the plaza and opened it every hour on the hour, bringing unending woe to the populace. Veracruz became known as the home of the *zopilote*, the Mexican buzzard, and at one time he was almost as numerous as the human population, and strolled the streets and plazas undisturbed because he was protected by law from any harm (he saved the city the expense of garbage removal). The *zopilote* is still resident in Veracruz, but not in such great numbers as in former years.

Veracruz has incredibly bad weather. So unhappy is the town's reputation that all over Mexico, whenever a spell of evil weather sets in, people invariably say, "It is the wind from Veracruz." The high humidity ages everything prematurely, including the people. There is a joke that goes: "In Veracruz even the *zopilotes* are mildewed."

The chief tourist attraction is, of course, a place of sadness and horror: the fortress of San Juan de Ulua, once an island but now connected to the mainland by a causeway. It is a grim castle built on a rock, a sort of Mexican Devil's Island surrounded by sharks. Someone has written sarcastically that the Spaniards brought God to Mexico but at the same time they brought San Juan de Ulua. It served for centuries as a prison for political offenders and its cells and dungeons and torture devices still exist. If a prisoner complained about the accommodations, the jailers sometimes lowered him into the water just far enough to permit the sharks to gnaw off his legs.

Veracruz has almost always been the jumping-off place for Mexican Presidents fleeing into exile. There is a story about a prominent Mexican who was notified one evening that the party had chosen him to be the next President. Before daylight he had packed and was on his way to Veracruz, where he chartered the fastest boat he could find and headed for safety in foreign lands.

Now, for the other side of the coin. All of the people I met back home who had been to Veracruz described it as the gayest and happiest place in all of Mexico. Mitchel Goodman, in the *Atlantic*, called the natives "an exuberant people — as gay and lively as any European equivalent." More than a hundred years ago Madame Calderón said they were the truest of patriots, holding their town to be superior to any other place on earth; they felt that way even in the city's darkest days.

Ignored by the great majority of tourists, Veracruz is nonetheless famous for both its food and its hospitality. The *Plaza de la Constitución* and its immediate surroundings combine to create one of the most delightful spots in the whole Republic. As for the food, Madame Calderón didn't like it the first time she stopped in Veracruz. She made a pun and called it "Spanish cooking vera-cruzified." And of the town itself she said, "To me nothing can exceed the sadness of the aspect of this city and of its environs." A couple of years later she came back and spent some time in Veracruz and fell in love with it, and changed her mind about the food, calling it wonderful.

As for me — I haven't been so excited about arriving in a place since the morning I got off the boat train in Paris.

January 23

As HE always does everywhere, Carlos spends a good deal of his time in gay banter with waiters and bartenders and desk clerks at the Mocambo, and I detect a frequent use of the word "Alvarado" which is usually accompanied by laughter. I asked Carlos about it and he described the fishing village of Alvarado, less than an hour's drive down the coast. "It is famous," he said, "because the people curse more than anywhere else in the world, even the women and children. They cannot speak one sentence without including one or two curse words, and some of them very bad, very dirty words. It is their ordinary way of talking, and they do not think there is anything bad about it." I asked him if he could give me a mild example of the way the Alvarado people talk. "Well," he said, "maybe there are two men, or two women, talking on the street, and they say good-by, and one of them will say, '*Adios,* and say hello to your son of a bitch mother.' "

Carlos told a story about the Bishop of Alvarado, who decided the time had come to preach a sermon against cursing. "You must learn," he told his parishioners, "to control your temper, you must not get angry at little things, and then you will not use such bad language all the time. Now, right at this moment, there is an innocent little fly on my hand. I can feel him walking around. I know that most of you would curse him if he were walking around on *your* hand. But he is only a little fly and he will do me no harm and he will go away, and anyway he is one of God's creatures, so why should I curse him?" At this point the Bishop glanced benignly down at his hand, and then exclaimed: "God Almighty! The son of a bitch is a bee!"

We must plan a trip to Alvarado. Even Nelle is eager for it, and has asked me several times, "When are we going to the dirty-talking town?"

We have started trying to spot the "General" who took our room. There's nobody around in uniform so we concluded that he's in sports clothes, the same as everyone else. In trying to pick him out of the crowd, we have usually settled on evil-looking men. This morning at breakfast we decided we had him located. Next to us in the dining room was a long table, set up for a family. The mother and four small children were present when we arrived and they looked like people of quality. Papa wasn't there, but I decided that Papa was probably the General. Then he arrived — a tall, trim, handsome man with a black mustache and an easy, soft-spoken manner. I reflected on Madame Calderón's observations about Santa Anna, "how frequently this expression of philosophic resignation, of placid sadness, is to be remarked on the countenances of the deepest, most ambitious, and most designing men." We were both convinced that this was our General and that a handsomer General never walked. His two little girls greeted him, kissing him on the cheek, and he sat down to his eggs, bacon, refried beans and *salsa*. He was just getting started when his wife notified him that the smallest child, a boy about three years old, wasn't eating properly. The General put down his tools, circled the table and took a chair beside the child. On the table was a toy telephone and the child said something to the General, pointing to the phone. The General picked up a spoon and began feeding cereal to the little boy. He'd thrust the spoon into the child's mouth, withdraw it, pick up the little phone, say *"Bueno!"* into it (the Mexican way of answering the phone), put it down, do the spoon bit again, then the phone, then the spoon. I thought, My God, I'll bet this man is as tough as Pancho Villa in the pursuit of his official duties. Wouldn't his underlings love to see him now! Wouldn't the professional crooks of Mexico City love to have a picture of this!

Today at lunch I asked the *Capitán* if I might have some enchiladas. He was very sorry. "We have enchiladas," he said, "but unfortunately we have no tortillas to make them with." A bit later I asked Carlos to find out if the milk came pasteurized in bottles, or in the big dirty-looking cans that are toted on muleback all over Mexico. *El Capitán* said the hotel gets its milk in cans. He said that a year or so ago in Veracruz they built a beautiful new plant for the pasteurization of milk. It had no more than gone into production when a mob descended on it, throwing rocks. They broke every window in the place and wrecked the machinery. They said that Providence decrees that milk should never be tampered with, that it should be consumed just as it comes from the cow, that putting it through all this machinery was offensive to God. And so the plant was abandoned.

Carlos has had a talk with the desk clerk, who said the General hasn't arrived yet from Mexico City. This particular clerk was one of Carlos's football players in the time when Carlos was a coach. He is a native of Córdoba, and there is a question I have to ask about that town. Carlos asked him if he would be willing to talk to me and then returned and said: "He says he will be happy to talk to you at great length but he must do it without looking at you, as he says he does not like your looks. He thinks you are a very funny-looking Gringo. He says he will talk without looking at you, but he will look at a bird or at a cloud or at his fingers."

Driving into town I told Carlos that I was most anxious to see San Juan de Ulua. Carlos replied that we can't see it, that it has been turned over to the Mexican Navy and is now used for the repair and refitting of naval ships, and the public is barred. I showed him a guidebook which said that tourists could visit the fort, so we stopped along the waterfront and Carlos talked to a man on one of the piers. When he came back he had a twinkle in his eye. "We cannot go," he said. "They do not allow tourists. For a while they did permit it, but the Gringos stole too many things, too many fittings and replacements, and there was fear that the Gringo tourists would steal the entire Mexican Navy. I did not say this — the *señor* on the pier said it."

So we wandered around town and Carlos encountered an acquaintance, a wizened old man with no teeth, wearing faded overalls, described to us later as being a typical *veracruzano* in his attitude toward life and the human race. Carlos told the old man that I had been trying to see the Governor of Veracruz. Was he in town? The old man said he was not. Where was he? The old man replied, "The son of a bitch has gone up north to show one of the other Governors how to steal better." (Actually, I learned later, the Governor was attending the inauguration of a fellow Governor in a northern state.) The ordinary people of Mexico almost always refer to politicians and political leaders as thieves. Of one particular leader who is reputed to have stolen immense sums I heard one Mexican say: "We really loved that man. He was so nice, so charming. Oh, if he had only taken about 10 per cent!" The politicians themselves have a code under which they never call one another thieves. They will refer to each other, in public speeches, as whoremasters and pimps and fragments of excrement and *sodomitas,* but they would never even hint at stealing.

I asked Carlos if we couldn't drive through the residential section. "There is no residential section," he said. Veracruz is a city of more than 100,000, but it has no residential section. Carlos said it, so it must be true.

Back at the hotel I heard reports that the General had either checked in, or checked out — I'm not sure which, but I know I'm still burned about him, and would dearly love to give him an *abrazo* with an icepick in my hand.

Then later in the day I met him and shook him by the hand. Carlos and I walked into the lobby — and there he sat, in a splendid green uniform with golden decorations. Carlos has no hesitation about approaching anybody and in a moment he was deep in conversation with the General. Then he called me over and introduced me. The General said *mucho gusto* and I said *mucho gusto* and Carlos said, "The general wants me to tell you that he did not take your room. It is just that he phoned from Mexico City and said he would like to have a nice room. It is the hotel people that took your room." So I said, "Tell him to forget about it — I am quite contented." The General spoke some more to Carlos, who then said, "He says that when you are in Mexico City you can have anything you want." The

General quickly uttered another sentence. "He says," Carlos added, "except money."

We had dinner at the Hotel Diligencias, an experience Helen Hector and others assured us was unforgettable. The hotel occupies the entire block along the western side of the plaza, with *portales* running the length of the building. The *portal* is a feature of Mexican architecture, especially around a plaza, and is a sort of arcade. Sometimes *portales* are for shops, but here they are for eating and drinking and are, in effect, sidewalk cafés.

There is a peculiar division of customers in the Diligencia's *portales*. The southern half of the area provides tables for those being served from the dining room; the northern half is for those people being served from the bar. The saloon side is more interesting, perhaps because of the domino players. Behind the sidewalk café, inside the saloon proper, are about fifteen tables with hard plastic tops, all occupied by men who slap down their dominoes with great Latin force and fervor. Antietam must have sounded a good deal like this. Anywhere on the premises, in fact, it is clear that this is one of the noisiest pleasure spots on earth. We occupied a table near the middle of the *portales*. A few feet from us was the sidewalk, swarming with people. A couple of feet beyond the curb were the car tracks for the open-air trolley cars; then one lane for auto and bus and bicycle traffic; beyond that the lovely little Veracruz plaza swarming with a graceful variety of blackbirds called *tordos*, birds that utter loud, shrill cries that sound quite human. Almost constantly, the voice of a girl comes over the hotel's loudspeaker system — paging people, I suppose, though she may be delivering commercials. At the northern street intersection a traffic cop stands on a box and blows his whistle. The cathedral stands on the south side of the plaza and its bells clang and bong at frequent intervals; the trolley cars bang and clatter and screech and jangle (I'm told they were bought years ago, second hand, from the City of New York); the *tordos* yell in the Indian laurel trees; the domino players wham away like machine-gun fire; countless urchins cry their lottery tickets; the cop whistles and the girl talks on;

there are fifty loud conversations going on at the tables; there are the vendors, who come in a steady stream, selling everything from Chiclets to weird-looking animals brought in from the jungles (no vendors are allowed to approach the domino players and interfere with their thought-processes, and I judge that an offender would be beaten to death with chair rungs); and then there are the marimbas. More of them in a moment.

We sat and sipped and ate and shouted at each other above the noises, and Carlos said, "This is a very quiet and restful place, Veracruz." After which he began twitching and jerking idiotically and rolling his eyes back in his head.

One of the marimbas was brought up and placed on the sidewalk directly in front of us. The three hammer-men took their positions and the maestro came over and talked to Carlos, who gave him some pesos. "I asked them," Carlos told us, "to play two very nice songs. One is 'Noche Criolla' and the other is 'Peregrina.' Later I will tell you the stories that go with these songs, but you will not understand the stories because you are a Jonkee *puerco*." And so they played and we took enjoyment from "Noche Criolla" and "Peregrina" as well as a song called "Mujer" and another called "You Belong to My Heart."

There are usually half a dozen marimbas going on two sides of the plaza. They will give you two request numbers for five pesos, but if you discuss the matter with them they might make it four numbers. The characters who do the actual hammering look as if they came out of the slums. They wear faded breeches and ragged shirts, open down to the navel, and busted shoes or no shoes at all, and they play with frozen, expressionless faces — but they make those marimbas sing. When we kept requesting the same Mexican numbers over and over, they began glancing in our direction in a shy manner, and Carlos said, "Oh, how they love to play these songs! And how they love you, because all the other Gringos ask for 'Three O'Clock in the Morning' and 'Deedy I Doody' and all the other estúpido music of the Gringos." ('Deedy I Doody' sounded familiar, but I couldn't think of how it went.) Our maestro, the man who circulates and collects the money, looked like Wallace Beery in his prime, smoking a big fat cigar, wearing a Laredo hat and much better-dressed than his hammer-men.

Among the vendors who parade through the *portales* are many children who sell Chiclets. One boy was so tiny that he hadn't even learned to talk yet, and went from table to table saying, "Chic! Chic! Chic!" I asked Carlos why so many people sell Chiclets.

"It is the cheapest thing to buy for them," he said, "and the easiest thing to sell."

"Why is it the easiest thing to sell?"

"The Mexican people, all the Mexican people, love Chiclets."

"Why?"

"Well," he said, "because a Chiclet is of many usages. You start off in the morning by chewing it awhile. Then maybe you put it in a hole in the screen to keep out the flies and mosquitoes. Later on you take it from the screen and chew it a little and then you put it in your wallet till evening. And in the evening you give it to your girl friend to chew a little. Then you put it back in your wallet. At night if you cannot sleep, all you have to do is take it out and chew it a little and then you will fall asleep real quick. A Chiclet is a very good bargain."

Driving back to the hotel, Carlos told the story of "Peregrina," something about a romance between an America girl and a Mexican governor; and he told about the composer of "Noche Criolla." I took some notes and then asked him about the folklore surrounding his profession. There are about fifteen hundred licensed guides operating out of Mexico City. There used to be one female guide, an attractive Mexican girl, but the men guides finally convinced the licensing authority that she should not be in the business — first, because she would have trouble changing a tire on a mountain road or fixing a carburetor, and, second, because sooner or later she would get into a situation with some male tourist that would be immoral. There is something amusing about this fear that the girl would become involved mattresswise. In Mexico the double standard is really double. Several times I've heard groups of guides, sitting around resort hotels, telling of their conquests among the lady tourists. They have a language all their own. "What you got with you?" one guide will ask. "Two whales," says the other, meaning two fat ladies. Or, if he says he has an attractive girl in his party, he might add, "I'm taking care of her bags," which means that he is making love to her. Carlos said: "These are very rude expressions and I would never use them and I do not approve of the others using them."

"Of course," I said.

January 24

THIS morning Nelle took a chair on the balcony and set to work sewing up a rent in a dress. Eighty per cent of the guests at this hotel are Mexicans and they normally don't fraternize with the Gringos, perhaps because of language difficulties. But now the Mexican women, coming and going along the balcony, stopped to speak to Nelle and to exclaim over what she was doing. They had never suspected that an American woman could do the same thing that they do — they believe that American women spend most of their time reading sex novels, drinking cocktails, and spurning the advances of their husbands. What a silly thing to believe, considering that it's largely true.

Various writers have remarked on the Mexican's inability to say he doesn't know the answer to a tourist's question. To a Mexican everything is "just the other side of the little hill," even though it be a thousand miles away. So it was that we got acquainted today with a large part of downtown Veracruz in our search for Francisco Broissin Abdala, head of the city's Chamber of Commerce. We walked along the main street, Independencia, asking people for the Chamber of Commerce; asking pedestrians, bread-boys, lottery vendors, cops, storekeepers, and each of them gave us directions which were wrong and we spent more than an hour going back and forth and up and down, and then we found our man. Señor Broissin was a short, bald fellow, speaking no English, so Carlos served as interpreter and I spoke of the multitude of different noises to be heard at the Diligencias. "Yes," said Señor Broissin, "we are very proud of these noises; they are the highest quality noises anywhere in Mexico." I suggested that he might undertake the job of cataloguing all the noises. No, he said, it would be too much — it would be a book of more than five hundred pages, and still some of the noises would be left out.

"Speak to him about the bridge," I said to Carlos. This had reference to a bridge which crosses over the tracks near the railroad terminal. It is a concrete bridge of most curious design. When we drove over it the first time, Carlos said he had been trying to find out for five years why it is shaped as it is, and nobody has been able to give him a sensible answer. It is about three hundred feet long with concrete side walls which curve sharply inward, then upward, then outward. Now Señor Broissin explained the bridge. President Avila Camacho came to Veracruz once and wanted to visit San Juan de Ulua. At the railroad tracks his car was held up for thirty minutes, and he was so irritated that he ordered a bridge to be built over the tracks. (Oh, to be a *Presidente!*) The engineers who designed the bridge foresaw a problem — the presence of big oil tanks in the railroad yards below. These engineers knew that human beings love to flip cigarette butts over the sides of bridges. They said that a human being will cling stubbornly to a cigarette butt for a hundred miles in order to flip it over the side of a bridge. So they designed their bridge to be unflippable-cigarettebuttwise.

"Not long ago," said Señor Broissin, "a Yucatecan came to Veracruz to see the sights, and when he went home he told his friends: 'Those dumb *veracruzanos* have built themselves a crazy bridge and now they are looking around for some water to put under it.'"

Señor Broissin also said that *veracruzanos* are the happiest people in Mexico because they have never learned how to worry and they are amused by the simplest things. This was graphically demonstrated fifteen minutes later on Independencia. The management of a store had called in a couple of men to install a small showcase on the front of the building — a plain wooden box about two feet square with a glass front. When we arrived on the scene four men were positioning the box against the wall, one wielding a *metro,* or yardstick, and the other three gesticulating and shouting and making squaring-off gestures. At first a dozen kids gathered to watch the proceedings, then adults began stopping, some of them shouting advice, and minute by minute the crowd grew, spreading into the street and hindering traffic. I would say that they were all obtuse oafs, except that I was among them.

On the way back to the Mocambo I told Carlos that I had been reading about those fascinating characters of the past, the *arrieros,* the men who drove the mule trains through Mexico in the time before there were railroads or trucks. The *arrieros* were the freighters of Mexico, and while they were a hard-drinking, tough breed of men, they were highly respected because they were almost the only Mexicans who got around and knew every part of the country intimately.

Meaning it in a complimentary way, I said to Carlos, "I think the guides are the modern *arrieros,* because they are traveling constantly, and know all the intimate details of every town and village in the nation." Apparently an *arriero* wasn't as socially acceptable a creature as the books suggested. "So!" cried Carlos. "So, you Jonkee baster! I am now a muledriver, a pusher of burros! Get the hell out of my car and walk, you . . ." And he used Alvarado-type language to describe me. I quickly changed the subject and began talking about the legend of Indian beardlessness. I said I had a theory that many Mexicans wear mustaches because they think it indicates a preponderance of Spanish rather than Indian blood. "That is true only of the Mexican women," said Carlos. I then called attention to the fact that he, Carlos, had only a few whiskers, maybe four or five on each cheek, and Nelle said, "I should think it would be much easier to shave." "No," said Carlos, "it is more harder to shave. I forget where the whiskers are, and I have to look all around and find them."

Back at the hotel we were standing beneath a deck on which the General and his wife were taking photographs. I could see the General sighting through the view-finder, and suddenly he lowered the camera and said something in Spanish, and his wife answered, and Carlos interpreted. The General had said: "When we get back to Mexico City I am going to burn that skirt and that blouse. You have been wearing them for fifteen years and I am getting sick of them." To which his wife had replied: "You are nothing but a big bluffer. Shut up."

At lunch today Carlos, as is his custom, asked the waiter for a toothpick. When he had it in his mouth he looked at us and said, "There is much good vitamins in toothpicks."

We loafed around the terraces most of the afternoon. One group of tourists got into a big argument on the subject of religion. I stayed out of it. Nobody won.

The Mocambo is a hundred yards from the beach, yet the hotel has four swimming pools. This afternoon a buxom *mittelnorteameri-cano* lady in a bathing suit went to the hotel desk and inquired: "Which swimming pool has the thick water in it?" The question has been repeated all over the place, but nobody seems able to figure out what the lady had in mind.

We have become acquainted with a Mr. and Mrs. Stoteweller from Oklahoma. Mr. Stoteweller is the most hen-pecked man I've encountered in . . . well, in a year or two. He is thin, ascetic-looking, close to seventy, and a nice man. I first took special notice of him when, sitting with a group of tourists, someone spoke of Guadalajara. Mr. Stoteweller's head jerked up. "Please!" he said. "Please don't say that word! Let *me* say it. Guadalajara. Guadalajara. Guadalajara. God-a-mighty, that's purty!" It sounds silly, but that man's pleasures in life were so few that he got enjoyment out of speaking a lovely-sounding name.

Later, in the presence of his shrew, he said that they were going to Yucatán. "When we get there," he said, "I want to go on to Quintana Roo. I want to go even if I only make it to the border and put one foot over the line, so I can go home and say to all my friends, 'I have been to Quintana Roo.' "

Mrs. Stoteweller now spoke sharply: "You're insane. You're not going to do any such thing. Just put it out of your mind and try to act your age."

I feel sorry for Mr. Stoteweller — among other things he has to sneak away from his wife in order to take a drink at the bar. She is made in the classic mold of the virago abroad. She believes that she is constantly being cheated. She abuses the waiters from soup to dessert, and sends almost every dish back to the kitchen, announcing loudly that it is not fit for a dog to eat. It takes no practiced eye to determine that she is an egocentric, ignorant woman, wholly unsympathetic toward Mexico and the Mexicans. I abhor violence, yet I would love to see her publicly whipped. This afternoon when she was taking a nap her husband crept out to the bar for an odorless double vodka. He beckoned me over and told me that he had found out an interesting fact — that hotel employees have special names for beds. A double bed is a *cama matrimonial* while twin beds are *camas americanas*.

Late this afternoon we went to the home of the American consul, Joseph Schutz, for cocktails. The consulate is a small but handsome establishment a few feet from the Gulf of Mexico and the consul's house is immediately behind it. Mr. Schutz is a young man with a lovely French-born wife and a small son who speaks three languages. I wanted to know what it's like to be a consul in Mexico, especially in a city like Veracruz, where the lower classes are almost as primitive as the tribes of the deepest jungles. Did he encounter much anti-Gringo prejudice? Not much, he said; only on special occasions. Such as? And he told the story of Red-whiskers and George Washington's Birthday.

A few years ago some wild rumors began circulating among the poor people of Veracruz, rumors that Mexican babies were being kidnaped and sold to Gringo doctors for vivisection, and that other babies were being snatched off the streets by American engineers who found that their blood was excellent for binding the cement used in the construction of bridges. A Veracruz radio station broadcast a denial of these stories, but that only gave them greater circulation and by now the whole town was in an uproar.

Into this explosive situation came an innocent screwball — a beachcomber with no interest in beaches, a man from Texas with little money, an ancient Cadillac, shabby clothes, weighing three hundred pounds, wearing a big red beard, and owning a don't-give-a-damn attitude toward the world and its inhabitants. He rented a room in a cheap section of town and began acting eccentric. He ordered a quart of milk daily but never used it and let it stand around his room and turn sour until both the room and its occupant smelled like a herd of goats. His sole interest seemed to be the collecting of skeletal remains of animals and the back seat of his old car was filled with bones and skulls. Somehow he came into possession of a dead iguana, that giant lizard seen so often in this country. This one was about two and a half feet long and he wanted only the skeleton so he hung it on the radiator of his car to dry out. Now the whispering began among the poor people — here was the Gringo monster who was not only kidnaping their babies, but openly and wantonly displaying the corpses in public. Before long a crowd began collecting in front of the house where Red-whiskers lived, and then the stones began flying through the windows, and the cops came and got the Gringo out and took him to the police station. The police immediately summoned Consul Schutz, who had to pass through a crowd of more than a thousand muttering, threatening Mexicans to get into the station house. The prisoner was haughtily indifferent. "Nuts to these bastards," he said to Schutz. "Nuts to the bastards outside, and nuts to you, and nuts to everybody." (This man missed his calling — he would have made a capable novelist.) The crowd continued to swell. The Mayor arrived in a sound-truck and tried to disperse the people.

The Mayor was a brave man and got out of the truck and faced the mob, just as in the movies. A brickbat hit him in the chest and he had to take shelter. The cops were not altogether certain that Red-whiskers hadn't kidnaped some babies, so Consul Schutz simply asked them, "Are there any babies reported missing?" There were none.

All this happened on George Washington's Birthday, a day when it is customary for the American consul to entertain local dignitaries at cocktails. The party was in progress but Schutz couldn't get out of the police station for another hour. Then, when the mob began concentrating its attention on the old Cadillac, shattering its windows, Schutz managed to slip away and get to his party. The Mayor showed up briefly, complained of a pain in his chest, and went home. The next day Schutz got Red-whiskers out of jail and advised him to leave town. "Nuts to you," said Red-whiskers.

Two days later the police called and said the Gringo was in the sand dunes south of town, sending up smoke signals. Schutz drove out to the dunes and found Red-whiskers trying to cook his own meals over a campfire. The consul told him that he was going to get killed if he insisted on hanging around Veracruz. The man said he had no money for gasoline, and Schutz happily gave him twenty-five dollars. He never heard of Red-whiskers after that.

It all made me think that the job of American consul in Mexico might be fun, but I found out later that the work consists mainly of accumulating volumes of statistics concerning imports and exports and other such nonsense.

January 25

THIS is the day we chose to go to dirty-talkin' Alvarado. I was eager to see it, and to listen to its citizens even though I wouldn't be able to understand them; I have always kicked against the pricks (Acts, ix: 5) and admired eloquent cussers. I dispute those who say that cussing is a practice indulged in only by people who lack imagination. What about Mark Twain?

Before leaving the Mocambo this morning a new friend named Moby Dick (Carlos gave him that nickname and it stuck) told us we should try to locate a famous pilot in the neighborhood of Alvarado — a huge man with a Zapata mustache, a sombrero, two large pistols and a small airplane. Moby Dick said this man flies his plane on private missions, is inclined to frighten passengers by pretending to fall asleep at the controls, and spits contemptuously at bigger planes when they go past him, shouting that their pilots have improper relations with their mothers. (When we got to Alvarado we found that this man operates farther south, in the interior.)

Riding down the coast Carlos told a story which I hesitate to believe — which I know, in fact, to be a lie — about an American promoter who came to Veracruz, heard about Alvarado and its celebrated cussers, and figured out a way to capitalize on the town. He knew that Mexicans will celebrate any kind of an event, even getting a tooth pulled, by throwing a fiesta, so he organized an annual Cussing Fiesta in Alvarado (he had once promoted a hog-calling tournament in Mississippi). There were special dances in which native girls, in colorful costumes, acted out strings of cusswords. There were great fireworks displays in which oaths and obscenities were spelled out in flame. There was a huge floral sign at the entrance to the town saying, BIENVENIDOS YOU BASTARDS. A dozen new dirty songs were composed for the celebration and, as a grand finale, male and female citizens of the town cussed for the championship.

"I tell you," said Carlos, "I do not like Gringos because they are dumb, but this one put on the nicest fiesta we ever had in Mexico."

He also discussed The Awful Obscenity. This is an expression in widespread common usage throughout Mexico and can best be described as a horrifying insult to one's mother. It has five syllables (its English equivalent has only four) and the number five, in consequence, is a dangerous thing to toss around in Mexico. The Awful

Obscenity is uttered frequently on automobile horns. It is not uncommon in the cities to hear, first, five short blasts on a horn, then the screech of brakes, and two drivers leap from their cars and begin slugging each other. I asked Carlos to give us a demonstration. We were deep in the country, not even a *zopilote* in sight, but he glanced around to make certain no Mexicans were near, and then he gave the five taps on the horn.

Carlos is a fine cusser himself if the occasion demands it, and he doesn't lack imagination. He told me that as a writer I might be interested in the way the Alvarado newspaper handles its stories. As an example he quoted one such story: "The ------ fishing boat of the Martinez family, the dirty ------, came back to this -- --- port at noon yesterday with more ------ fish than the ignorant --- - ------ have caught in a ------ year."

Arriving in Alvarado we found it to be a sun-baked little town lying at the mouth of the Papaloapan River. We strolled along the main street, which appears to be one long avenue of pool parlors. I doubt if anywhere on earth there are as many pool tables concentrated in such a small area, and every one of them was in use. Carlos said the language of the pool players would roast meat. We strolled along the wharf nearby and a small boy came along with a fish he had caught. Carlos spoke to him in Spanish and he answered, according to Carlos, "Just look at this ------ fish that I caught with my own -- -- - ------ hands." Nelle now saw an opportunity to try out her rudimentary Spanish. She mixed English words with Spanish and said to the boy, "You . . . take . . . *pescado* . . . home . . ." She paused for several seconds, groping, and then finished the sentence, ". . . *tu madre?*" I flung up my hands and cried, "My God, don't say that! Don't use those words in this town!"

We bought a few trinkets in the market as souvenirs of the dirtiest-talking town on earth, and headed back for our hotel. On the way Carlos remembered another story. He said that once there was a convention of all the birds of Alvarado, and the big event of the convention was a flying contest.

"The yudge was an iggle," Carlos said. "A hock was the first flyer and went ziss, swiss, ziss, swiss. The yudge said pretty good but not good enough." Next was a canary, which sang "Three O'Clock in the Morning" while flying. Then a pigeon did a marvelous job, and the yudge said, That looks like the best. Among the spectators was a parrot. Suddenly he took off and astonished the crowd with his feats in the air. When he finally landed the yudge went up to him and said, "Señor, I believe you have won the —— prize." The parrot said, "I don't give a damn about that — I just want to get my hands on the —— — - —— who stuck a hot cigarette up my behind."

"So," said Carlos, "you see even the birds of Alvarado are the same as the people."

During our brief visit in Alvarado he told us that the birthplace of Agustin Lara, the man who wrote "Noche Criolla," could be reached by boat up the Papaloapan River, but I wasn't interested in making the trip.

January 26

AT BREAKFAST today Moby Dick said he had been to the fortress of San Juan de Ulua yesterday. I jumped Carlos about it, and he still insisted the place was off limits to tourists. We drove downtown, however, and out the causeway, and found no trouble gaining admission. There was a fat Mexican loafing around the entrance and he proved to be a guide; so, just to humiliate the cabrón Campo, I hired him. His name was Romero and he was remarkable because of his use of the word "Christ!" as a punctuation mark.

As we moved from dungeon to dungeon and from rampart to rampart, Romero talked a steady streak, but the information was not of the highest quality. Right at the beginning he turned to me and said, "I am once in your country, living in Flatbush Brooklyn. Christ!" A few minutes later he said, "And what do you suppose happen in 1814? Christ!" He didn't see fit to enlarge on the subject.

In the dungeons Romero had a tendency to concentrate on the matter of sanitation, or the lack of it. Dungeon Number 1 and Dungeon Number 2 were the only dungeons with latrines, he said, and he insisted on showing them to us. He took us into the torture chambers and then into the dungeons called Heaven, Hell and Purgatory. Along about here Nelle remarked that human beings can be pretty horrible in their treatment of one another.

"Ah," said Romero, "these was not people, these was only politicians. All politicians deserves worse than this. Christ!"

By now I decided that his use of the word after almost every sentence was a sort of concession to us as Gringos — in his Brooklyn days he had probably heard the expression a number of times; now he had decided that its use here would affect us sentimentally, reminding us of home, and we'd give him a big tip. I asked him if by any chance he came from Alvarado and he said he didn't, but that his mother was a native of that town.

In one of the dank corridors he stopped to tell us about a General Barragran, who had something important to do with the fortress at one time.

"The General," said Romero, "wrote his will, and willied his eyes to his home town, his heart to the city of Guadalajara and his gots to a convent in Mexico City."

"His what?" asked Nelle.

"His gots," said Romero.

"Why did he willy his gots to a convent?" I wanted to know.

"It is a way," Romero said, "to show his faith in the Church. Oh yes. He willied his tongue, the most important part, he willied it to the chapel here in the fort."

Nelle asked, "Is it here now?"

"Is what here now?"

"His tongue?"

"Was here for many years," said Romero, "and then . . . Say, listen, what do you suppose happen in 1814? Christ!"

"But the tongue . . ." Nelle insisted.

"Somebody es-stole it," he said. "It was never found, the tongue. Christ!"

And so we took our departure, never having found out what it was that happened in 1814, and not caring very much.

January 27

UNTIL you have been to a town and looked at it with your own eyes, it is never much more than a dot on a map, plus what you'd heard about it and read about it, and it never adds up to the image you have in your mind. It usually falls far short of expectations, far short of the mental image. But not Veracruz. It is much the same as I visualized it, except that it is considerably better. We had to leave it this morning, and I regretted the departure and resolved that, if they hold off dropping the H-bombs for a few more years, I'll return.

We headed back toward Puebla through flat, rich country where the men ride horses instead of burros. We stopped in one town, hoping to call on the mayor. Someone in Veracruz told us that this particular mayor had the ugliest ears in all of Mexico, perhaps in all the world. I remember that I asked for a rough description of these ears, but my informant said they beggared description, that I'd have to see them for myself. We arrived in the town this afternoon and asked around about the mayor, but learned he had gone to Fortin. I was sort of glad, because it would have been a difficult kind of interview; I couldn't just say to the man that I wanted merely to look at his ears awhile.

We lunched in the Town of the Ugly-Eared Mayor and Carlos said the menu included fried grasshoppers and that if I were a competent reporter I'd eat a few of them. I told him I was not a competent reporter.

We paused in the city of Córdoba and made some inquiries concerning certain leaders of the Confederacy during the War Between the States, but nobody understood what we were talking about, so

we gave it up. It is a fact, however, that quite a few Confederate generals and other important Southerners fled to Mexico at the conclusion of the war rather than knuckle under to the hated Yankees. One of these, General Joseph Shelby, led five hundred Missouri cavalrymen across the Rio Grande at Eagle Pass on July 4th, 1865. They buried their battle flag in the river and Shelby ripped the plume from his hat and cast it into the river. Generals were real hammy in those days, as they are today. Shelby went on to Córdoba, where he was joined by General Sterling Price, General Stephens of Lee's staff, General Lyons of Kentucky, General McCausland of Virginia and Governor Allen of Louisiana. These men went into the freighting business in Mexico, but that's all I know about them. Another bunch of hardshell Confederates settled up around Tampico and Tuxpan.

We stopped overnight at Fortin and swam in the most famous pool in the world, the one in which the water is covered with floating gardenias. No sign of the Ugly-Eared Mayor.

January 28

IN PUEBLA we discussed taking a few extra days for a trip down through Chiapas to the Guatemalan border. By a strange coincidence I have been reading a book by Carleton Beals and today I came to a passage about a certain Don José Avellaneda, who got out of favor politically and fled for his life toward Guatemala. Beals wrote:

> A pleasant Dantesque region! No longer in any immediate danger from the federals, but the tropics themselves lowered deadly menace. . . . Mosquitoes might bring malaria, even yellow fever. The chiclero fly might deposit its larvae in the nasal membrane, whereupon nose and cheek would rot away. Other insects pierced near the temple, devouring the optic nerve; others in the hip or beneath the toenails. If you put your hand on some inno-

cent tree, it might come away with a viscous substance that shriveled the skin. The brackish water reeked typhoid. Deadly snakes lay among the leaves. There were wild animals, too.

I read that and got up and went immediately to Carlos's room and dug him out of his siesta.

"Carlos," I said, "I've always been a sort of town boy. I like a town. Never cared much for the open country. The good material for a writer is in the towns. Why don't we stay pretty close to the towns? By pretty close, I mean right *in* the towns. And I mean fairly big towns. Let's head for Mexico City."

To which he replied: "What you are, you are chickens."

A bartender at the hotel here told us a story about a Gringo who drank two bottles of beer. The beer was two and a half pesos per bottle and after a while the bartender, under the impression that the tourist wanted to pay the check, went up to him and said, "*Cinco.*" The Gringo responded, "Yer welcome."

January 29

WE DROVE over to Cholula today to have a look at all those churches. There are supposed to be three hundred and sixty-five of them and some of the books use that figure, but a few years ago some energetic researcher decided to count them, and it came out that there are really only about two hundred.

This is the place where the Spaniards really got tired blood. They had resolved that every time they came upon a heathen temple they would rip it down and erect a True Church over its ruins. So one day they arrived in Cholula, and I imagine they got real depressed over what they saw. But they sighed and rolled up their sleeves and went to work and did what they had resolved to do, and they even erected a large basilica on top of the Pyramid of Quetzalcoatl, one of the biggest pyramids in the country. After they had finished this job and built all those other churches, the Spaniards wiped off the sweat and then looked around and decided they didn't like the town, so they left for Puebla and today if you want to live in Cholula, very likely they'll let you have a church of your very own. And one to sleep in.

Cholula is the town where the Indian maiden (maiden!) Malinche performed another one of her feats of duplicity against her own people. Cortez and his troops and Malinche, who was his mistress, had marched down from Tlaxcala. Cholula was a big town then and Montezuma's agents had persuaded the citizens that they should, on signal, rise up and massacre the Spaniards. But Malinche found out about the plot and tipped off Cortez. He had his thousands of Tlax-calans hidden in the woods nearby, so now he called them in and *he* did the slaughtering. It is no wonder that the very name Malinche was hated by the Indians for centuries. Today that hate no longer exists, for it has been found out that duplicity is so fundamental to human life that it has become almost noble, as in the advertising industry. Now there's a beautiful mountain named for Malinche, and the historians are digging for the details of her story on the theory that she was one of the most interesting and influential women ever to live on our continent.

If Malinche was the most interesting woman, then Quetzalcoatl was the most interesting god, and Cholula was his town. He may have started out as a real person, a priest of the Toltecs, but then he became a god and ruled the Toltecs for more than a hundred years. One day another priest-god, jealous of Quetzalcoatl, told him to look at himself in a mirror. Quetzalcoatl was shocked at seeing how many wrinkles he had and how old he looked; his enemy then told him that if he drank a whole jug of pulque, it would make him look young again. It didn't make him look young, but haggard, and while he was drunk he was beguiled into the hay with his two sisters. When he sobered up he was so ashamed that he went a-journeying and spent the next twenty years in Cholula.

Quetzalcoatl wore white robes, had white skin and blond hair and beard. Orozco has painted him as looking like Charles Laughton in a long white nightshirt and with wild blond hair and whiskers. He did a lot of important things in his time. He showed the Indians how to make jewelry, although most tourists give this credit to William Spratling. He was against sacrificing human beings or any other living creatures. He once turned himself into an ant and crawled inside an anthill and stole a grain of corn and presented it to mankind. He then showed the Indians how to grow corn with ears so big that a man couldn't reach around them with both arms. If that sounds impressive, it's nothing alongside his feat in inventing the weaving of fabrics, because he taught people how to grow cotton that came out of the ground already dyed in half a dozen brilliant colors. What a boon it would have been to our own South if that method of cotton growing had been preserved! Says one plantation owner to another: "Whut yall a-growin' this yeah, Amos?" And the reply: "Ah thank ah'm gonna put in some reds and some yellers and mebby a few hunned acres uh pupples."

Quetzalcoatl eventually left Cholula and journeyed to Yucatán, where he was known as Kukulcan and where he built a lot of magnificent ruins; at Chichén Itzá there is a pyramid-temple a hundred feet high dédicated to him. Finally he left Yucatán and went up the coast to Veracruz, and made a boat out of snakeskins and sailed out to sea, promising that he'd be back. He hasn't been back. Snakeskins are no good for making boats.

We spent half an hour exploring the tunnels that run all through the base of Quetzalcoatl's pyramid at Cholula — a very dull and damp and depressing experience. If the pre-Conquest Indians did their worshiping in such places, even worshiping such a great fellow as Quetzalcoatl, they must have been approximately as intelligent as our own snake-handlers. And if the Indians really believed that Quetzalcoatl did all those things about corn and colored cotton, it is easy to understand the personalized relationship that exists today between many Mexicans and their saints.

Madame Calderón told of a saint's statue in a Veracruz church and how the young ladies of that city, when desirous of getting a husband, would enter the church and bombard the statue with stones, and if they made a sufficient number of direct hits, they would get their mates. A similar belief is connected with Saint Anthony of Padua's Day, June 13. On this day if a girl begs thirteen centavos from thirteen men and burns thirteen candles, she'll get a husband. A few years ago a twenty-four-year-old girl complained that she had been trying this system over and over. "Saint Anthony pays no attention to me," she said. "I won't go to him any more. If he wants to help, he knows where I live."

In various parts of Mexico the people are grateful to their saints when things are going well, but they get real angry when things turn bad. As late as 1944 some villagers near Cuernavaca were praying to their saints for rain. When no rain came, they undressed the statues (Mexican religious statues often wear wigs and real clothing) and put them out in the fields to swelter in the hot sun, saying, "Now, see how you like it!" When there was too much rain, these same people carried the statues out and threw them into a swollen creek, saying, "So you like much water; well then, have some!"

The Mexicans, especially in smaller villages, often talk to their saints in the same language and the same tones as they use on each other. The Virgin of the Conquest, *La Conquistadora*, has charge of rain in some areas. Sometimes she supplies it so copiously that it ruins the crops, whereupon she is marched about the countryside and roundly scolded: *"Mira lo que tu hijo ha hecho!"* (Look what your son has done!) There is another story of a man who stole some money from a church. Later he returned and knelt before a statue of the Virgin and began talking to her. A priest was in the choir loft, out of sight, and heard the thief apologize for taking the money and promise that he would repay it as soon as he could get it. The priest called out in sonorous tones, "You are going to repay it now!" Whereupon the thief glanced upward and said, "Shut up. I am talking to your mother!"

In Mexico there are many nonreligious people, but they all say the same thing — religion is a good thing for the masses, it keeps them subdued, keeps them in submission, keeps their passions in check. I've heard the same thing said many times in the United States. The Greek historian Polybius, who wrote before the time of Christ, said that ". . . as every multitude is fickle, full of lawless desires, unreasoned passion, and violent anger, it must be held in by invisible terrors and religious pageantry." It certainly works in Mexico, as it does everywhere else. The history of this country is as bloody as that of any other; the Mexican story is a story of cynical selfishness, of cruelty and torture beyond description, of incredible villainy in high places and low, of graft and corruption on a Gargantuan scale. I might add that I have never been cheated so steadily in all my life as during the few weeks I spent in Italy.

3

Peregrina and Don Quixote

SO WE drove on to Mexico City, and along the highway talked again of Mexico being the Land of Tote. Everywhere we've been in the Republic the picture is the same — tote, tote, tote. Everybody totes something. No provincial Mexican ever goes anywhere without carrying something, and in the family groups, seen along the streets and highways, everybody totes, down to the smallest walking child. Carlos has learned the word and loves to cry out, "Tote!" when he sees someone toting.

January 30

BEFORE we left on our trip to Veracruz I was trying to read a Mexican newspaper and I came to a feature article and was able to puzzle out its subject matter, which was: Do animals have a sense of humor? The topic interested me, and I decided to have a translation made. In the Hotel Reforma there is a pleasant-mannered young employee named Luis who often speaks to me about his efforts to learn English. So I gave him the newspaper article and my English-Spanish dictionary and asked him if he could do a *traducción* for me. He accepted the assignment with great enthusiasm and now, on our return, I found the translation waiting for me. Here it is, exactly as Luis typed it:

Have Animals the Ability to Laugh?

Have animals sense of the humor? Are they capable of appreciating situations amusing? Do they have the ability of entertaining others? The specialists in psychology animal never able have been to agree, but is evident that yes exists a sense of humor among the animals or, at least, that is what say the persons who have passed many years studying them.

For example, the coyote always has been known for the jokes it spends and all the world knows its tricks, such as that of not letting sleep the travelers lonely with its howls.

One time I saw how a coyote persecuted with its cries a bull furious. When the horned one started to charge it, the coyote begin to run, seated itself at certain distance from the bull with a moué that resembled much a smile and recommenced its serenade.

The guard of a park zoo told to me of a young orangutan that was a comedian innate; when he saw that the crowd him observed front of his cage, he put like a hat his eating dish and started walking crazy like asking an applause.

The kittens of mountain lion which I had in my house had all the habit of to jump over the legs of the ladies when they were most unaware, throwing at the time a howl peculiar to underline the effect of their unexpected attack. After, they walked with the tail raised, giving themselves airs of great importance and apparently very satisfied of the scare that they had given to the ladies.

Other example, more known, of the curious humor of the cats is the instinct that makes them play with the mouse before of to kill it and eat it. This, which is a torture for the mouse, undoubtedly is a diversion for the cat; the same diversion that have many boys to frighten and even hit their companions more small.

The observers specialized in the treatment with the animals say that undoubtedly the puppies of dog laugh when they play among themselves and these games go accompanied of an expression in the eyes, very similar to the sense of the humor among the humans.

The bears manifest their contentment with a movement special of the muscles that are under the skin, in the way that presents waves progressive and the hair of the animal seems that it raises alternately in all its body.

The psychologists who search the origin of the sense of the humor among the humans, find this reaction very interesting because those wrinkles are similar to those which form themselves in the face of the people when they laugh.

Other curious example of the astuteness of the coyote is that which to me told a rancher friend mine. It treats of a female coyote which had now many days of to steal his chickens, for which the rancher decided to go out to give it to hunt, carrying with him his dog. After two days, he saw go out running the coyote, followed from close by the dog, and put itself in a place rocky; my friend had the shotgun ready for to go in aid of the dog but soon it he heard throw injured complaints and when he took himself near to see that which to the dog happened, the dog he found standing in an anthill, to which he had been led by the perfidious coyote who, meantime, have time to escape.

January 31

THIS afternoon I dug out an accumulation of notes about Cortez and took them downstairs to a table in the Bar Jardín and started going through them, trying to get them organized.

Along came a gorgeous, heavy-chested blonde, who could have been either a Hollywood actress or a prostitute, and a sleek and dapper Mexican escort. They took a table behind me and for the next half hour I only pretended I was studying my notes.

I wrote down several things that I heard them say. One came from the lips of the blonde: "I'm tired of hearing it referred to as 'making love.' Most of the time there isn't any love connected with it."

A bit later I heard the man say: "To hell with San Francisco. All the men in San Francisco wears vests."

And another delicious bit from the blonde: "Sure I'm oversexed, but I don't call it that — I call it just right."

There were other sapient remarks but I've forgotten them and I didn't accomplish much with Cortez. I did, however, scratch out a few paragraphs about the great man.

After the conquest of Tenochtitlán, Cortez imported from Europe the olive, the grape, the orange, the almond, the hog, the chicken, the cow, the sheep, the burro, sugar cane and silk. At the same time he brought smallpox, whooping cough, diphtheria, syphilis, and fear of the Evil Eye.

Cortez has long been regarded as one of the great heroic figures of history and part of this reputation is based on the fact that he burned his ships so there could be no turning back. Today's historians say that Cortez came to Mexico against orders, in ships which were actually stolen; he was therefore a criminal, and the death penalty awaited him if he ever returned to Cuba. He *couldn't* go back, he had to stay in Mexico, and that's why he burned his ships.

Cortez is often described as an extremely devout man, which leads me to believe that in those days they didn't have a sin called adultery; at least Cortez hadn't been told about it. He was a sinner of the first magnitude, an adulterer, a barbaric torturer, a sneak, a liar, a thief, a brute, a murderer — but his apologists justify all this by saying, "We must remember the time and the place — he was a part of his time." I don't recall their ever saying, when they come to describe the barbaric practices of the Aztecs, that Montezuma was a part of his time. Oh, well, in the old days things were different and in some respects better. Sir Lancelot has been held up to us as a model of chivalry, bravery and fidelity. Yet he adulterated the wife of his friend, King Arthur, right under Arthur's nose. God knows what he did when he was out on the road searching for the Holy Grail.

Max Miller tells about a book published long ago, in 1856, by Robert A. Wilson, who was an Indian authority, an engineer, and a judge in California. Wilson went to Mexico as a tourist and stayed to conduct certain investigations, for which he was qualified both as engineer and as an authority on Indians.

"Spanish historians," Wilson wrote, "and all early Spanish writers upon New Spain, except the two brigands, Cortez and Díaz, were priests. With them truth was not an essential part of history. By the law of all countries, the Conquistadors had outlawed themselves by levying unlicensed war; but as they bore a painting of the Virgin Mary on one of their standards and the cross on the other, it would be impiety to place their conduct in its true light."

Thus it was, says Wilson, that they lied like diplomats in their written reports, describing cities that never were and civilizations that never could have been. He argued that the Aztecs were a small community of Indians, much like the North American plains and mountain tribes, living primitively in huts and getting their livelihood by hunting and fishing.

I have sprung Wilson and his theories on a lot of different people in Mexico but thus far I've found nobody willing to accept him.

February 1

MR. STOTEWELLER, the henpecked husband we met in Veracruz, phoned today and said they were at the Hotel Bamer and asked us to come by for a drink. When we got to their suite Mrs. Stoteweller took Nelle into the bedroom to show her some trinkets while her husband and I stayed in the living room. He told me in a low tone that he was quite happy — that his wife was not speaking to him.

They had been out to the pyramids that morning and their guide had told them about the Aztec god, Mejitli, who was born of a holy virgin. "Down here," said Mr. Stoteweller, "they always call a virgin a burgeon." The guide said that Mejitli was born with a shield in his left hand, an arrow in his right, a plume of long green feathers on his head, his face painted blue, and his left leg adorned with feathers. At this point Mr. Stoteweller had made what he thought was a passable joke. "When I get back to Oklahoma," he had said, "I'm going to tell all the young married ladies about this Mejitli. I'm going to tell them that I don't want to hear any more complaints out of them about how painful it is to have a baby."

His wife withered him with a few well-chosen words, and then began giving him the silent treatment. He told me that he had been unable to fulfill his ambition to set foot in Quintana Roo — she wouldn't permit it. He said she was also mad at him because of the fun he had deliberately misusing Spanish words. For example, he would say, "Well, I guess I'll go upstairs and take a hacienda." Or, "Look at that beautiful siesta over yonder." I thought it was very bad grace on the part of Mrs. Stoteweller to object to her husband's Spanish. I had already noted her difficulties with the language; she spoke of Cuernavaca as "Kerna-vacka" and she called Oaxaca "Oh-axe-acka."

Mr. Stoteweller revealed that during their travels he was reading Prescott's Conquest of Mexico. He got out his copy and opened it to a marked page and showed me an Aztec word: AMATLACUILOLITQUIT-CATLAXTLAHUITLI. It means, "the reward given to a messenger who bears a hieroglyphical map conveying intelligence."

"I've got that word all written out on a slip of paper in my wallet," said Mr. Stoteweller. "I hope someday I'll get to use it, that a messenger will walk up to me with a hieroglyphical map conveying intelligence. I want to be ready for him."

A bit later we were standing at the window, looking down into the

Alameda, when Mr. Stoteweller suddenly pointed at something.

"Look!" he exclaimed. "Look at that statue down there, right next to the sidewalk. As sure as I live and breathe, it's a statue of a woman givin' a man an enema."

"Charles!" came an angry shout from behind us, for the virago had come into the room. She was in a fat fury, glaring at him, and now she said, "I'll never travel with you again as long as I live." He didn't respond as I would have responded. We decided we had an engagement elsewhere and left, feeling a great sympathy for Charles Stoteweller of Oklahoma.

February 3

YESTERDAY some words Carlos had spoken in Veracruz came back to me — words concerning the song "Peregrina" and a girl named Alma Reed. Now I remembered that I had read a brief account of Alma Reed's story in Erna Fergusson's book, *Mexico Revisited*. I went downstairs to Maxine Smith's office and she had the book, and I reread the bit about Peregrina.

"She's right here in Mexico City," Maxine said. "She writes a big piece in the *News* every Sunday — you must have been reading her things without connecting her name with the song."

I found it in the phone book: REED, ALMA M., ELBA 31. I called her and she said she would be happy to see us late this afternoon.

We walked out the Paseo from the hotel until we came to Elba, in that area where all the cross streets are named for famous rivers, and turned left and walked a block and a half to No. 31.

I have interviewed hundreds of individuals, many of them of great prominence, but I don't think I was ever so tensed up as I was standing at the door of Alma Reed's apartment. If there ever was a living legend, she is it. No . . . a legend is a fiction, and Alma Reed's story, the story of Peregrina, is true. It is history, and I intend to write at some length about it because it is not known in the United

States, even though it is one of the great romantic tragedies of our continent.

Her apartment is in a row of buildings with stores on the ground floor. We were admitted by a Mexican girl who escorted us to the far end of a darkened room, and in a few moments Alma Reed joined us. I have been going around the last few days gathering information about her and about her history, so I was not surprised to find her dressed in a brocaded costume, the skirts almost sweeping the floor. Several times in our long conversation I tried to trap her into revealing her age, but she was onto me, and I never found it out. She retains strong traces of the beauty for which she was famous; the "clear and divine" eyes of the song are a wonderful blue and her skin is unblemished. Much of the time, when she is talking, especially if she is talking about Felipe Carrillo, she closes her eyes for long periods.

After she had told her story and answered many questions, she showed us over the house and got out photographs of herself, taken when she first came to Mexico, and a big photograph of Felipe, and a lot of souvenirs of Orozco.

Her story begins in San Francisco in 1921 when she was on the staff of the *Call*. She was a tall, brown-haired girl — a beautiful girl in a city of beautiful girls. She had been educated in a convent, and she had been married briefly to an industrialist who had become hopelessly ill soon after the wedding with the consequence that the marriage was annulled.

The dominant person in Alma's life was her father, a man of strong liberal tendencies, a businessman and a scholar, who believed in labor unions, in woman's suffrage and in full racial equality. Much of this liberalism was transmitted to Alma. On the *Call* she conducted a column under the byline of "Mrs. Goodfellow." The aim of the column was to help people who were in trouble.

Alma knew nothing whatever about Mexico. Her father spoke Spanish and she had picked up a little of the language from him. As Mrs. Goodfellow she soon found out that there were many Mexicans in California and that most of them were destitute. As a social worker of sorts, she became associated with a group that was interested in prison reform. She visited San Quentin and became acquainted with Warden Johnston. Her chief concern was for the men in the death cells and she got permission to visit them, write letters for them, or just talk to them.

Then she found out about Simón Ruiz. He was a sixteen-year-old Mexican boy from Sonora, whose father had been killed in the Revolution. He had come to California and found work as a carpenter's helper at Bakersfield. He was a quiet, hard-working boy and he was sending most of his wages home to his mother. He was scarcely aware of the fact that Mexicans were regarded by most Californians as lower than beasts of the field, and that the town he had chosen, Bakersfield, was a center of Ku Klux Klan activity. One day Simón's foreman called the boy a name, an argument developed, and Simón knocked the man down. His head struck some lumber and three weeks later he died. The boy was charged with murder and put on trial with a court-appointed lawyer who apparently had little use for Mexicans himself. The boy was swiftly convicted and sentenced to hang — but nobody bothered to translate the judges' words for him, and he was hauled off to San Quentin without any knowledge of the doom that awaited him there.

Alma Reed's anger flared when she heard that Simón Ruiz was to be hanged in a few days. She went to a prison guard who was usually assigned to the execution rituals and from him she got the procedure, grisly step by grisly step. She began writing her story on the ferryboat that carried her back to San Francisco, and it was spread over the front page of all editions of the *Call*. People began telephoning and telegraphing the Governor in Sacramento, demanding a stay of execution, and he granted it. Altogether there were four reprieves as Alma continued her crusade.

She was finally told that she could not save the life of Simón Ruiz unless she got the law changed, the law which provided hanging for any person fourteen or over. So she went to Sacramento and got a bill introduced changing the hanging age from fourteen to eighteen. After a long fight the bill squeaked through and Simón Ruiz was saved.

Alma Reed immediately became a shining heroine to the Mexicans of California. More importantly, she became a shining heroine in Mexico itself. Relations between that country and the United States were not good at the time — the Mexicans despised the Gringos almost as much as the Gringos despised the greasers. But here was something — a beautiful Gringa, battling furiously and successfully to save the life of a lowly Mexican boy. The Mexican press whooped it up for Alma, and then she received an invitation from President and Señora Obregón, asking that she come to Mexico as their guest, assuring her that all Mexico was at her feet.

She decided to accept. Her mother, in the manner of mothers, said, "You'll be murdered in your bed." Her father, who had traveled in Mexico, agreed to her trip with some reluctance.

She traveled by train with a small dog for companion. Her first taste of Mexico came at Ciudad Juárez, across from El Paso. She looked at the dirt streets lined with saloons and populated by people who populate saloons. She remembers glancing back apprehensively at the American flag on top of an El Paso hotel on the other side of the river. She thought of turning back, and she almost did. But in the end she stayed with the train and rode south toward Mexico City.

In the station at Aguascalientes she was fascinated by a group of *mariachi* minstrels who were singing a refrain, "Alma de mi alma." They were singing "Soul of my soul," but she thought they were serenading her and she became so excited that she began buying handfuls of opals from the vendors on the platform.

At the station in Mexico City a delegation of important Mexicans met her, along with a crowd of cheering people. She was swept into a large open touring car and paraded to the Hotel Regis in the heart of town. She was escorted to a suite of rooms jammed with floral pieces, and she fell into a fit of girlish giggling when she found her bathtub filled with bird cages — a bird in a cage is considered in Mexico an even more sentimental gift than flowers.

The following three months were months of almost melodramatic excitement. Mexican generals besieged her, sending more flowers and more bird cages, and some offered out of the goodness of their hearts to take her on long trips in their private railroad cars (every Mexican general had a private railroad car, if not a private railroad, in those times). The newspapers wrote about her almost every day; President and Señora Obregón entertained her at Chapultepec. The young bloods of the capital, handsome sons of the rich, took her to balls and garden parties.

At this time she met, almost casually, the artist Orozco, whose career was to be so greatly influenced by this Gringa *periodista*. She also heard talk about a man who was Governor of Yucatán, but she paid little heed to it.

After her return to San Francisco Alma did an interview with Adolph Ochs of the *New York Times* and made such a favorable impression on him that he engaged her as a *Times* correspondent. Later she heard that the Carnegie Foundation was sending an expedition to Yucatán to explore and excavate the Mayan ruins, and she asked Mr. Ochs if she might go on the trip, explaining that archaeology had long been one of her hobbies. She was ordered to New York and in mid-February sailed with the Carnegie expedition.

On board the ship she met a Yucatecan landowner who told her of Governor Carrillo Puerto, describing him as a horrible man, "a crimson dragon with green eyes," and urging that she attack him in her dispatches back to the *Times*.

Instead, she fell in love with him, and he fell in love with her.

As a race the Yucatecans are small in stature but Felipe Carrillo was a big, athletic man, over six feet tall. He had devoted his entire life to the task of freeing his people from the bondage imposed upon them by the Spaniards. Not so long ago the whole of Yucatán had been owned by less than a hundred Spanish families and these genteel *hacendados* were possibly the most savagely cruel slave-masters in history. The Mayas had reached the point of doglike servility where a laborer would crawl to kiss the hand of the overseer who had just lashed him to a bloody pulp. The *hacendados* had an aphorism: "The Indians cannot hear except through their backs."

Almost singlehandedly Felipe Carrillo changed all that. The Revolution, which had swept the rest of Mexico during the last ten years — the years of Zapata and Villa and Carranza and Obregón — had finally penetrated to the Yucatán peninsula. It had taken longer to reach Yucatán because of the State's unique geographical position and because of the iron-fisted control of the *hacendados.* Yucatán was cut off from communication with the rest of Mexico by land because of jungles and impassable swamps. The trip was usually made by rail to Veracruz, thence by ship to Progreso — the port of Yucatán. Even then the ships were not able to dock at Progreso, and passengers and freight had to be transferred to smaller craft.

Obregón's soldiers had given Yucatán its first honest election since the Conquest and Felipe Carrillo was chosen Governor, 60,000 votes to 4000. He embarked at once on a vigorous program of social reform. He built schools and more schools and still more schools; he seized the uncultivated land from the huge haciendas and distributed it among the Indians; he built highways from the villages to the cities, so that farmers might get their produce to market quickly, and he built more highways to the Mayan ruins so that his people could visit them and understand their great heritage. The Leagues of Resistance, which he had organized before he became Governor and which were a sort of underground movement against the *hacendados,* were turned into night schools for adults. He renewed the native arts and crafts, which had been suppressed by the Spanish overlords. He built a model prison, embodying ideas so advanced that New York State sent a commission to study them. He liberalized the laws governing marriage and divorce, he gave women positions in government, he legalized birth control and established the first birth control clinics in this hemisphere.

With all these things, and many others of commensurate importance, he became the greatest hero Yucatán had ever known — he was all but worshiped as a god. He had a strange personal magnetism which drew people to him and caused them to fall silent in his presence; yet he remained a big, amiable, boyishly shy man on most occasions, and he refused to live or work in the splendid Governor's palace, preferring a plain desk in one of the League offices in Mérida.

Alma Reed met this "monster" soon after her arrival in Mérida with the Carnegie group, and almost immediately he asked her to go with him to Kanasín, a model village which he had built; they spent hours together in Kanasín, during which he told her of his many plans for the future of his people. When she got back to Mérida, Alma wrote in her diary: "He is a miracle of goodness and of beauty."

After three weeks in Yucatán, devoted chiefly to inspection of the ruins at Chichén Itzá and Uxmal, she returned to New York with the first real journalistic report on those ruins as well as on the enlightened government of Felipe Carrillo. There were daily letters and telegrams from Felipe, and she fell victim to a strange premonitory feeling that she should forget about this man. She went to Adolph Ochs and asked him to send her to Turkey to interview Kemal Pasha, but he told her she still had work to do in Mexico.

This time her ship paused at Progreso but she did not disembark. Felipe sent out a launch decorated with floral arches and salutations spelled out in floral designs and carrying his secretary, who urged her to come to Mérida. She refused and went on to Mexico City, and Felipe was right at her heels. Within a few days they had become engaged to marry. The wedding was set for January 14, in San Francisco. There followed an idyllic month in the Mexican capital, sightseeing and dancing and dinner parties with all the famous names of the country, for Felipe Carrillo was by now a national hero, possibly the most popular man in Mexico.

Felipe returned to Mérida after announcing an All-American Press Congress to be held in that city. Alma traveled with other correspondents, boarding the battleship *Jalisco* at Veracruz. The ship sailed into a raging storm during which Alma, in her cabin, heard for the first time the sad and lovely strains of the song, "Peregrina."

Felipe had gone to Yucatán's foremost poet, Luis Rosada Vega, for the lyrics, and then to the State's most famous composer, Ricardo Palmerin, for the music. Today the song is sung and played from Sonora to Quintana Roo; it has spread to other Latin-American countries where the people are familiar with it. Everybody in Mexico knows it, for it is not only a love song; it is the song of Yucatán and its sadness. It contains, according to one critic, "a curious sense of impending nameless sorrow . . . all the tragedy, the haunting mystery of Palmerin's native Yucatecan earth — the distilled cry of oppressed peoples through the centuries."

Maxine Smith translated the lyrics for me as follows:

PEREGRINA

Wanderer of the clear and divine eyes,
And cheeks aflame with the redness of the sky,
Little woman of the red lips,
And hair radiant as the sun,
Traveler who left your own scenes —
The fir trees and the snow, the virginal snow —
And came to find refuge in the palm groves,
Under the sky of my land,
My tropical land,
The little singing birds of my fields,
Offer their voices in singing to you —
And they look at you,
And the flowers of perfumed nectars
Caress you and kiss you on lips and temples.
When you leave my palm groves and my land,
Traveler of the enchanting face,
Don't forget — don't forget — my land,
Don't forget — don't forget — my love.

The poet, Rosada Vega, was once asked about the circumstances under which he wrote the words. "I just put down what Felipe said," he replied.

And now on the Mexican battleship Alma heard the song for the first time; Felipe had secretly sent his favorite quartet to Veracruz and had them smuggled aboard the ship, under order to play and sing "Peregina" outside her cabin at a certain hour. And they did it, even though the waves almost washed them overboard.

There were parties and balls and fiestas in Mérida, for Felipe was not only host to the Press Congress — he was celebrating his engagement. The other journalists departed, but Alma stayed on for a month. Felipe had acquired a lovely but modest home which he called Villa Aurora. He had installed furniture and Alma remembers the difficulty she had suppressing screams of laughter when she saw the special room he had fixed up for her exclusive use in taking care of her hair.

There was a ceremony at Chichén Itzá in which Alma was given a Mayan identity, *Pixan-halal. Pixan* means *alma,* or soul, and *halal* is the Mayan word for a kind of reed growing along the water's edge.

In October Alma said farewell to Felipe and left for home to assemble her trousseau and spend some time with her family. In December she heard of an incipient revolution in Mexico, started by the disgruntled de la Huerta. Later she heard that it had spread to Yucatán and all communication with that State had been cut off.

Back in Mérida Felipe was finding himself in deep trouble. The de la Huerta forces, with the connivance of the *hacendados,* had replaced the federal garrison there with a contingent of their own troops from the north of Mexico. These troops were equipped with machine guns and commanded by a hard-bitten, villainous colonel named Ricardo Broca.

Felipe had always believed passionately in the philosophy of pacifism and he clung to it now, even though he was told that the time had come to arm his people or lose everything he had accomplished.

At last he agreed, and sent an agent off to New Orleans to get arms and ammunition.

Now the *hacendados* began circulating false rumors that Obregón had been shot and that de la Huerta had taken over. Word also reached Felipe that a bribe of two hundred and fifty thousand dollars had been offered the garrison on condition that the Governor be seized and killed. Felipe decided the time had come for action. He summoned three of his brothers and six of his chief lieutenants and they crept away from Mérida in the middle of the night, headed for the coast, where they planned to take ship for Cuba and hasten the business of acquiring arms.

As they moved toward the coast the faithful Mayans came out from their villages in great numbers, armed with machetes, offering to fight the enemy. Felipe said no — the machete was no match for the machine gun — they should wait until he came back with munitions.

The party arrived at the coast. They waded out to a launch which was to carry them to a larger boat. In the water, Felipe carried his hat above his head — inside it he had pasted a photograph of his Peregrina. The Mexican in charge of the launch proved to be a traitor — he pretended that the boat's engine was disabled while he signaled ashore, and a squad of soldiers came in view. Felipe's brothers and associates wanted to shoot it out, but he forbade it, and so they were taken, and marched back to Mérida and lodged in the Governor's own model prison.

On the evening of January 2, an attorney was admitted to Felipe's cell and told him that he had influential friends, that he could have his freedom to leave the country if he would pay one hundred and twenty-five thousand dollars — just half the sum that had been posted for his death. He scorned the offer, so he and his friends were brought before a fake court-martial. He was told to plead but he refused, saying, "I am the Governor of the State — I do not recognize your court. You are outsiders, and I will be judged only by my own people."

When it became apparent that the whole proceeding was rigged against him, he made a dramatic plea for the lives of his brothers, insisting that they had merely been loyal soldiers. "Cut me to bits," he said, "but spare my brothers and my friends."

He was returned to his cell, knowing there would be no escape, and there in the night he was taunted and tortured further by the appearance of a group of singer-musicians near the cell window, singing a whiny, nasal version of "Peregrina."

At dawn Felipe and the others were led out and herded into a bus and driven through the streets of Mérida to a cemetery. There the ten men were lined up against a wall. A squad of riflemen moved into position for the execution. Yet the strange and wonderful magnetism of Felipe Carrillo was still at work; the soldiers of the firing squad were nervous and jumpy, obviously unhappy over their assignment. Felipe left the wall, walking slowly and with great dignity toward the soldiers. He handed one of them a ring — a Mayan wedding ring — which he had acquired for use in the ceremony in San Francisco. "Please see that *Pixan-halal* gets it," he said, and the soldier nodded.

Felipe returned to the wall, said good-by to his brothers and his friends. Colonel Broca, the arrogant bribe-taking commandant, gave the order to fire. The first volley was directed over the heads of the men against the wall, the bullets spattering plaster. The soldiers had refused to shoot Felipe, and Colonel Broca, in a rage, screamed to the riflemen in the second rank to cut down the soldiers of the firing squad. Thus there was a horrifying delay. Then the second squad, standing over the bodies of their compatriots, executed the ten.

Of this moment Ernest Gruening has written: "Thus perished the most enlightened, the most courageous, the most lovable man in Mexico. Her tragic history of blood and tears has offered no nobler, no sweeter figure as a sacrifice to human freedom."

In San Francisco, Alma Reed was told of reports out of Mexico that Felipe had been shot. She refused to believe it. She told herself it could not possibly be true, that such a thing could not happen to so great a man.

Back in Mérida the Mayas pondered the problem of getting word out to Alma. Finally they wrote a cablegram to her and one Indian swam out to an English ship and asked that the message be sent. It was sent, but it was addressed to PIXAN-HALAL, SAN FRANCISCO. Alma didn't get it until long after the *New York Times* had notified her that Felipe was dead.

She went back to Mexico as soon as the revolt had been put down. In Mérida, while a large and weeping crowd stood by, she walked to Felipe's tomb and placed a single rose on it. The concluding words of "Peregrina" ran through her mind as she stood there, and she murmured, "I'll not forget."

Thereafter Alma Reed traveled and studied in Europe. Then, in New York, she became acquainted with Orozco and fought for his acceptance in the United States. She was responsible for the great Mexican's murals at the New School for Social Research, at Dartmouth College, and at Pomona College in California. Not long ago she told that story in a fine book, *Orozco*.

Eventually she went back to live in Mexico. She is known and revered wherever she travels in the Republic, and always she is saluted with the strains of her song. She rides buses and trains and planes from one end of the country to the other, gathering material for her articles, attending dinners given in her honor, attending conventions of Mexican scholars and scientists. One of the most knowledgeable correspondents in Latin America, Paul Kennedy, told me: "Whenever I need to know the true facts on any Mexican subject, whether it's art or history or archaeology or language or geography or witchcraft or anything, I phone Alma. She has never failed me yet."

In the time when she and Felipe had talked of their future, he said that his work would soon be done in Yucatán, that he had brought his people forward to the point where they would be able to take care of themselves. He said that he was almost ready to step out of office and then, together, they would write a fine book, setting down the full story of all that had happened in Yucatán.

Alma Reed is now at work, alone, on that book, and it will be called, of course, *Peregrina*.

February 4

FROM eating large quantities of hot *salsa*, I felt this morning like the world's largest mammal* and so I decided to stay in bed. After an hour or two, however, I grew restless and suggested that we go downstairs and hire a car and take a ride for an hour, say through Chapultepec Park. One of the guides at the entrance gave us a price of thirty pesos an hour and off we went. Soon after entering the beautiful and historic park the guide stopped the car and pointed off to the left and said, "Is ofer there Rosas, is great Mexican composer, is composer this song famous all over the world, song call 'Ofer the Wafes.'" I expressed surprise at hearing that a Mexican wrote "Ofer the Wafes" and the guide continued: "Everybody in the world, all contries, say is wrote 'Ofer the Wafes' in their contry. All is liars. This song is wrote right here." He extended the long bony index finger of his right hand and jabbed it toward the ground for emphasis. "Right here!" he repeated, jabbing. "Rosas is in lawv with Mexican girl. She don't like him. She saize, Go away don't bother me you bom. So he saize, Okay my dear, I will get dronk and go ofer the wafes to Cuba and you will not see me never again. And she saize, Go ahead you big dronk. . . . And he did. He was Mexican man, come from Guanajuato."

I began to think that we were in the presence of a most interesting character. A short distance farther on we stopped at a fountain, or series of fountains, part of the aqueduct built by the Aztecs. The guide said that he would tell us the whole history of the Aztecs "in

* The world's largest mammal is the sulphur-bottom whale.

only few words" if we would care to stop. We walked over to the fountains and he began a discourse about a fellow named Netza-hualcoyotl — "means the name, Lost Coyote" — and I decided that some of this should go into my journal. I asked the guide for his name. He straightened his back and said, "I am Don Quixote." Gears meshed, wheels spun, click-clack, clack-click, and it registered. Back in New York someone had told me that when I got to Mexico City I should not fail to look up one of the town's great characters, a guide known as Don Quixote. I had forgotten all about him and now, purely by accident, I had drawn him out of a pool of about fifteen hundred licensed guides. His real name is Gregory Zamulio, but apparently he's the only one who knows it. He is thin, with a shock of black hair, a black mustache, leathery complexion; he is slightly stooped, a bit shabby, and with two striking characteristics: (1) he visualizes all history in terms of conversations between fa-mous people, and (2) he emphasizes his words with that bony fore-finger, making emphatic jabbing motions toward the ground, and as he proceeds, his head keeps cocking around to the left and his stoop grows more and more pronounced. "I am pure Aztec Indian," he told us. "I am founder of the guide service, first of all guides in Mexico. I have been in front of Hotel Reforma since before Hotel Reforma was builded." He said he was a painter of murals and a composer of music as well as a guide. He finished off the complete history of the Aztecs, none of which I understood very well, and then drove us to the "Bath of Moctezuma." It turned out to be a small swimming pool with a fence around it. "This," said Don Quixote, "is called Bath of Moctezuma. Is wrong. Is big lie. Was actually builded by Cortez for La Malinche. Now I will tell you the story of La Malinche." He began at the seacoast, where he had Malinche meet Cortez. When she addressed Cortez "in Espanish" he threw up his hands to heaven and cried out, "O Lord is a miracle you have made!" Then Cortez addressed La Malinche, "My dear, how do you learn Es-panish language so good?" To which she responded, "My dear, there is a fellow from Cuba titches me Espanish language long time ago.

Señor, my dear, I will go with you and I will terpet so you will defeat the Aztecs that I no like." "And Cortez saize, Okay, my dear. Thank you very much." And now Don Quixote concluded, "This is why he builded for her this bath. What I am telling you is the truth."

The hour was up, but I suggested that we keep going, so we went up the hill to the castle. He showed us the room where the historic carriages are exhibited — two of Maximilian's, the beautiful golden one which was for Sundays, and the less expensive one which was for going to work on weekdays. Also the rude black funereal-looking carriage which Juárez used in his wanderings while Maximilian was in power.

In front of the golden coach Don Quixote lowered his voice to what might be described as a loud whisper — there were other tourists around. "Not very long ago," he said, "we had a little trobble with France. France saize to Mexico, Mexico, you bring back the things that are belonging to us. Mexico saize, What things you mean? France saize, The golden carriage of Maximilian. You bring it back. So Mexico saize, Who saize? . . . And France saize, We saize. And Mexico saize, Okay, we bring back the golden carriage if Napoleon saize; if HE saize, then we bring back. . . . But they could not because everybody is dead. This is the truth. Pretty good, yes?"

Pretty good.

We went to look at the apartments of Maximilian and Carlota, and Don Quixote told another long and involved story about a *capitán* serving Juárez: "Benito Juárez saize to him, You know this Carlota? You go over there and you make lawv to this Carlota because you are very handsome, and find out what is going on. . . . So the *capitán* saize to Benito Juárez, Okay. So the *capitán* comes over to this costle, and knocks on the door, knock, knock, knock, and the servants open the door and bow and saize, How do you do, what do you want? . . . The *capitán* is now become very nervous so he saize, I want to see Maximilian. But Carlota comes into the room and sees him, how big and handsome, and she saize, Come in. Have some tea. . . . So they have some."

After that the story was never quite clear, but I do seem to remember that it had some kind of unhappy ending.

Now Don Quixote pulled a daring little off-color joke on us. He showed us Carlota's marble bathtub. "The tourists look at this tob," he said, "and they say, Where is Maximilian's tob? And we say, Well, they either do it separately or at the same time. . . . Then next door in Carlota's bedroom we show them Carlota's bed, and the tourists say, Where is Maximilian's? And we say, The same as the tob. . . . Pretty good, yes?"

Pretty good.

On the roof terrace Don Quixote called our attention to the murals of the Muses, which are in the open air. Again he dropped his voice and recited: "When Don Porfirio Díaz is president, all these ladies is nude. No clothes on. Not any. What I am telling you is the truth. So one day Señora Carmen Romero Rubio de Díaz, the wife of Don Porfirio Díaz, she is taking a little walk right along here where we are taking a little walk, and she looked up and she sees these ladies and she is shock. So she claps together her hands and yells out for her dear hosbon, and Don Porfirio comes out. My dear, she saize, these are terrible ladies and if they are not destroyed these dirty pictures, then do not ever spick to me again as long as you live. But Don Porfirio holds his hand over his mouth to hiding the smile, and then he saize, My dear, these-a paintings was already made before I ever had any idea I would be Presidente. I do not think I can destroy them. So she saize, My dear, you destroy them. So he saize, My dear, I have a great idea. These ladies it is true is not got on much clothes, and it gets a little cool up here, specially in the night. I think these ladies would get very cold so maybe I will do them a kindness and put on them a few clothes. Enough only to keep warm. Not many, just a little. . . . So now you see what he put on them. I am telling you the truth." I must observe that Don Porfirio didn't put much on them — just some thin, gauzy veils and in every case one breast is veiled and one exposed. I must remember to ask some authority if *dos tetas* constitute immorality, while *una teta* is okay.

Don Quixote is a most solemn man, even when making his little jokes. At one point he got me more confused about Montezuma and Moctezuma than I already was. "It is a mistake made by American tourist to call Moctezuma by name Montezuma," he said. "Is two different people. In fact, is three of them."

We left the park and had him drive us through the Pedregal residential area, where he said, "I will show you the biggest and finest house of all, one of the houses of Miguel Alemán, but it cannot be seen." On our way back to our hotel I wondered how many hours we owed him for and I asked him what his watch said. "My watch does not say," he replied, "because I do not have a watch. I can tell the time by the shady of the people and the trees." So I asked him what time it was now. He glanced at the shady of the people and the trees and said, "Five-thirty." A few moments later I spied the shady of a clock on a store building. It was four-forty.

We came to a small park and he said: "This is a little park we have, we call it Cholly Limburg Park. It is for Cholly Limburg that went in the air to Paris." And when we arrived back at the hotel I found, much to my surprise, that there wasn't a trace of my sickness left.

February 5

LAST night I couldn't get to sleep, tossed around for what seemed hours, and I was blaming it on the altitude when Nelle said, "Just think of some simple thing — something very colorless and unimportant."

"How do you mean?" I asked.

"Get your mind off all this Mexican color and think of something real simple, something without any color."

"Okay," I said, "you name it."

"Well, think of . . . think of dust."

"Dust?"

"Yes, dust."

"My God, how can any sensible person lie in bed and think of dust?"

"Go ahead and try it — it'll relax your mind."

"Well, all right. Dust. Dust. Dust on my shoes. Dust in the streets. Dust on the furniture. Feather duster. Dust. Dust. Dust storms. The drought in Texas. Getting worse. Texas needs water. Invades Mexico. Token resistance. Texas takes over Mexico. Shivers installed in National Palace. Lyndon Johnson becomes owner of Reforma. Sam Rayburn takes over Alemán's holdings. John Mc-Quown gets the Alameda. All Texans are now Mexicans. Start talking big. Start threatening. Washington sends note. Tex-Mex say nuts to you, you big bully. United States invades and conquers Mexico. Diego Rivera pledges allegiance to the flag and to the Republic for which it stands. I take over Sam Rayburn's holdings. Listen, this is getting me nowhere!"

"Well," she said, "think of something else besides dust."

"Like what?"

"Oh, like, like . . . canned corn."

"Too colorful," I said, and shortly afterward fell asleep.

In the drugstore this morning Nelle overheard a Gringo trying to tell the clerk that he wanted medicine for a condition of constipation. The clerk was doubly confused, because such a condition is remarkably rare among tourists and because of the word itself. In Spanish *constipación* has two definitions — one being the same as our own, the other meaning a cold in the head. The clerk was trying to give the American various medicines for a cold in the head, and the customer was uttering loud protests and Nelle stood by, pretending interest in some hair nets, anticipating the moment when the customer in desperation would try sign language to illustrate his trouble and she was wondering just how he'd go about it. He never did.

She reported back to me that when she walked out of the hotel she almost tripped over a white duck, waddling around near the entrance, acting as if he wanted to go in and register. I went out to have a look and located the duck some distance down the street, pecking at a mudhole. I conferred with one of the bellboys, who said the duck had been around for a long time, and was known to some people as Donaldo and to others as Oswaldo. He said the duck belonged to a shoeshine boy down the street, and we went down to talk to him. He denied ownership and said the duck belonged to the lady at the corner newsstand. So we went to the lady and she said the duck had no name. "Okay," I said. "We will call him Señor Duck."

Lunch today was quite exciting, because Maxine introduced me to Denise Darcel, who is singing at the Reforma's night club. I told her that I loved her dearly and she flashed those dimples at me and my blood turned to jello. Jello is the way a Mexican says yellow, except when he's talking Spanish, in which case he says *amarillo*.

Tonight we walked over to the new Hotel Vista Hermosa, a beautiful place with much marble and onyx all around. We sat in an upstairs dining room and had passable Mexican food and I made some notes from the English side of the menu, where the dishes included: Cardenal Pouched Eggs, Crowfish Cream, Raviols Beef Juice, Italian Spaguetti, Red Shoper Grilled, Stuff Chicken Leg with Musrons.

Our table stood by a huge window and we could look across to the statue of Cuauhtémoc which stands before the Hilton, at the point where Insurgentes comes into Reforma. Cuauhtémoc, the Aztec leader who succeeded Montezuma, is one of the greatest of all heroes in the eyes of the Mexican people, and when they have a celebration at this statue they put up a big sign which says SEÑOR MEXICO, which means that he is Mister Mexico. Aristocrats and pseudo-aristocrats and pretenders to aristocracy complain that the city has this big statue to a miserable Indian and no monument anywhere honoring Cortez. They fail to realize that their complaints merely irritate a population that is 90 per cent pure Indian or part Indian. Cuauhtémoc was, from all accounts, an exemplary young man, noble and handsome and courageous. Cortez marinated his feet in oil and then burned them until they were charred stumps in an effort to get Cuauhtémoc to tell where he had hidden a lot of non-existent gold. Later on Cortez strung him up to a giant ceiba tree. Just before he died, the handsome Indian glanced down at his charred feet and then spoke his final words: "I knew what it was to trust your false promises from the first. I knew you intended this fate for me. Your God will demand of you why you killed me so unjustly."

Mexicans know those words. For Cortez, no monuments.

Tonight we violated our rule against night-clubbing and went to the Chanteclair room and paid a cover charge of thirty-five pesos because I wanted to hear Denise Darcel sing and I wanted to look at her shape some more. She represents something pretty important to me — my own personal revolt against the fashion which says dames should be skinny. Back home the models and the actresses and the debs and the beauty pageant winners are little more than walking skeletons. I'd hesitate to pay court to them for fear they'd rattle and wake up the neighbors. Denise was lovely, shapewise.

After a while I observed, at a nearby table, one of the most picturesque drunks I've ever had the pleasure of watching. He was a Mexican and quite handsome. When his party of eight arrived he was being supported by two other men, who eased him gently into a chair, where he sat staring fixedly at the tablecloth. Now and then he would get up and start out of the room, and he always walked sideways. It was clear to me that, in his stupor, he walked sideways because he realized if he did it would be impossible for him to have a head-on collision with another person or a wall or a pillar (one learns so many things from travel!). He never made a sound all evening, never spoke a word so far as I could detect. At one point two men got up, seized him by the arms, and started leading him out, which was a difficult task because even under escort he insisted on walking sideways. I thought that would be the end of him, but they brought him back; and in a little while, damned if he didn't take one of the ladies to the dance floor, sideways, and waltz with her. An altogether admirable character.

Charlie Bowers, the manager, stopped by our table and somehow I happened to mention Señor Duck down on the sidewalk, and Charlie turned a trifle red, and spoke some words in anger, so I changed the subject. I asked him if it were true that his beautiful wife is a niece of Lázaro Cárdenas and he said it was true, and added that he sometimes has fun kidding her about it. I've noticed that almost everyone to whom I mention the name of Cárdenas seems to grow uncomfortable. This is a strange thing, considering the way American writers praise the man consistently and call him the greatest living Mexican.

After Charlie Bowers left, Nelle asked me about his nationality and I said I thought he was an American, but that someone had told me he was a Carthaginian of Hungarian extraction.

February 6

LUNCH today with Freddie Vosberg, once a professional dancer on Broadway, now executive assistant manager of the Reforma. Freddie quit show business to operate a chain of restaurants and wound up in Mexico City. He and a man named Joe White ran several top eating houses here and then, in 1946, they came up with a big idea. There were no hot dogs in Mexico and it was obvious to them that those screeching, yowling, hair-tearing fans at the bullfights were of the same breed as the fans at American ball games; wherefore, those fans would go crazy for hot dogs. The world's largest bull ring, Plaza Mexico, was to open soon, so the two men applied for and got the concession to sell hot dogs. Immediately they were shocked to discover that there were no frankfurters in Mexico. They were desperate, so Joe White flew to New Jersey and acquired equipment for manufacturing franks. Back in Mexico City they threw together a small factory and started turning out hot dogs, and then they discovered that Mexico didn't have the kind of bun traditionally identified with the delicacy. Back to the United States flew Joe White to get molds and recipes. So on opening day at Plaza Mexico, with 55,000 fans present, they had a corps of boys in white uniforms, each with a tray of dogs, mustard and piccalilli. Printed on one side of the trays were the words, *Hot Dogs,* and on the other side, *Perros Caliente.*

The trouble started at once. At first the crowd merely jeered the boys. There were cries of, "Now the obscenity Gringos are trying to take over our bullfights!" Then came violence. Some of the boys were seized and thrown down flights of stairs, and their boxes were shattered and their frankfurters hurled into the bull ring. Freddie and Joe White started the day with 15,000 hot dogs, and ended it with 14,820. There was no place to store them and the next bullfight was a week away. They took them to their apartment and filled their own refrigerator, then went to their neighbors begging for icebox space. All that week they threw hot dog parties, calling in everyone they knew and even asking strangers to come and eat dogs.

Some of the newspapers took up the cry that the Gringos were trying to muscle in on Mexico's sacred institution. But Vosberg and White refused to back down, and in a few weeks the bullfight fans had begun to buy hot dogs, and then other concessions were negotiated at baseball parks and at the racetrack.

"The Mexicans," said Freddie, "like the hot dog done in American style, but now there are Mexican hot dogs — they make a sweeter roll, a dog of a yellowish color, and they douse it with hot chile sauce." I remembered now having seen, in Mexico City, a sign in a small restaurant window: HOOT DOGS.

Freddie also told us that Mexicans won't drink anything cold. They believe that any cold liquid, passing through their throats, will fetch on a sickness in the tonsils. Yet they are probably the greatest consumers of soft drinks in the world; sometimes it seems that the ordinary Mexican is not a complete human being without a pop bottle fastened to his lips. Because of their partiality for luke-warm beverages, it is often necessary in smaller establishments to specify *"fría"* when ordering beer, if you want it cold. I mean *"fría, por favor."*

4

The Road to Taxco

February 7

CARLOS de la Big Smile arrived on schedule and off we went this morning down the Cuernavaca highway which is becoming as familiar to us as the Saw Mill River Parkway back home. Just at the edge of Cuernavaca we doubled back on a small paved road, heading for Tepoztlán. Carlos waved a hand toward the fields and said, "The soil around here is very rich — so rich that in some places if you plant beans, it comes up strawberries." The road was narrow and winding and in bad repair, but many stories go with it. One that Carlos told concerned a handsome, athletic playboy of Cuernavaca named Malacara (which means Bad Face), who got himself involved with a country girl. Malacara was already married, so the girl's parents and uncle came to him and warned him that if he ever tried to see her again, they would kill him. Malacara decided it was time to break it off, and he did. The girl, however, hadn't had enough and tried to communicate with him, but he wouldn't see her. Love now turned to hate and the girl begged him for just one more meeting for the purpose of talking it over, and he agreed. The girl then went to her folks and told them that her former lover had talked her into meeting him at their old trysting place beside the Tepoztlán road. That evening Malacara and the girl drove out to the spot. The girl started whipping off her clothes. The father, mother and uncle closed in.

They seized Malacara and beat him to death with clubs; then they erected a cross, nailed him to it, and burned him. Imagine. Just for having a little fun.

Arriving in Tepoztlán, we drove up a narrow, precipitous street to the Posada del Tepozteco. A tall, graying man with a slight stoop came out to the parking area to help with the bags. He proved to be Larry Brookwell, who opened this hotel three or four years ago. I remarked on the length and steepness of the hill and he said, wryly, "Yes, we like it that way — it keeps the shoe salesmen away." Later he told us that the cobblestone hill had been a handicap because tourists refused to use it, so he got permission from the town government to lay two concrete strips at his own expense. His workmen had just started the job when a native lady of quality who lived at the top of the street set up a howl, saying that Brookwell was destroying the town's personality. The Mayor told Brookwell to pay no heed to her, that she was a chronic complainer, and Brookwell remarked jokingly, "Maybe we won't let her walk on my concrete." After the job was finished a cop called on Brookwell and asked if he had seen the sensational new *pronunciamento*. Down at the municipal building a notice had been posted for all to see. The village constitution had been amended and the new clause specified that the complaining Señora should never set foot on either of those concrete strips, on pain of imprisonment in the town jail.

Carlos saw us settled, and then returned to Mexico City, and we had a look around at the hotel, once the country residence of Eduardo Villaseñor, a leading Mexican banker who was once Consul General in New York. At one time or another he and his wife had been entertained at the leading haciendas all over Mexico, and when they came to build this place they made each of the twelve rooms an exact copy of a room they had loved in one or another of the haciendas. Our room had been the library, a spacious chamber with a picture window facing the cliffs. From the front terrace the views are stupendous. Below lies the famous village itself, and on either side are the most spectacular mountain cliffs I've seen anywhere. High on these cliffs stands the pyramid of the Aztec tribal deity, Tepoztecatl, the god of pulque. There is a vertical trail leading from the village to the pyramid, and many tourists undertake the climb. The caretaker is an eighty-one-year-old Indian and every day he makes the climb, carrying a case of Coca-Cola. This job is an example of Mexican mulishness. The old man insists upon carrying the Cokes in their wooden case, whereas if he carried them in a bag slung over his shoulder the task would be much, much easier. He says no. For years he has always done it the other way. *Es la costumbre.*

The village of Tepoztlán has been probed and prodded and investigated and psychoanalyzed and studied under a microscope more than any other community on earth. Thirty years ago it was an isolated village of Aztec Indians, speaking Nahuatl (Gnaw-wattle), self-sufficient and content to be blocked off from the rest of the world. No wheel had ever turned in its streets, and such outside supplies as were needed were brought in by burro or on the backs of the people. Then along came Robert Redfield, an anthropologist and social scientist from the University of Chicago. He undertook a long and thorough investigation of the village and its people, and published a book on his findings. Stuart Chase read the book and headed for Tepoztlán and did another investigation, and *he* wrote a book on the subject. Years later, after World War II, another anthropologist, Oscar Lewis of the University of Illinois, arrived with a squad of helpers and did a fresh investigation, more painstaking than the others. It is possible, through these books, to learn almost everything there is to know about this village — including even the sex habits of its people.

February 8

TEPOZTLÁN has been described in the guidebooks as "delightful" and "charming" and "unspoiled." It is none of these. The streets that are paved with cobblestones must have been put down by drunken workmen; thick dust lies heavily over everything; the central plaza has not a particle of charm and is shabby and dirty, and everywhere — in the streets and in the plaza and in the market — are scraps of food and other garbage. The town is delightful and charming only when one views its historical aspect.

We spent a good part of today wandering around, looking at the junk heaps which are called buses and which run between Tepoztlán and Cuernavaca, and the smaller junk heaps which are the village taxicabs. We explored the deserted Dominican convent. I have heard about a professor in a Midwest university whose hobby is "collecting ancient convents" in the Americas. Just a year or two ago he finally arrived at this one, went through it, came out and issued a judgment: "This is the finest god-damned convent I've ever seen." I was interested in the fact that Zapata made this convent building his headquarters for quite a while during the Revolution, stabling his horses in the kitchen. At least five of Zapata's generals came from Tepoztlán, and every political campaigner who comes here automatically makes a strong mention of Zapata, just as our political speakers find it essential to make a strong mention of God.

Even a brief reading of the social studies will show how superstitious the local people are, how willing they are to believe anything they hear. During World War II the fascistic Sinarquistas came in and set rumors going that the Germans were winning great victories for a special reason: Emiliano Zapata was still alive and was riding at the head of Hitler's troops. Because they believed this story, many Tepoztecans were bitterly opposed to Mexico entering the war on the side of the Gringos. For a while they resisted conscription, and when the Mayor's son was drafted a posse was formed to intercept the bus carrying the lad off to Cuernavaca. He was taken off the bus and hidden away, but federal troops came marching in, the mayor was put in jail, and the villagers finally resigned themselves to the inevitable.

While Zapata is the historic hero of Tepoztlán, the more modern hero is a man named Angel Bocanegra. He was a member of Squadron 201, made up of Mexican fliers who fought valiantly in the

Pacific. When the squadron came home its members were received as great heroes. President Avila Camacho gave a public reception for them and, during it, invited each of the fliers to ask for anything his heart desired. Almost all of them asked for large sums of money, but when it came Angel Bocanegra's turn he said: "I live in a village that is very poor and cannot afford a decent school for the children. I would ask that my village be given a nice school." The crowd roared its approval, and Avila Camacho issued orders that the school be erected double-pronto, and it was, and it stands there in the center of town today, named Escuela Squadron 201.

Lázaro Cárdenas arrived unannounced in the village one day, on foot. He walked in and set up a temporary office in the atrium of the church, and asked the Tepoztecans to bring their problems to him. (This was the type of thing Cárdenas did all through his presidency.) Most of the citizens told him their greatest need was a paved road to Cuernavaca. He gave it to them, with consequences that some people consider good, and others bad. For a long time Larry Brookwell had the only telephone in the village and the only electricity. Now there are seven phones and most of the people are beginning to itch for electricity. The buses take the young people to the city of Cuernavaca and they have learned about movies, and going steady, and mop-haired crooners, and permanent waves, and all the other civilized things.

The town is still primitive enough for me. The telegraph office is operated by a man who can neither read nor write but who has learned to type out the letters as they come clicking over the wire. When he gets in trouble he yells across to the school and one of the pupils is sent over to get him untangled. The post office is a box in a little adobe shed which is stacked full of big sacks of chicken feed. Not long ago the room was a carpenter's shop. Letters often fell into the sawdust on the floor and the customers who were expecting mail would come in and sift through the sawdust until they found it. There is a blackboard outside near the door, with a dozen or so names scrawled in chalk; the customer passing the shop looks at the blackboard; if he sees his name he goes in, gets his letter, and the postmaster then hands him a little rag which he takes outside and uses to erase his own name.

The village government in Tepoztlán functions in much the same flamboyant manner as the governments of all Mexican villages. Village officials love to issue ponderous *pronunciamientos* — long and complex documents that are stamped, beribboned, sealed, sworn to upside down and backwards, and even read in public to the ruffle of drums — and such a document may be a regulation forbidding a specific chicken from trespassing in the plaza bandstand.

One day Larry Brookwell discovered that Tepoztlán had a tailor who was quite competent, so he had the man make him a pair of pants from English gabardine. The pants turned out so well that Larry ordered three more pairs, buying the gabardine himself in Cuernavaca. Weeks passed, and no pants. Finally he went down and demanded action. More weeks passed. *Nada.* Larry knew the manner in which local government functions, so he went to a law clerk and together they drew up a magnificent document, resembling both in tone and in bulk the Charter of the United Nations. They took this to the municipal authorities. Now the wheels of government ground so loudly that they drowned out the barking of the dogs and the grunting of the pigs and the honking of the burros and the crowing of the roosters. The whole thing came off with a sort of thunderous series of quick ceremonies, with marching and countermarching of troops through the streets, as if it were a bill to impeach the President of the Republic. Larry got his pants in a hurry and I got the impression that government operations on a local level here are almost a burlesque of government.

Tepoztlán is one of the villages where retroactive arrest is employed. This is an interesting and ingenious device for getting urgent municipal work done. A section of street needs to be repaired, or the municipal building needs a new roof or a coat of whitewash. The mayor sends the police into the streets. They seek out known masons, if masons are needed, or carpenters, or painters, or diggers, and they say to each of these men, "You are hereby arrested for the last time you were drunk, whenever it was." The prisoner is then sentenced to "hard labor" for the number of hours or days his services are needed.

The people of the village are vastly amused by the Gringos, especially by their struggles with the Spanish language. Yet they will never laugh in a tourist's face. I was in the plaza when three schoolboys came along. I wanted to locate Angel Bocanegra, the war hero, and now began asking these boys the whereabouts of the Bocanegra *casa*. All I got was a lot of babbling and a lot of pointing in two or three different directions. So I thanked them and walked away and in a few moments turned and looked back and there they were, doubled up with laughter. I found out later that Bocanegra drives one of the buses to and from Cuernavaca.

Tepoztlán has the look of poverty, yet the social scientists speak of the town's "rich people." A "rich" Tepoztecan is one who owns a house, or maybe two or three houses, and has a few pesos hidden away. These people almost always go to great lengths to conceal their affluence; they pretend that they are poor almost to the point of starvation, they dress poorly, they even go out and take day labor on the farms to emphasize the extent of their poverty. They don't want their friends to know of their prosperity, because the friends will want to borrow, and more importantly, they don't want the tax collector to know that they have anything. This somehow makes me think of home.

Larry Brookwell is really a rare specimen — a hotelkeeper who entertains an active distaste for some of his guests, and lets them know it. If he doesn't like your looks or the way you talk, you might as well move on to some other town because he'll do you no favors at his *posada*. One of the richest of all American heiresses, a character of international repute, walked into the lobby recently. She was wearing an Indian sari of brilliant orange, a pound and a half of jewelry in her head area, and shoes with golden heels set with sparkling gems. There were several guests at the other end of the little lobby and they stared at this creature and began whispering to one another, because they recognized her. She became indignant, turned to Larry and said, "I demand to know why these awful people are staring at me and whispering about me." Larry looked her straight in the eye, and said, "Well, I suppose it's because you look like something that just escaped from a circus." She whirled and clattered out of the place on her golden heels, never to return.

There was the case of a chubby tourist lady who walked into the lobby, spread her arms in a gesture meant to suggest rapture, and exclaimed, "Who, oh who, is the artist here? I have a feeling for art!" Larry looked up from his desk work, gave her a long, hard stare, and then said, "Madame, you have lost your marbles."

Back in Westchester our friends the Maulsbys had told us about Larry Brookwell. Now he described a recent letter he has had from the Maulsbys in which they said they were thinking about living in Mexico some day and operating a small hotel about the size of the *posada,* and thus "becoming semi-retired." Larry has never recovered from that expression, "semi-retired." He works steadily from daybreak till all his guests have gone to bed at night, performing every kind of chore imaginable. He is the hotel's mechanic and maintenance man, keeps the books, handles reservations, answers a thousand questions a day (many of them pretty silly), takes care of the correspondence, which is quite heavy, settles the problems of the hired help, tinkers with misbehaving toilets (he shares my opinion that the whole of American industry stands condemned for the stupid mechanism of the standard toilet), sells trinkets and rebozos and shirts and stamps and archaeological items to the tourists, does the marketing in Cuernavaca, puts on a white jacket and tends bar at cocktail time, deals with the village government, tries to keep his ten-year-old daughter amused, hangs pictures, prints signs — and so on and so on — while Mrs. Brookwell is kept occupied supervising the kitchen and dining room. All during the day, whenever I've come upon Larry perched on a ladder or toting furniture or tinkering with a toilet, his comment has been: "I'm semi-retired. That's right, semi-retired. Good God!"

In the midst of all this interminable labor he found time to dig out a pamphlet, the text of a speech by Villaseñor, the banker who built this house. The speech was delivered before the Anglo-American Institute and in it Villaseñor told about a test paper in zoology written from the point of view of an ant. The ant divides the animal kingdom into two classes: (a) the kind and gentle animals, such as the lion, the tiger and the rattlesnake; and (b) the ferocious animals, such as the chicken, the duck and the goose.

There was also a lovely anecdote about Villaseñor's Mexican friend who went to England and was cross-examined by an immigration officer at Plymouth. "What is your Christian name?" asked the officer. "Jesús," said the Mexican. To which the officer protested, "But, my good man, that's not a Christian name!"

I caught Larry at lunch today and had a chance for a long talk. We discussed the marvelous arched brick ceilings in the *posada* and other architectural matters, and he said that in the early years of the Conquest the church-builders didn't know the proper technique for putting on a roof; therefore they built the four walls of the church, filled the enclosure with dirt, built the roof over the dirt, then dug the dirt out of the church. This is very interesting information but I don't believe it.

He knew I was interested in parrot stories (he has a parrot that can speak better Spanish than I can) so he told one which he said was true. In Acapulco the natives will capture small parrots and teach them to yell a certain obscene word. When the bird has learned this dirty word, he is set free. He flies back to the jungle and teaches all the other parrots to yell the obscenity (this is a fine example of the famous Mexican educational program known as *each one teach one*). When all the birds in the jungle have learned the word, they organize themselves into flights of several thousand parrots, sweeping low across the town of Acapulco and shrieking their obscenity in unison. This is an amusing story, but I don't believe it.

Larry spoke at length of the Indian temperament:

"Water supply has always been a problem in the village," he said, "especially in the dry season. During the dry season the natives let their street faucets run constantly and when somebody objects, they say the pigs have got to have mud to wallow in or they will perish. I have a saying that no Indian ever turns off a faucet or closes a door. And every Indian will resist progress almost to his last breath. When they finally brought in a gasoline engine and set up a mill to grind the corn for tortillas, that mill represented the emancipation of the local women, who always had spent most of their waking hours grinding the corn by hand on their *metates*. It took a long time to convert those women to the mill. They used all kinds of excuses — they said their husbands complained that the tortillas tasted like machinery and they said that a woman who abandoned her *metate* lowered herself in the eyes of her neighbors. You've seen the old man who sweeps the terraces here with that bundle of twigs. Once I got to feeling sorry for him, trying to keep things clean with a handful of tree limbs, so I sent to Sears-Roebuck and got him a nice factory-made broom. He wouldn't touch it, and stayed with his twigs."

A dignified-looking businessman from Indiana arrived today. He takes color movies, and told us of an adventure he had when he was here five years ago. A big fiesta was in progress down in the village and during the festivities two native men, loaded with pulque, went at each other with knives. This was great drama for the Hoosier's camera and he began hopping around on the periphery of the fight, his camera buzzing steadily. Suddenly one of the combatants became aware that a Gringo was photographing the battle. He whirled away from his foe, raised his big knife, screamed a few drunken curses and charged. "I took off like a shot," said the Hoosier, "and went over benches in the plaza like one of them hurdle-jumpers, and I made it to the police station ahead of him or he'd have killed me for sure."

Later I told Larry about this man's experience and he said that the ordinary American tourist has a positive genius for bumbling into unpleasantness in Mexico. He told about a Texan who had recently been here, a big man who talked big and drove a big Cadillac. After a day or two he departed for Acapulco. Larry saw him, however, a few days later in Cuernavaca. One arm was in a sling and he was bruised and bandaged elsewhere. He had been driving along the highway when half a dozen Mexicans appeared on the road, trying to wave him down. "No goddam bandits gonna get me!" he growled and stepped on the gas . . . and drove straight into a dynamite explosion.

There is an attractive young woman, Mrs. Blank, who is here with her husband, and today she and Nelle were down in the village. Mrs. Blank had to go. They hurried over to Bocanegra's school, but it was closed. Then, in desperation, they knocked on the door of a little house. Inside they found a pleasant Mexican woman to whom they said, with some urgency, *"Damas, damas, damas!"* The woman no comprende. Nelle, who is usually handy at such things, began making signs. The woman now summoned her daughter, who led Mrs. Blank out through a rear yard where two women were doing the washing on rocks (these were well-to-do people, it seems, and had their own rocks), and through a bamboo fence. Mrs. Blank now proceeded into a cornfield where she encountered an enormously pregnant sow lying on her side and delivering slow, unmelodious grunts. Soon Mrs. Blank returned to the house, where she found the mother and daughter glaring at her coldly. Neither she nor Nelle could understand why the temper of the women had changed. Maybe they had misunderstood Nelle's sign language; maybe they thought the Gringa just wanted to have a look at the pregnant sow; maybe they spied on her and saw her violate that most sacred of all village institutions, the corn patch, or *milpa*. In any event, back at the *posada*, from that hour on, Mrs. Blank was known by the affectionate name of *Señora Milpa*.

February 9

SINCE we are in the home town of the principal deity of pulque, I have been gathering a little information about that beverage.

When the maguey is about to flower a worker cuts out the heart, covers the incision with side leaves, and all the juice which normally would flow into the great stem now goes into this basin. It continues flowing for several months and must be drained three times daily. A man using a long gourd pipe sucks the juice out. Many of us, on first hearing of this sucking process, have been revolted, but it turns out that the juice leaves the gourd before it arrives at the man.

The liquid is drained into pigskins, and these are carried by burros to the brewery, which is usually in a big shed. The fermentation occurs in large vats made of oxhide, and above the vats is always an image of the brewery's patron saint. There is much praying over the vats while the maguey sap is converting itself into booze, and the workmen take off their hats when they enter, just as if they were in church. In some regions no woman is allowed to come near the fermentation sheds, for her very presence would contaminate the brew, especially if she were pregnant, which she very likely would be.

Tepoztecatl was primarily the god of pulque but he did other things which lead me to believe that he was usually loaded with his own foul nectar. Once his people were being attacked by enemy Indians so he brought on a terrible earthquake to scare off the foe. This is like drinking a jigger of strychnine to ward off a headache. Tepoztecatl's miracles, in fact, were all pretty queer. Once the Spaniards were trying to hoist a bell into the tower of the Cuernavaca cathedral. They couldn't make it, but Tepoztecatl turned himself into a sandstorm and came roaring over from Tepoztlán, and when the air finally cleared, the bell was aloft in the belfry. The suggestion here is that it was put there by a sandstorm. Sometimes I get a little confused over the things people believe.

Pulque was a ritual intoxicant among the Aztecs although they drank it socially, too. Excessive drinking was controlled by the "rule of the fifth cup." The fifth cup was always reserved for the priests and is said to have caused them to dance. If anyone drank more than four cups, he was in trouble with the law. Only the old men among the Aztecs were allowed to get intoxicated. The young men who got drunk were clubbed to death — the poor young men in public, the rich young men in private. It is ever the same — the rich get all the good things in life.

I have not as yet partaken of pulque because I have heard that there are processes employed in its fermentation that resemble the processes employed in the production of a certain Mexican wine, which I mentioned earlier. I have heard that in some places naked Mexicans are hired to get into the vats and leap around real briskly to keep the stuff stirred up. Even without such processes I somehow have no great appetite for a drink that is sucked out of a worm-infested plant by a Mexican using an old gourd pipe, that is hauled away in pigskin containers and fermented in oxhide vats. Even the fact that it's prayed over doesn't move me. The only thing I like about pulque is the fact that it has produced a beautiful Mexican toast, often heard in the lowlier *pulquerías:* "Have a drink! Have a drink and *be* somebody!" It belongs with that other Mexican saying: "Tequila makes a man ten feet tall and eight feet wide."

February 10

AT EARLY breakfast in the dining room I had a long final talk with Larry Brookwell. He said that the changes wrought in the village by the paved road are as nothing to the changes that are coming soon. He said that he has acquired the land and the financial backing for a second hotel on a nearby hillside. He showed me a picture of an ancient Spanish castle which will be the model for the new building. He said that an express highway will soon connect the village with the superhighway to Mexico City, and that a small airport is being planned between Tepoztlán and Cuernavaca. Before many months a power line will bring electricity to town, and the present highway to Cuernavaca is to be widened and straightened. And so it would appear that this famous and picturesque village, studied and written about so much, will soon be losing the last traces of its primitive character. In parting I asked Larry what the Indians of Tepoztlán had thought about the social scientists and their researchers when they came swarming into town. Did they understand that they were being studied scientifically?

"No," said Larry, "they had no idea what those people were doing. They just shook their heads and said, 'More crazy business by those dumbhead Gringos.' "

We rode to Cuernavaca in one of Tepoztlán's rattletrap taxis, driven by a man of the most horrible aspect — whiskered and ragged and bleary-eyed, with so many scars that I judged he had spent half his life in brawls. He was accompanied by a younger man, also very tough-looking. However, the whole front seat area was a forest of Virgins and saints and crucifixes, and the two men, in spite of their frightening appearance, were both quite gentle in manner and voice.

In Cuernavaca the usual Sunday afternoon mobs swarmed in the main plaza, around the hotels and the open-air cafés, around the Cortez Palace, and the peddlers and beggars were falling over each other trying to get to the tourists. For some reason the noise and clamor of Cuernavaca grate on the nerves, unlike the noise and clamor of Veracruz, which is music. We had just about decided to move on to Taxco when I thought about the Reachis. I telephoned the house and went through the usual mad routine. First the kitchen maid answered and she began screaming, *"Americanos! Americanos!"* Then Mama Reachi came on, all excited, and when I asked for Colette, Mama cried, "Sure! I fix you enchiladas!" I kept repeating Colette's name until I made myself understood to Mama, who then yelled, "Wait! I callum up! Hold on the phone!" There followed Mama's physical attack on some kind of inter-com system which she is never able to operate, and she ended up, as always, shouting at the maid to run and tell Colette to get on the phone. Finally I got Colette and she said we should come right over and have dinner with them.

Don Santiago was not at home and a domestic crisis had arisen. The cook and Mama Reachi had got into a quarrel over Mama's right to taste things and criticize in the kitchen. The cook quit, and then the yard boy quit, which was the first intimation the family had that the yard boy was probably carrying on with the cook.

Mama and I watched a play on television. It was about the Egyptians in Biblical times, played by Mexican actors speaking Spanish. It was quite obviously a burlesque of some kind, but Mama couldn't make up her mind whether to weep or to laugh. When the commercials came on she mocked them, and shook her fist at them, whining their singsong messages about cigarettes and chocolate and so on. During the play she would jump up and run to the screen and point to one of the characters and try to explain about him. "This Mosey!" she would say. "You know Mosey? He make Ten Commands." Or, "This Princess. Ho, ho. What she don't know gonna happen!" From this I judged the show was either a repeat, or a serial.

The dinner was Arabic, featuring rice and tomato and eggplant. At one point I got up and said "Con su permiso" and started for the bathroom, and Mama cried out, "Ho, ho! So you go see Meester Johns?" She spent the rest of the evening apologizing for this outburst, which she considered distressingly vulgar. "I am so shame!" she kept saying, and in her halting English explained to me it was "something I hear once in Californey."

Mama talks in three languages and sometimes a single sentence will be a complexity of all three. She was trying to tell me how to make a certain kind of enchilada and she was groping for a word; finally she just threw up her hands and exclaimed, "I all mix up!" The talk turned to Mexican history. The two girls from Lebanon had been studying and now Natasha brought up the subject of Madero and made the flat statement that he was a fine and noble man. Mama glared at Natasha from behind her spectacles. "Who say?" she cried. "Who say?" Natasha replied, "I say." And Mama shouted, "I hate!" Natasha demanded to know why Mama hated Madero. "Make revolution," Mama shouted. "Make everbody poor peoples."

Santiago came in late and we talked some more about Cantinflas and arranged that I should go with him to the Churubusco studios tomorrow.

February 11

SANTIAGO picked me up at the hotel this morning and off we went in his green Thunderbird, roaring up the *autopista*. In the car Santiago spoke of a hundred-dollar bet he had made once with a Hollywood screen writer, involving the height of mountain peaks in Mexico and the United States. Santiago claimed Popocatépetl as the highest and collected the money. So I said, "You ought to send it back to him. Orizaba is higher than Popo." He looked at me pityingly. "You goddam Americans," he said, "give me a pain. You come down here and stagger around for two weeks and then you try to tell me — me, a guy born and raised in this country — you try to tell ME that Orizaba is higher than Popo. God in heaven!"

"Okay," I said, "look it up when we get to the studio."

"*You* look it up!" he roared. "*You're* the one making the big crazy statement, so *you* look it up!"

At the studio I went into Cantinflas's office, where there were several sets of encyclopedias. I got down the *Britannica* and found the figures showing Orizaba to be higher than Popo, and then I called Santiago in. He glanced at the book, then almost flung it to the floor. "That poor excuse for an encyclopedia!" he said. "You couldn't prove anything with *that* goddam mess of a book!" So he got out the Mexican encyclopedias and searched through them, flipping the pages angrily, and finally he had to surrender and admit that I was right.

Sad to relate, I had made a serious tactical blunder. I should never have pressed the point about Orizaba, but I did, and I made more blunders as the day went on.

While Santiago took care of his affairs in his office across the hall, I got acquainted with the contents of Cantinflas's office. He is a great hero to the Mexican masses and he has grown wealthy, yet his office was not one tenth as plush as its counterpart in Hollywood. There was a large portrait of his mother back of the desk and two portraits of himself on other walls. There was a small portable television set, a dictating machine and a leather chair for guests.

His private bath was no better than those in some of the lesser hotels. The bathroom was tiny, the toilet seat was about to fall off, and the plumbing at the basin was so loose that when I turned the handle the spigot moved with it. On the toilet box stood a large bottle half filled with eau de cologne, and beside it a big red comb with several teeth missing. The tilework on walls and ceiling was cracked in places.

After a while I went over to Santiago's office and got into a chair in a corner and observed several conferences involving motion pictures. Another producer came in and he and Santiago engaged in a long and excited conversation in high-speed Spanish, with much pacing back and forth and arm-waving. I managed to detect an occasional word, but I didn't get the sense of the talk until I heard the phrase, "Tremendo box-uffus!" and then I knew that it was the same as in Hollywood.

A movie critic from one of the big Mexico City papers came in, and he and Santiago went at it for the better part of an hour; when they had just about concluded, Santiago turned to me and said, "I'll bet you wouldn't have any idea what we've been talking about."

"Yes I have," I said. "He's been telling you how to make movies and you've been telling him how to run his newspaper."

"Very clever!" he said, and there was a note of unpleasantness in his voice. Orizaba was still eating at him. Mexican witchcraft caused me to apply a bit of salt to the wound.

"And another thing you were talking about," I said, "was how Popo is higher than Orizaba."

I shouldn't have said it.

He had been talking to me, now and then, about the possibility of my writing a series of stories for Cantinflas movies and now, as we drove away from the studio, we were even working out a story line for the first script. Then I mentioned something about my agent, and about money, and Santiago regarded me as if I had slapped him across the face. He told me that I didn't understand — that if I turned out to be the man to write English-language stories for Cantinflas, my fortune would be made, I'd be rich beyond estimate. The intimation was strong that I should do the first story for free, and I demurred.

Santiago was in a fairly black mood when we stopped at the Lebanese legation, a large and handsome house on a corner of the Paseo de la Reforma. In a few moments I was awash with Lebanese, who were speaking in Arabic, French, Spanish and *pocito* English. Two brothers of Colette and Natasha were there, one being a member of the legation staff and the other on a diplomatic mission from Beirut. There was an excited discussion about a fishing line which Brother Joe had bought when he stopped off in New York. It is a fishing line which the President of Lebanon wants very badly. But when Brother Joe was in Cuernavaca he misplaced the fishing line at the Hotel Jacaranda. Colette and Natasha had been told, by telephone, to rush over to the Jacaranda and find that fishing line if they had to search all day, and then bring it up to Mexico City. The chargé d'affaires began bouncing around, doing something about serving Turkish coffee, and his wife came in and got all excited because we had to leave, and I spoke up and asked the name of the President of Lebanon and what kind of fisherman he was and what was so special about that lost fishing line. Diplomatic mum set in, and somebody changed the subject, and so we departed amid fevered exclamations of distress because we could not wait for the coffee. Santiago set the Thunderbird thundering on out

Reforma and I asked why Lebanon should have such a large and elegant legation in Mexico. He said that long ago, during periods of political troubles in the Near East, some Lebanese were obliged to decamp, and these political exiles settled in Mexico because Mexico had certain resemblances to Lebanon in climate and topography. They liked Mexico and prospered here, and wrote to their relatives and friends, and more came until today there are about 60,000 of them in the Republic. For the most part they are merchants and manufacturers and bankers. Some of the biggest stores in Mexico City are owned by Lebanese, and it is generally conceded that they have been good for the economy of the country.

Far out on Reforma we came to a gateway of beautiful varnished wood set in a long white wall. Santiago spoke into an inter-com and soon a servant opened the gate and we were admitted to a fantastically beautiful residence, the principal home of Mario Moreno, better known as Cantinflas. After we had wandered about, indoors and out, for a while, Santiago mentioned that I had seen no more than a tenth of the whole, that back toward the rear was a theater, and I think he also said there was a chapel somewhere on the premises. The grounds occupy two levels with an abrupt drop of about fifty feet from the main house to the lower lawns where there is a swimming pool, *frontón* court, steam baths, and more.

Back in the house, we settled down in the library (far too elegant a room to ever read in) and in a few minutes Cantinflas came in wearing slacks and a black turtle-neck sweater. He looked younger than I thought he would, a charming and handsome man, and he spoke in a soft voice. His English is not too good, but we managed. Santiago had already told him about the possibility of my becoming his writer — but in view of recent developments, I didn't want to press the point. I said I'd like to write a magazine article about him, but that I'd rather not sit with a notebook, asking when and where he was born, what he likes for breakfast, and so on. He agreed with me and said that type of interview was always a bore. I suggested that if he were going traveling soon, I might go with him and we could do our talking in transit. He asked if I would like to go with him in his private plane to his house in Acapulco the week end after next, and stay two or three days and just sit around and talk. I said that would be my idea of a good way to do it. So he said we would make the trip unless some big deal came up to interfere.

Santiago and I left on a note of high good will and drove downtown, turning left at the House of Tiles and ducking into a cavernous garage under an office building. We stepped from the car and into an elevator and were hauled to the top of the building where we entered the Bankers' Club. The place was somber and solemn and conservative, with paneled walls and heavy furniture and not much light. The men wore business suits and vests and most of them had gray hair, or were grayed-up at the temples, and it was all precisely the same as bankers' clubs in the United States. Santiago said the club serves the best food in Mexico. He did the ordering for me, including a dish of long red chiles that had been toasted. They had a wonderful, inviting aroma but when I took my first bite the roof of my mouth tried to escape right out the top of my head. Santiago now had the laugh on me, and he exercised it, flinging back his head and haw-hawing over my oral pain. "Let me show you how it's done," he finally said. He seized one whole toasted chile and crumpled it into his soup, very businesslike, smacked his lips in anticipation, then took a big spoonful of the soup. In three seconds tears were streaming down his face, he started to pant like an exhausted dog, at the same time shaking his head violently from side to side; when he could use words he grumbled that they had fooled him with chiles from Guatemala. I could tell that Santiago was having a real bad day. After lunch he introduced me to "the richest man in Mexico," whose name I didn't catch, and then to "the most dynamic industrial leader in Mexico," whose name I missed. He then suggested that we cross the street to the Palace of Fine Arts, saying there were some Orozco things he wanted to see.

We roamed through several exhibitions and now and then he would ask for my comment on certain paintings. Then we came to the Orozco canvases, and to the portrait of a man. "What do you think of that?" asked Santiago. "What *should* I think?" I asked. "Well, do you know who it is?" I studied the portrait, trying to place the face, thinking of various contemporary political figures, but finally I said I had no idea who it was. It had to be, of course, a portrait of Santiago Reachi painted by Orozco. It was dumb of me not to know it, and I recognize his right to show pride in it; if Orozco had painted my portrait and it was hung in this famous palace, I would be out in the Alameda collaring strangers and dragging them in to look at it.

But Santiago was now showing signs of irascibility. I had offended him four times: I made the mistake of Orizaba, I made the mistake of mentioning money in connection with writing a story for him, I made the mistake of backing away from the Guatemala chiles, thus impelling him to take them on, and I made the mistake of not recognizing him in the portrait. He was definitely out of sorts, and when a mousy little man, a guard, approached him and told him to put out his cigar, that smoking was forbidden, Santiago flew into a rage. "People of refinement and intelligence and taste," he almost shouted, "come here for relaxation and enjoyment of these beautiful works of art, and you nasty little bureaucrats and Hitlers want to show off your authority, and spoil the whole thing!" At this point I made my final blunder of the day, siding with the little attendant and saying that Santiago was dead wrong — that the rule said No SMOKING and that he should not smoke.

Driving back to the studio he didn't talk much. A producer and a director who had been quarreling over something were waiting for him to arbitrate, so I retired to Cantinflas's office and studied a picture history of the Revolution. Later a young man came along and asked me if I'd like to watch a beautiful actress from Brazil, named Laura Hidalgo, doing a bedroom scene. We arrived on the set one minute after Laura got out of the bed and put on a robe. So I went back to Santiago's office and found the feuding producer and director screaming curses at each other, and threatening murder, and Santiago was howling at them to behave themselves, and I felt that I was once again in Hollywood. At last Santiago told the director that if he'd go ahead and do what he didn't want to do, then some time within the next year he would let him make the life of Zapata. The director was overjoyed, and hugged Santiago, and shook hands with the producer, and left. Santiago and the producer then had a big laugh, and from their talk I judged that whenever there is trouble with a temperamental director or producer, a sure way to calm matters down is to promise the unhappy man that he can film the life of Zapata later on.

February 12

CUERNAVACA continues in my estimate to be a scatterdemalion town, at least in its public portions, and so I phoned Hacienda Vista Hermosa for a room and engaged a cab to take us out there later today. I read for a while in Cuernavaca history and got to wondering how Dwight Morrow ever reconciled his J. P. Morgan background with his reputed sympathetic attitude toward the Mexican Revolution. Perhaps he didn't. Dr. Eyler Simpson, who wrote one of the most authoritative books on the Mexican economy, said: "I make no pretense to passing any final judgments on Ambassador Morrow's actuations and policies in Mexico. I simply note the fact that coincident with his presence in Mexico, the life went out of the revolution." Reading about Morrow gave me the urge to look at the Rivera murals again, so we walked over to the Palace of Cortez. In the crowd on the balcony were about a dozen Indians, most of them shabby and barefooted, and as they looked at the historic figures on the wall, I felt that they knew much more about the whole thing than I — that the meaning of the paintings was embedded deep in their souls. And then I realized that I was indulging in a sort of hophead, poetic thinking, a form of romanticism that writers should guard against, but usually don't. If the truth be known, those Indians had no slightest inkling of what those murals signify, for they know nothing of history, including their own, whereas I have studied Prescott and Bernal Díaz and I've even read Madariaga's life of Cortez, and as for the Aztecs — Don Quixote gave me the lowdown on them that day in Chapultepec Park.

The young man who drove us to Vista Hermosa spoke no English, so Nelle and I were reduced to talking with each other. At one point we came around a curve and saw a herd of cows up ahead.

Nelle cried out, "Oh, look at the *leches!*"

"Good God, woman," I objected, "they are not *leches!* They're *cavas.*"

The driver seemed to sense what we were talking about, and spoke one word: "*Vacas.*" What I had said was: "Good God, woman! They are not milks, they are wine cellars."

Vista Hermosa is one of our favorite spots in Mexico; if the food were just a trifle better, it would be the perfect resort. It began as a hacienda for the production of sugar, having been established by Hernando Cortez himself. After about a hundred years it passed from his family, continuing as a sugar mill. Then in the Revolution it was destroyed by Zapata. Some of the walls were left standing and the huge, cavernous hall that is now the dining room is pretty much as it was originally. Otherwise, the whole thing is a restoration.

The swimming pool, with the remains of the ancient aqueduct passing overhead and creating a waterfall at the entrance to the dining room, is the center of activity and the place to meet unusual people. This evening, for example, we fell into a poolside conversation with a couple who said they live in "a wonderfully restricted community in New Jersey." I asked what they meant by restricted. "We don't allow the New York type," the woman said. It soon developed that a hatred for the "New York type" all but dominates their lives, although at the moment they were almost too busy despising the Mexican type to worry about the New York type. They spoke of several resorts in Mexico "where the New York type ruin everything" and warned us away from those places. They asked about the hotels we had been in and in each case wanted to know, "Do they have good American food?" When the poolside waiter brought me a glass of beer, the Jersey gentleman, who snuffled between his words and wore a porkpie hat, said, "Better count your change — they'll rob you blind." I remarked mildly that if there is one country on earth where they don't rob you, this is it. He chuckled and snuffled and said I apparently hadn't seen much of Mexico, and then his wife said, "I simply don't understand why they can't learn to cook a decent meal down here." I was so irritated by these people that I felt like beating their brains out with a limp tortilla. I thought back to Tepoztlán and the little old woman at the church. Paul Saunders and I were standing at the entrance to the church and the little woman came out, barefooted, wearing a rebozo, head bowed low. As she glanced up I nodded and said, *"Buenas tardes, Señora."* She responded in a soft, murmurous voice. She hesitated and then, before crossing in front of us, she said gently, *"Permiso."* She was quiet and gentle and sweet. She had probably been attending that church for sixty or seventy years, long before the loud and nosy Gringos ever came to the village. I think maybe I liked her better than that unhappy woman from Jersey. And as for the gentleman, the reason he wears a porkpie hat is that he's got a porkpie head.

February 13

I'VE been reading several little books produced by local writers for tourists in this area. In almost every town favored by tourists somebody gets out a book summarizing the history of the place and describing the landmarks. The English in most of these volumes is fascinating. I've been told that the blame lies with Mexican printers, who are rugged individualists with their own ideas of how words should be spelled and sentences constructed. I have a book containing this sentence: "If Mexico is a land of dractic contrasts, Cuernavaca can claim a good share of it." And another: "This pyramid was accidentally discovered during the Revolution when guns were placed on it because it resembled a hill thought inexpugnable, but the trepidation uncovered a part hidden beneath the vegetation. Morelos has a tremendous number of these covered pyramids which will be revealed when time is available to remove the grass which jealously conceals the past."

Sitting amidst the flowers, beside the pool, Nelle made an interesting observation — that our luggage is wearing out *on the bottom*. And she has discovered why: it's a combination of rough cobblestone courtyards and very short bellhops. I observed that this is the only hotel I know about that has room keys you could kill a man with — they are of wrought iron, nearly a foot.long, and hell to carry around. I also observed that after long effort I have finally mastered a Spanish word that I had trouble learning: *cenicero,* which means ash tray. The current Minister of Education is Señor Ceniceros, or Mister Ashtrays.

Today three twittery little ladies from Ohio came up to me and said they had heard I was a writer and they wanted to know if I was acquainted with their friend Cy Plunkett. I said I wasn't. "Oh," one of them exclaimed, "you ought to know him — he plays beautiful piano and writes for the *Saturday Evening Post.*" I said, "Under what name?" And the lady said, "Why, Cy Plunkett, of course."

We also met a Mexico City businessman who said he had recently returned from Europe. At the New York airport he bought a copy of *Time* magazine. President Ruiz Cortines was on the cover and the story inside was all about how honesty had come back to government in Mexico, and the *mordida* (bite) was no longer, and graft was a thing of the past. The businessman was very happy at this news, for he had been paying off under the table for many years. So at the Mexico City airport he flung open his bags and said to the customs man, "There it is, help yourself." The customs man began rolling his eyes suggestively; then he flipped over the lid of one bag and held his open hand underneath it. The businessman said, "Oh, no, my friend. We are now going to be honest under Ruiz Cortines — I read it, and it is so." Said the customs man, "What is the matter with you? You live in Mexico, don't you? Well, you can see my hand." So the businessman sighed and placed a fifty-peso note in the hand, and decided that the *mordida* will stay until the winds wither Popo down to a nubbin.

Nelle has a remarkable facility for striking up acquaintance with people who are precisely right for us. Today she came up with the Ernest Leuenbergers, who own the famous Swiss Chalet restaurant in Mexico City. They drove us over to Lake Tequesquitengo — a name that is harder to pronounce than ash trays and which means "Market for Saltpeter." Ernest, who calls himself Ernesto in Mexico, engaged a speedboat and took the wheel himself and treated us to an hour's circuit of the lake, pointing out the resort homes of various politicians.

For a long time there was a ghostly legend about this lake. Natives of the region often told visitors that sometimes, especially on moonlit nights, the tower of a church could be seen beneath the surface of the lake, and sometimes the dim outlines of an entire village, with big bells hanging from the limbs of the trees. The visitors, Mexicans and Gringos alike, always had a good laugh at this prime example of Indian superstition. As late as the 1940's Byron Steel wrote in his guidebook: "During the dry season one can imagine one sees the belfry of an ancient cathedral said to lie on the bottom of the lake." Along came the Era of the Skin Diver and some of these boys went down, and be-dagged if there wasn't a real pretty church down there, and a whole be-durned village. And who was responsible for its being there? Mine host, Hacienda Vista Hermosa. The old histories said that the lake was originally quite small, with a village devoted to the mining of saltpeter (they used it only to make soap and as a purge for cattle). At that time Vista Hermosa was a big plantation, much of its land under water. Its owners needed more land for sugar cane, so they began draining operations, funneling the water into Lake Tequesquitengo. The lake rose. The villagers hung the church bells in the taller trees. The lake continued to rise. The villagers fled. And many

years later I went zipping above the spire of the church in a speedboat. Anybody could have done it.

At Vista Hermosa I've been attracted by a big man with a kindly
face and an extremely sweet manner toward everyone. For a while I
took him to be a guide, because a guide is required to put on a kindly
face and a sweet manner even if he's got a hangover that would hos-
pitalize a rhinoceros. I watched this man as he strolled around the
pool and through the grounds or sat reading a book. At last I had
to find out about him and tonight as he came along I gave him a
buenas noches and invited him to have a drink. We spent the whole
evening with him and became quite friendly in a violent, argumenta-
tive sort of way. Señor M. is a prosperous automobile dealer in Mexico City, suffers from nerves, and is down here for a week of rest. He
speaks good English and describes himself as being of pure Spanish
blood. He hates Juárez. He loathes Lázaro Cárdenas. He despises
Franklin D. Roosevelt and Harry Truman. At my mention of Zapata
he flung up his hands. "A nasty, bloodthirsty murderer!" he cried. "A
destroyer of haciendas — beautiful country homes that took centuries
to build and beautify, and where there was a way of life that was
serene and lovely and happy."

Nelle asked him why Zapata is such a popular hero, with statues
and monuments honoring him everywhere.

"It is because of this awful government," said Señor M. "It is the
same as if the government of Illinois, and also the government in
Washington, decided that Carpface Al Capone is to be a hero, and
streets are named for him and statues and monuments erected everywhere, and poems and songs written in tribute to him. It would have
to be done because the government said so, but the people would
know better. The people of Mexico know better about the bloodthirsty Zapata."

All through our long conversation this pleasant man made deroga-
tory remarks about the Indians, always distinguishing between them
and "Mexicans." So I finally said, "The truth is, *you* are not a Mexican. You are a Spaniard and you don't like it here one bit, and if I

were in your shoes I'd pack up and go live in Spain, with Franco."
He didn't throw me in the pool or draw a knife on me — he was a
gentleman.

He revealed that he is a high-ranking member of an international
secret fraternal order and soon after that he began describing the
native dances and ceremonials in Mexico, saying that they were "the
most degrading and ridiculous performances in the world, proving
that the Indian is little more than an animal." I sat there and had a
long, hard laugh, for I have seen the annual conventions and parades
of his fraternal society, and I've heard about its initiation rites and
other secret ceremonials, and if ever human animal acted sillier, the
records don't show it.

When I brought up the name of Cárdenas I thought Señor M. was
going to have a coronary. "A pig!" he cried. "A filthy *puerco!* I spit
on him!" He said that expropriation of the oil was a criminal act and
Cárdenas should have had his neck stretched for it. "The filthy pig
broke an agreement," he argued, "and what kind of a world would
this be if we all went around breaking agreements? It is the same as
if I say to you in my house, I give you the right to hang your hat on
that peg over there for ninety-nine years. Now, suppose the very next
month I tell you to take your hat out of my house and never hang it
there again. What kind of a nice fellow would I be?"

I was getting sleepy, so I decided to tell him. I said, regarding the
hat, that I might be the kind of fellow who would come into his house
to hang my hat and foul up the house, arriving perhaps in the middle
of the night to hang my hat and waking up the entire household, and
I might even make passes at his wife and bat his children around;
that I might refuse to obey the ordinary rules of the household; that
I might demand that all members of his family step to one side, get
out of my way, when I came in to hang my hat.

He said I would never commit such offenses in his house, and even
if I did, *he* would not be the one to break the agreement — the way
that pig Cárdenas did. So I just smiled and we *hasta luego*-ed and
parted amicably and I noted in the moonlight that this man still had

one of the kindliest faces I've ever seen. I have known some rabid
and fiery radicals in my time and I always believed that they were the
real wrathful and apoplectic ones of this earth; they were models of
quiescence alongside some of these Mexican conservatives.

February 14

CARLOS arrived from Mexico City early this morning and before
we left I saw Señor M. gazing at a fountain, and I said good-by to
him.

"Where are you going?" he asked.

"Deep into the Zapata country," I said. "We are going to find his
birthplace, and I may even place a wreath on his tomb."

"He was an evil, bloodthirsty murderer," said Señor M.

"He was the general of an army," I responded, "and if he was a
bloodthirsty murderer, then Cortez and Pizarro were bloodthirsty
murderers, and the same goes for Robert E. Lee and Porfirio Díaz
and George Washington and Zaragoza and Ike Eisenhower."

He smiled and shook his head and said, "You are impossible. You
do not understand things." And so we headed south into a region
known to very few tourists — the land where Zapata made his revolution.

Before leaving home I read a biography of Zapata called *The Crimson Jester,* by one H. H. Dunn. Dunn was in Mexico ostensibly as a
newspaper correspondent but actually he was a spy for Porfirio Díaz.
He describes Zapata as cruel, ruthless, cunning, and "the most powerful and most destructive outlaw in the known history of the entire
world." He charges that Zapata executed 1100 men, killing 250 with
his own hands (you reckon he means strangling?). His personal loot,
said Dunn, ran into millions. He went through phony marriage ceremonies with twenty-six different women. He killed many of his cap-
tives by rubbing them with honey and spread-eagling them over ant-
hills. The book is one long recital of rape and torture and death. Dunn

wrote that he spent a lot of time in Villa Ayala, which was Zapata's headquarters, and that Zapata had his loot stored in a big concrete strong room there. I am now in a position to say that this man Dunn reminds me of the Ozark character who once in a great while would tell the truth and then lie out of it just to keep in practice.

As we drove toward Jojutla, Carlos told a story that is one of the best-known tales to come out of the Revolution. There was a Chinese peasant who got off a ship at Acapulco and started walking toward Mexico City where he had friends. He didn't know that a wild and crazy revolution was in progress in the South. He was captured by a band of armed men and their leader said to him, "You Zapatista or Federale?" The Chinese was bewildered but, being prodded for an answer, said, "Federale." Whereupon they beat hell out of him, for they were Zapatistas. He struggled on toward Mexico City and again he was captured, and the leader said, "Zapatista or Federale?" This time he played it smart and said, "Zapatista." And they beat hell out of him, for they were Federales. It happened a third time, with a third beating, and then came the fourth capture, and the leader said, "You Zapatista or Federale?" This time the Chinese didn't hesitate, but cried out, "You say first!"

We stopped for a while in Jojutla (Ho-hootla) and ate some *jicama* and looked at a little bridge which they say Cortez helped build with his own hands. Carlos said that Jojutla is the home of the *calzón*. Elsewhere in Mexico the word means underpants, but here it means the simple, white, wrap-around pants worn by Zapatistas, by farm hands, and by Vista Hermosa bus boys. Nelle insisted that I should have a pair, so we proceeded to the market and found a stall where clothing was for sale.

"*Calzones, por favor,*" Nelle said to the woman in charge.

"*Para usted?*"

Carlos laughed, and I caught on. In saying, "For you?" the woman had been taking a sly dig at tourist ladies and their costumes; no Mexican woman would ever consider wearing *calzones*.

"No," said Nelle, "*para Señor.*"

The woman looked me squarely in the face, turned around to a pile of clothing, snaffled out one garment, folded it, and wrapped it in a piece of newspaper. Clearly a talented woman — she could look into a man's eyes and tell the size of his pants. My *calzones* came to nine pesos, or seventy-two cents.

Driving on toward Tlaltizapán I happened to notice two workmen sleeping at the side of the road. They were lying crosswise in a shallow ditch, their behinds resting in the ditch and their feet and head elevated on either side. They looked very comfortable, and it occurred to me that such a roadside scene may have inspired some furniture designer, touring in Mexico, to think up the contour chair. Those men in the ditch were in exactly the health-giving posture that I assume when I tilt back in a chair that cost me a hundred and twenty dollars.

Tlaltizapán is the village where Carlos saw his father for the last time. It is a small town. The plaza contains many huge laurel trees which cast the whole park into deep shadow. The town was one of Zapata's favorite headquarters and in the plaza we came upon a concrete platform, presumably for orators, with a crude painting of Zapata above it. Carlos had not been here in many years. His father was a young officer, recently graduated from the military academy, and he had been sent down at the head of a detachment of troops, under instructions to capture Zapata if possible. Zapata captured him instead and he was brought to this town and sentenced to death. His family was notified in Cuernavaca that they would be permitted to visit him. Carlos, who was about five, and his older brother and their mother were transported to Tlaltizapán by handcar.

"I remember," Carlos said now, waving a hand over the plaza, "that this place was all full of horses, tied to the trees. And now, let me think — now I will show you where my father was prisoner."

He led us around to a one-story building, now a cantina, and pointed to the window through which he and his mother and his brother said farewell to his father. "Oh, he was angry," Carlos said. "He was more angry than sad, and he already knew he was to be shot. And he was shot as soon as we left for Cuernavaca."

Soon we were on the road again and Carlos stopped to ask a group of workmen some questions about Zapata's birthplace. On the opposite side of the road I suddenly saw a strange tableau. About a hundred feet away stood six figures, having the appearance of statues of naked Indians. But they were real Indians. There was a small stream there and they had been bathing. Tourists are rare in these parts and they had been taken by surprise. When they suddenly realized that our car had stopped and that there was a woman in it, they didn't scamper for the water or the bushes. Instead they froze in their tracks, standing motionless, trying to escape our notice, and they were covering themselves with their hands. I was the only one who had seen them and I didn't say a word. Then Carlos put the car in gear and Nelle suddenly spotted them. "Wait!" she shouted. "Look over there in the field!" But Carlos and I, being Great Moralists, outvoted her and we drove on.

So we came to Villa Ayala, which is supposed to have been the town most closely associated with Zapata. Here his family lived and here he had his base of operations. It wasn't much of a town but we stopped and I spotted an old man drowsing on a bench in the little plaza. Carlos cross-examined him about Zapata, with special reference to any landmarks that might remain in the village. The old man said there was nothing here connected with Zapata. Yes, he remembered the General quite well. What kind of a man was he? He peered around, looking to right and left to make sure nobody was listening, then he waggled his hand in the gesture which means "so-so" and said, "Some good, some bad." The old man's cautiousness delighted Carlos, who said, "You see, Zapata is dead forty years and he was such a no-good mean baster the old man is still afraid to talk."

Just beyond the village we came to a field, and in the middle of it stood a heroic statue of Zapata — heroic in size but not in quality. It appeared to be made of plaster of Paris and then painted in gaudy blues and reds and whites and blacks. There were a few burros grazing around the base of the statue and off to one side half a dozen hogs stopped whatever they had been doing and stared at us as if we were from some foreign land. We turned up a road here, the poorest byway in the history of engineering, covered with two inches of powdery dust, full of deep potholes and jagged rocks, twisting and turning past shabby adobe shacks. Twice we had to stop and chase sleeping pigs out of the road and finally, after almost destroying the car, we arrived at Zapata's birthplace. The remains of the adobe house are now enclosed by a concrete shelter which is painted a brilliant blue, with bars across the front painted a bright yellow. The barred gate was padlocked and there was a cow lying against it, but we could see inside. The ruins of the house looked as if it might have contained four tiny rooms, but only the walls are left now and they seem to be going fast. It seems worth noting that the three monuments we saw in the heart of the Zapata country — the painting, the statue and the birthplace — are all shabby and cheap, done by unskilled but loving rustic hands, which is perhaps as it should be. The people of this region are of the same stripe as the soldiers who rode with Zapata. In 1914, when Zapata led his army into Mexico City, the people of the city were so frightened that they locked themselves in their homes. They were astonished that the peasant army was the best-behaved of any invading force in the city's history. Instead of looting and burning and raping, as everyone expected, the Zapatista soldiers appeared at back doors, hat in hand, asking politely for a bite to eat. They took over the National Palace for a while and the peasant guards spent most of their time making faces into the big wall mirrors, while the officers played with the elevators like children. One group of Zapatistas, lounging in front of the palace, saw a fire engine clanging toward them. They had never seen such a monster before and, thinking it was some new terrible instrument of war, they raised their rifles and with deadly accuracy picked the firemen off of it.

We drove in to Cuautla for lunch. Cuautla is a big town with an equestrian statue of Zapata, a church that has been converted into a railroad station, and a famous watering-place. I saw a chart of the major Mexican spas, and Cuautla leads all the rest with cures for circulatory ailments, diabetes, heart trouble, skin disease, stomach trouble, nerves, and rheumatism. The chart said you have to go to some other spa for sterility, whatever that means.

Before returning to Vista Hermosa we took a quick look at a village near Cuautla, called Yecapixtla. The name is Aztec and means "Where People Have Sharp Noses." We rode around, looking closely at the people, and found their noses to be quite dull.

February 15

BEGINNING the long climb to Taxco we came to a stretch in the highway where small boys and girls held up live iguanas and yelled at us, "Peecha, peecha, peecha!" Carlos explained that they charge tourists one peso to pose for photographs holding the iguanas. Later on the children take the dragon home where it furnishes meat for the evening meal and after that they make a pocketbook out of the hide.

On the outskirts of Taxco we stopped to visit with Carlos Manning, who operates a silver shop and is head of the federal police in this district. At Manning's place I fell into conversation with a tourist couple from Milwaukee who were just getting ready to pull out for more northerly climes. I noticed that the lady was shaking and asked how things had been going.

"Oh, dear," she quavered. "We're trying to get out of this awful place. It's the children selling things, and begging — they're driving me insane. I'm so nervous I can't sit still. It's worse here than Cuernavaca. They grab hold of you and drag you around. I'm going to have to take a whole bottle of tranquilizing pills." I knew, from our previous visit to Taxco, what she was talking about, but I do believe she was exaggerating a trifle; if she really suffers from a steady procession of strident and baldly deceitful peddlers, then I can only conclude that she never looks at television back home.

We sat in Taxco's colorful Plaza Borda while Carlos went looking for Leslie Figueroa. Leslie is a fabulous character and a great person. Long ago she was a chorus girl in New York and a newspaper woman in Colorado and Indiana. She was the first American to buy a house in Taxco and now she owns about twenty of them, renting them out to people who want to stay awhile. She is the author of *Taxco, the Enchanted City*, which has been selling like tortillas for years.

Leslie took us up cobblestone hill and down cobblestone dale to one of her houses, Casa Clarita, waved a hand at it and said that we could have it as long as we wanted to stay. It has a broad terrace with a fine view of the town, and its own cook, named Vicenta. Leslie confided to me that Vicenta, who is maybe sixty and maybe seventy or even eighty and who has a wonderful Mexican face, was once Obregón's cook at Chapultepec Castle. This, of course, is a great thrill to me.

We returned to the plaza and then climbed some more cobblestones to Casa Figueroa — the studios and art school run by Leslie's husband, Fidel Figueroa. Fidel is a painter, native of Taxco, and Mexicans don't come any handsomer. His Casa Figueroa occupies a historic palace which was built in the sixteenth century by a Count Cadena. The Count was Taxco's magistrate and every Indian who couldn't pay his fine was put to work as a laborer on the construction of the palace. When it was finished, the Count sentenced other Indians, male and female, to terms of domestic service in his big house.

Casa Figueroa stands just a few steps above the plaza and Fidel took me outside to a stone railing which he said was "The Balcony of the Poors." In colonial times the poor people, meaning the Indians, were not permitted in the plaza during the hours when the gentry were promenading; the "poors" were, however, permitted to stand on this balcony and look down at their betters. Standing there I thought of the day in 1811 when the great Morelos, son of a poor carpenter, an Indian with some Negro blood in his veins, came into Taxco and ordered thirteen high-born and wealthy Spanish gentlemen shot, and it was done in front of the building across the plaza now occupied by a drugstore. Maybe they had it coming.

Carlos departed for Mexico City and Leslie cobblestoned us back to her house where we had lunch on the terrace — the best overall view we've had yet of Taxco. Every building in town has a red tile roof. Leslie explained that after José de la Borda grew rich from the Taxco silver mines, he got homesick for his native town in Spain. He remembered best the tiled roofs, so at his own expense he had all the thatched roofs of Taxco changed to tile roofs, and the tradition was established.

Leslie pointed out a house farther up the mountainside and said it was occupied by people who raise and butcher pigs.

"In Taxco," she said, "we have a breed of humans known as pig rustlers, and those people up the hill keep two fierce dogs to scare off the rustlers. Not long ago the family went away for a day or two, and in came the rustlers. They fed the dogs meatballs loaded with Nembutal. They poured tequila into the slop troughs and all the pigs got so drunk they couldn't grunt or squeal. The rustlers were driving the pigs away and had got as far as the convent, right below us here, when a cop happened along. He noticed that the pigs were reeling and staggering around and so he arrested the rustlers. They took the thieves off to the human jail and the pigs off to the *puerco* jail. Yes, we have a special jail for vagrant *puercos*. Pigs are not supposed to wander around the streets, so once in a while the cops start a campaign and begin picking them up. The way a cop gets a pig to the *puerco* jail is by handling him like a wheelbarrow. He seizes the two hind legs and compels the pig to go forward on his front legs. It is a common sight in Taxco."

At dusk we proceeded to our little house, Casa Clarita, and Vicenta had dinner ready. We met her grandniece, Estefana, a child about ten who is being reared by Vicenta. Dinner was served on the terrace — lamb chops, creamed onions, salad. Vicenta is accustomed to serving Gringos and there was no hint of Mexico in the dinner, so I asked her for *salsa mexicana* and heard her going at it in the kitchen with mortar (*molcajete*) and pestle (*tejolote*). When she brought the *salsa* to me I found it mild, but didn't say anything, and then we spent half an hour trying to talk to her about Obregón. She acted out the assassination of Obregón and made it appear that the killer came up behind him, and she showed how his head fell on the table, and she seemed quite sad about it. I mentioned Zapata and, mostly in sign language, she indicated that he always wore his wagon-wheel sombrero at table, and all he ate was stacks and stacks of tortillas with chiles on the side.

Vicenta is paid the equivalent of eight dollars a month and is contented. She promised that tomorrow she would make some enchiladas for us. I said, "Like para Obregón," but she just smiled and I'm sure she didn't know what I meant.

February 16

NOISES seem to be magnified tremendously in Taxco because of the topography and they blend to produce what is known as "The Symphony of Taxco." It is made up of many different sounds, only one of which jangles my nerves. The burros, the dogs, the chickens, the siren at the mine and the church bells seem to harmonize all right, but I could do without the cornet players. There is a high school just below our terrace and every kid in that school is studying the cornet. They carry the horns around with them all day, and take them home with them, pausing now and then to let go a couple of blasts. My prejudice against the cornet has now grown as powerful as my prejudice against the Scottish bagpipe. To the deepest abyss of hell with them both!

Leslie told us today of the period in which she and Fidel ran Bar Paco — the drinking establishment which occupies a balcony overlooking the plaza and which is the best place in all Mexico to

Observe Life. Fidel ran the business at night and Leslie stayed at home and read — she spends several hours each day with her books. One evening Fidel came upstairs and told her there was an American writer in the bar — he got the name wrong, "Shinnerick." Leslie said she had never heard of him, went back to her reading, and missed meeting one of her heroes, John Steinbeck.

Bar Paco is a fine establishment but I object to some of the phony legends surrounding it. I have read and heard stories about how Cole Porter wrote his *Mexican Holiday* on that balcony, and Covarrubias sat at one of the tables and worked on *Mexico South,* and Thornton Wilder wrote most of a play there, and Steinbeck dreamed up *The Grapes of Wrath* while drinking Bar Paco tequila, and so on and so on. I know something of the writing trade, and I know a thousand writers, and I say that nobody ever wrote anything at Bar Paco except, maybe, an I. O. U.

Leslie has furnished me with a number of books I hadn't been able to locate at home and today I read *Tempest Over Mexico,* by Rosa E. King. Mrs. King came to Cuernavaca in 1905 and had the misfortune to open the Bella Vista Hotel in the fateful year of 1910. She writes of life as she observed it on the haciendas in the time of Díaz — the luxurious living of the *hacendados* and the misery of their Indian slaves. She tells how the youthful Zapata was employed at one of these haciendas and how he was assigned the job of taking some horses to the owner's Mexico City residence. When he got there he found that the horses had marble stalls and were petted and pampered, and he compared this treatment with the treatment of the Indians and he began to suspect that something was out of balance. Then when the *hacendados* moved in and seized his father's cornfield, he decided the time had come for action.

Mrs. King saw both sides of the Revolution at close hand, because Cuernavaca was occupied by the Federales, then by the Zapatistas, then by the Federales again, and so on, and many of the officers on both sides were quartered in her hotel. She writes about how Zapata's soldiers often had to leave the army and go home for a while to cultivate their cornfields. When they were caught the Federales made them dig their own graves, then shot them alongside the excavations.

> The government [Mrs. King writes] made every effort to paint the Zapatistas as monsters . . . with tales of atrocities committed by the rebels. I think this was largely propaganda, but if there was some truth in the tales, the acts were retaliation for the cruelty of the Federales, who should have known better, and if I had been one of those ignorant, hounded people, I think I should have acted as they did.

This from a woman who underwent the horrors of the "death march" from Cuernavaca, which is described in great detail in her book. Cuernavaca was under siege, with only remnants of the Federal force in town. The people were starving and had already eaten the last of their horses and mules. The railroad had been cut and at last the Federale officers announced that the only escape would be to walk to Mexico City. Eight thousand men, women and children set out, struggling toward the capital, hungry and wet and cold, and all along the way Zapata's snipers harassed them. Many died of exhaustion and hunger, many of bullets. Carlos and his mother and brother and grandmother were on this march. The grandmother was killed by a stray sniper's bullet and her body left behind, never to be found. Mrs. King suffered as much as the others, but she was one of about two thousand who finally made it — two thousand out of eight thousand who started. Because of Zapata she went through one of the most heroic and horrifying death marches of history, and she came out of it admiring Zapata and believing he was right. She died a few years ago in Cuernavaca at the age of ninety, still believing it.

A stone's throw from our Casa Clarita is a house called Villa Ayala. It was so named in tribute to Zapata by Leslie's daughter, who lived in it while working on a biography of the agrarian leader. She did an enormous amount of research but died before she could get her book written. The house was also rented for a while to

Leon Trotzky. Leslie said: "He was the most frightened man I've ever seen. He kept himself locked in the bathroom most of the time, and had armed guards all around the house."

We sat some more in the plaza, Observing People, among them the begging children who unnerved the lady from Milwaukee. Some years ago the town government took cognizance of this problem. Each cop was given a long switch. If he caught a child on the streets during school hours, he switched him all the way to the schoolhouse door. This solved the problem of truancy, but not of begging because the children redoubled their operations after school and on holidays. The worst of the lot are the ragged little girls, ten or twelve years old, who borrow a neighbor's baby and tote it around the plaza, pretending it is their own, and softening the hearts of elderly ladies. An artist told me that these little girls are marvelous actresses and that one of them belongs to a family of beggars who are so accomplished at their trade that they own four houses. Many of the children approach the Gringo with hand extended, crying "Neeckel, neeckel, neeckel." Leslie has a way of coping with this nuisance. She extends *her* hand and says, "*Peso, peso, peso.*" Old-timers tell me that the way to repel beggers and peddlers who refuse to give up is to wag an index finger at them, slowly moving it back and forth and scowling at the same time. This usually sends them away; but if it doesn't, then you yell at them, "Vayase!" That means "Hit the road!"

February 16

WE HEARD today that William Spratling, whose name is almost synonymous with modern Taxco, crashed in his private plane this morning. The report here is that he was taking off from his ranch, about five miles south of Taxco, intending to fly to Mexico City. In the cockpit he had a couple of boxes of fresh strawberries which he was taking to a friend in the capital. The plane was badly damaged

in the crash and the people from the ranch who saw the accident
were certain Spratling had either been killed or badly injured. They
rushed toward the wreckage just in time to see him emerge. He was
calmly picking strawberries out of his hair and eating them.

Spratling is the Silver King of Taxco, the Tulane professor who
came here for a visit in 1930 and stayed to create a major change
in the life of the town. He revived silverworking and other arts
and crafts among the natives and today most of the silver shops in
Taxco are run by his former employees and pupils. Among the
Spratling legends I like best is the one concerning the Eskimos.
Ernest Gruening, author of the best modern history of Mexico, was
a good friend of Spratling and knew of Spratling's success with the
natives in Taxco. Gruening, as Governor of Alaska, wanted to do
the same sort of thing with the Eskimos. He proposed that Spratling
send him a group of Taxco Indians to teach the Eskimos, but there
were legal difficulties, so Gruening sent his Eskimos to Taxco. Spratling put them up at his ranch and soon he was having his problems.
The Eskimo boys couldn't eat the local food and Spratling had to
make frequent flights to Acapulco and bring back fresh fish — they
wanted it raw. The heat bothered them too, and one lady told me
that when they got loose in town all females except those over eighty
had to take to the storm cellars. My understanding is that the project
was not an unqualified success.

Leslie is a realist and sees things clearly. Most other people, when
they criticize the behavior of American tourists, always soften the
blow by saying that only a few act badly. Not Leslie. She says that
at least 50 per cent of them are unpleasant, unreasonable jerks. She
deals with them constantly in her business of renting houses, and
she meets hundreds of them who are in Taxco for only a few days.
In addition to that, she has traveled all over the world and still
spends a good part of each year in foreign lands. She's full of tales
about her tenants and some of the crazy things they've done. One
woman said she didn't want the servants who came with the house
she was renting, "because I always call in a caterer when I want to

entertain." Leslie told her, "That's all right, but you may have to wait a while before your call gets through to San Antonio." Another woman complained bitterly because the Mexican cook she had drawn was unable to make baked Alaska.

Years ago Leslie was working on a newspaper in Nevada when she met a multimillionaire industrialist and married him. He took her back to a small city in Indiana and installed her in a mansion that looked like the White House. He was thirty-five years her senior and he and all his friends expected Leslie to play the part of a conservative, aristocratic lady, but Leslie's unorthodox ways kept the town standing on its ear. Nevertheless she stayed with her husband until his death. She was touring in Mexico in 1941 and arrived in Taxco to spend a few days. "Fidel was the second man I met in Taxco," she said. "I had no more idea of marrying him than I had of marrying Mussolini." She went back to Nevada where she had a ranch, and Fidel followed her, and they were married.

We had lunch today with Leslie and Dorothy MacDonald, once a newspaper writer in San Francisco and now a permanent resident of Taxco. We talked about bullfights, and both Leslie and Dorothy said they don't like them; but they suggested that I soft-pedal my criticism of them, lest somebody decide that the Moment of Truth has arrived for me. We went to Dorothy's house, which is near our own and which is called Casa del Corazón, or House of the Heart. She said that there are only half a dozen houses in town with telephones. Most people don't want them. Communication is by notes, carried by the servants. The Mexican girls love to tote notes back and forth across town — it gives them a chance to visit their friends in other houses and to catch up on the latest gossip.

Dorothy said that mail service is fairly good in Mexico, but never as efficient as in the United States. Sometimes, however, letters are mailed and never heard of again. There was one post-office employee in Taxco who was walking along with a bag of mail one afternoon, seemingly contented with his lot in life. Suddenly he stopped at the edge of the deep *barranca* which runs through the town, seized the mailbag in both hands, raised his eyes heavenward, and cried out in anguish: "Letters, letters, letters! And never a one for me!" Following which he dumped all the mail into the *barranca*.

When we arrived home this evening Vicenta was waiting with enchiladas and frijoles. They were good but I wouldn't say they were of Presidential caliber. I tried to talk to her some more about the eating habits of Obregón, and she got through to me with the information that she worked for three presidents — Obregón, Carranza and Huerta. Later she was in our room and found my *calzones* and brought them out, shaking with laughter and saying, "Zapata something something something," which probably meant that Zapata wore them all the time. I have read that these white wrap-around pants served as gonfalon and oriflamme for Zapata's troops and the Federales had a habit of shooting every person they found wearing them. I have not had my pair on yet, on the grounds that I don't know how to operate them.

The dogs of Taxco are an exceptional lot. They don't have anywhere to go but they always act as if they did. They come through the plaza, heads down, going at a slow but purposeful trot, looking neither to right nor left, much as if they had been working on the other side of town and were now on their way home for lunch. The quality that they appear to have is doggedness. One woman told us that the Mexicans don't keep dogs as pets, but as servants, with the job of guarding them against all enemies, including the invisible. She said that it is never wise to try to pet a Mexican dog because most of them are inclined to be vicious toward strangers. They are also inclined to be smarter than most dogs. I have read somewhere, possibly in Sybille Bedford's book, about the dogs of certain villages in the Guadalajara region. These dogs hang around the railroad station and when a train comes in, they leap aboard, and start racing through the cars, looking for food scraps dropped on the floor by the passengers. If the passengers of one particular train have been real sloppy about their eating, and the scraps are plentiful, the dogs will stay aboard until the next stop. Then they get off and, presumably, wait for a train going back. Almost as smart as commuters.

The annual Blessing of the Animals at the Mexican churches is a thing we've unhappily missed so far. It is a colorful and touching ceremony, with men, women and children bringing all kinds of domestic animals and pets to the church. Chickens, pigs, ducks, burros, dogs, cats, mules, parrots, cattle, turkeys, monkeys — decorated with flowers and colored streamers and some even wearing a fresh coat of paint — are blessed by the priest, and he usually speaks of the community's gratitude to the animals for the hard work they do and the food they provide. I imagine that if the pigs and the chickens and the cows and the ducks and the turkeys understood the implications of this last compliment, they would not be inclined to cheer and applaud. Once in a while the animals, made nervous by the hubbub, get out of hand. The trouble usually starts when the priest raises the aspergillum and sends forth a shower of holy water, and some of this holy water hits a pig. There is nothing like a shot of holy water to set a pig on edge, and he tries to get away from his owner. The dogs go for the pig, the chickens and turkeys and ducks fly in all directions, panic seizes the mules and burros and calves and cows and people. Sometimes the padre is bowled over in the stampede, and sometimes the frightened animals get inside the church and overturn pews and do other damage.

Everywhere you go in Mexico you find beautiful tile, but there seems to be more of it in Taxco than in most of the smaller towns, probably because of Fidel Figueroa. As a young man he lived in Puebla, the tile center, and he is a tile artisan as well as a painter. In this country a bathroom is not a bathroom unless it is tiled, and that includes all public conveniences, or terlets. I have been in many such places which were indescribably bad and overpowering, yet the floors and walls and ceilings and accessories were done in beautiful tile. The Mexican people, rich and poor alike, attach no importance to such conveniences. I'm convinced that all their pipes and plumbing fixtures were manufactured and installed by the Aztecs.

Leslie puts good bathrooms in all her houses and introduced a feature that was confusing to the natives; because the Mexicans don't have the entrances to their bathrooms inside the house — it is necessary to go outdoors first, the way we have it in many of our filling stations.

February 17

THERE are nearly two hundred Gringos living in Taxco, many of them being mining engineers. Quite a few are elderly people who came here after they retired. As they have grown older and less vigorous, some of the retired people now find themselves in a quandary. They bought little homes up on the steep hillsides and now it is almost impossible for them to get downtown and back. The cobblestone streets were designed for the hooves of burros and are certainly picturesque, but they are hell on human feet. And no matter where you go in Taxco, you are always ascending or descending, and panting and puffing, and stopping now and then to rest.

We were scheduled to return to Mexico City today but we are enjoying Taxco and Casa Clarita so much that we've decided to stay a few days longer. It is evident that Vicenta has pledged herself to never speak a word of English in her life. I have been pointing to things, such as meat and spoon and table and tree and saying them in English, but she clamps her mouth shut and simply nods her head, frowning at such outlandish sounds. If we want to talk to her, we can damn well talk in God's own language, *español,* and if we want to understand what she has to say, then we'd better learn *español.* Soup is *sopa* and not soup.

I keep a phrase book and dictionary close at hand and today I talked to her some more about Obregón and Carranza and Huerta. I thought we had this whole subject pretty well settled, but suddenly I discovered that Vicenta has not understood me at all, and I have not understood her. In the course of today's talk about her work in Chapultepec Castle, she suddenly exclaimed, "No, no, no, no!" fol-

lowed by an enfilade of hot Spanish, and seizing the front of her
skirt in both hands, she began making vigorous scrubbing motions.
God in heaven! She was not Obregón's cook at all — she was his
washerwoman! She had never been his cook or anybody else's cook
at the castle. I thought about last night when she served the enchiladas and how I kept saying to her, "Enchiladas à la Obregón?"
and "Enchiladas à la Carranza?" She must think I'm the champion
ninny of all the ninnies in Christendom. Now she managed to in-
form me that Obregón and the others always had *hombres* for cooks,
and the *hombres* were French . . . meaning that those perfidious,
double-dealing, hypocritical Presidents never had enchiladas and
frijoles.

The whole thing has been a keen disappointment to me. It had
been important that the former cook of Mexican presidents was
cooking for me. Nelle insists that I should not be upset about it.
"After all," she said, "she washed the shirts of Obregón and Carranza
and Huerta, and now she's washing the shirts of you, I mean now
she's washing your shirts." To which I replied bitterly, "You do not
understand. It is not the same at all. There are certain spiritual
nuances involved that only a sensitive and artistic person like myself would feel. Shirt-scrubbing is not the same as cooking."

There are a number of American artists living here and I had a
long talk with one of them, a man who wears cowboy clothes, in the
plaza today. He said that the basic fascination of Taxco, over and
above the colors and the light, is that you lose all sense of the
passage of time. He no longer carries a watch and both clocks in
his house have long since run down. He usually can never remember
what day of the week it is. "I get up when I feel like it," he said,
"and eat when I'm hungry, and sleep when I get sleepy. I haven't
heard the jarring sound of an alarm clock in years. I hope I never
do."*

---

* The Mexican's indifference toward time and its divisions seems to me
to be reflected in the fact that the names of the days and the names of the
months are not even capitalized; January is *enero*, Wednesday is *miércoles*.

He also told me about a gag in one of Cantinflas's pictures. The comedian is standing on a corner with a friend and they are discussing where they should go for the week end. The friend says, "Let us go to Taxco." But Cantinflas says, "No. It would be foolish for us to go to Taxco as we cannot speak any English." This joke brought tremendous roars from Mexican audiences all over the nation.

Another story concerned a beautiful Mexican girl who works in one of the local silvershops. Several years ago she went to her employer and asked him if she would lose her job if she had a baby. The employer knew she was not married and asked her if she were in love with someone. She said she was not. "I do not know," she said, "who would be the father, but I want very much to have a little baby girl of my own. I must keep my job, so I will not do it if you tell me I will lose my job." The proprietor of the shop considered the problem for a few moments and, impressed by the girl's straightforwardness, told her to go ahead. (I think *my* solution would have been a little different.) So after a while the girl selected the man and in due course had the baby, and it was a little girl. She returned to her job, where she is a good worker; she supports the baby and loves it, and, most important of all, she has not lost caste in the town.

At dinner tonight I didn't clean my plate. Up to now, when I thought I was eating Obregón-endorsed comestibles, I ate everything with fine relish. I ate more than I really wanted. From now on, if I don't want it all, I intend to say so.

Early this evening we were sitting at Bar Paco, looking down into the plaza, Studying Humanity, when a funeral came around the corner. Six men had a black coffin on their shoulders and the mourners were marching behind. The pace was brisk and businesslike as they swung around another corner and disappeared. I asked a waiter why they hadn't crossed over to the church and why there was no padre in the procession. "Many do not have," he said, "because the church and priest costs twelve pesos, maybe more. Many do without." He also explained that vehicles are never used in Taxco funerals; the procession moves on foot to the cemetery, which is a

long way out from the center of town. Leslie has written about Taxco
funerals and says that, when the family can afford it, musicians
accompany the procession. These musicians are usually amateurs,
knowing only a few numbers, which they play slowly and mourn-
fully; among those numbers are such old favorites as "Roll Out the
Barrel," "Ain't Gonna Rain No Mo'," and "Happy Days Are Here
Again," all played as dirges.

February 18

I WANDERED around town today looking for the barber shop
where I had the experience with the pig, and at last I found it, and
glanced through the door, and saw that it had been somewhat mod-
ernized, so I strolled on and came to another shop, just around the
corner — a hole in the wall on Taxco's main shopping street, with
wooden chairs that must have been imported by Borda himself. The
barber was a little old man with a three-day growth of beard (the
trademark, apparently, of Taxco barbers) and a haggard expression.
He had six pairs of clippers laid out on a shelf, some of them a
little rusty-looking, and as he picked each of them up he always
stared at it a moment as if he had never seen it before, and as if it
might be dangerous. He worked on me with flamboyant gestures,
flicking and whipping out his arms the way Art Carney does it when
writing a letter or playing the piano. There was a sign on the wall
saying, SE PROHIBE ESCUPIR, which means, IT IS FORBIDDEN TO SPIT.
I obeyed.

As in the other shop, this barber totes his water in and heats it
in an old coffee urn, using a wood fire, and the presence of the urn
made me think of the mother and five daughters who opened a
beauty parlor in Taxco. The oldest daughter was sent up to Mexico
City to learn the trade and when she returned, she taught all she
knew to the other daughters (each one teach four). Mama was appointed engineer in charge of water supply in the shop. The water

system consisted of a tin tank fastened to a wall, and the rubber tubing from a douche bag attached to it. There was a metal clip on the tube which controlled the flow of water and Mama sat all day with the clip in hand. When one of the girls wanted water she called out, *"Ahora!"* (Now!) and Mama pressed the clip and the water marched. Their equipment and their methods were crude, but they prospered, and finally they decided to improve their plant. They put up a beaver-board wall to hide Mama from the customers; she sat behind this wall with the metal clip; the tube ran through a hole in the wall, and whenever the girls wanted water they would rap on the wall twice, and when they wanted it shut off, they would rap once. Much more Elizabeth Ardenish.

Cobblestoning my way home today I came face to face with the most beautiful Indian girl I've ever seen, even on a calendar. She had perfect features, flashing white teeth, huge dark eyes, and a shape that would drive a man to a life of crime, and she wore a cheap but colorful dress. She looked up at me and then lowered her eyes as we passed and I had the same feeling that comes with sticking a finger accidentally into an electrical socket. At Casa Clarita I told Nelle about her, and suggested that she go downtown and try to find her. "It's obvious," I said, "that she's a poor girl, and I think it would be real thoughtful of us if we offered to let her use our extra bedroom. I could find out a great many interesting things from her." Nelle said she didn't think that Leslie would approve, she didn't think that Vicenta would approve, she didn't think that Estefana would approve, and she knew damn well that *she* wouldn't approve. She gave me a definitive, conclusive, determinate no. An author's research work is often made difficult by people who do not understand him. I don't know how I *ever* get anything done.

Some years ago there was a man from Philadelphia who came to Taxco, decided he liked it, and stayed two years at one of the leading hilltop hotels. He scorned the Spanish language and demonstrated his contempt by learning exactly two words in two years. The first year he learned *"muy"* and the second year he learned to put *"bueno"* after it. At the end of two years he developed sacroiliac trouble and found that he needed to have some planks put beneath his mattress. He was making plans to return to Philadelphia when the hotel owner learned of his problem. "You don't have to go back to Philadelphia," said the hotel man, "just to get a few planks put in your bed. My God, we're not quite that helpless here."

The ailing Gringo was somewhat surprised to learn that planks could be put under a mattress in Mexico. And it was done — a perky little Mexican chambermaid brought the planks into his room and soon had them where they were supposed to be.

Within three or four days the man's back had improved considerably. He was most happy about it, and when the chambermaid came into his room he felt that he should express his gratitude, so he stepped over and began patting the bed and he said, *"Muy bueno!"* The girl flung up her hands, cried out, "Oh, no, Señor!" and raced out of the room. He could not understand her alarm, and he was embarrassed over the fact that he had frightened her. He felt that she may have misunderstood him, and he remembered someone having told him that any time you can't get a point across to a servant, money talks. So the next day he hung around until the maid came into his room again. This time he gave her a sort of exultant look, pulled out a five-peso note, extended it toward her, patted the bed and said, *"Muy bueno! Muy bueno!"* The girl screeched like a wounded yak and fled straight to the front office and complained to the management. Happily, it was all straightened out in the end. Moral: Learn at least *three* words.

There are two systems that can be followed by Americans who want to stay in Mexico for several years, or for the rest of their lives. Tourist cards are good for six months, and must be renewed at the border twice a year. Apparently they can be renewed again and again, indefinitely, but it would be something of a nuisance. The other way is to acquire the status of an *immigrante,* which involves depositing a sum of money with the government. This is a guarantee, I suppose, against your becoming a beachcomber. One American woman here in Taxco said that when she finally got her *immigrante* papers, and asked her Mexican lawyer about her status, he said, "You have all the rights that I have except three: you cannot vote, you cannot run a saloon, and you cannot operate a whorehouse. The law says it."

In the plaza today we met Natalie Scott. If Spratling is the King of Taxco, then Miss Scott is surely the Queen. She was a newspaperwoman in New Orleans years ago, and knew William Faulkner and Sherwood Anderson . . . and Bill Spratling. After Spratling came to Taxco, he sent back a glowing description of the town and Natalie got the fever. At that moment she didn't have enough money to get to Taxco, but she started anyway. At Laredo she took almost all the cash she had left and bought an old horse and saddle. She rode from Laredo to Taxco on that horse, and the story goes that as she came up the little cobblestone hill that opens into the plaza, the old horse dropped dead.

She has lived here ever since, and now she is known to multitudes of Americans as well as Mexicans. She raised the money to establish La Guardería de Niños, a day nursery where poor working mothers can leave their children during the daytime hours. She is the author of a little Mexican cookbook which we have found very useful.

From Natalie and from other sources we have learned about a woman who lived in Taxco until a few years ago, when she returned to her native Los Angeles. Mrs. Hapless was a friendly, intelligent, respectable woman and everybody liked her. If this were a sensible and well-ordered world, life would have run smoothly for her. But it isn't and it didn't. Somehow, in Taxco, *things were always happening to her.*

She lived alone, except for a cook, in a small rented house. She was kind and considerate toward her servants, but for some reason they never stayed long. There came a time when she was without a cook for several days. She managed everything except disposal of the garbage. At that time garbage had to be carried to the *barranca* and thrown into it. Mrs. Hapless went out and found a small boy and engaged him to carry her garbage to the *barranca*. When he returned to her house she had no centavos, so impulsively she gave him a peso. His huge, soft, dark eyes grew even wider as he looked at the peso, for this was the most money he had ever had in his life. By the next day Mrs. Hapless had engaged another cook, but the boy showed up at her house and, in a deep, sepulchral voice for such a small one, asked, *"Hay basura para la barranca?"* (Is there any garbage for the ravine?) He seemed crushed that there was no *basura para la barranca*. Thereafter, for almost a year, he haunted the footsteps of Mrs. Hapless. He had a way of appearing in unlikely places, coming up silently behind her and saying in those lugubrious tones, *"Hay basura para la barranca?"* She'd hear it in Bar Paco, on the terrace at Rancho Telva, in the plaza, even at private parties. And the climax came when a former servant of Mrs. Hapless died. She went to the house to pay her respects, and circled the room shaking hands with the relatives and speaking her condolences, and then she arrived at the flower-banked casket, and stood looking for a moment, and then from back of the floral pieces came the deep, sad voice: *"Hay basura para la barranca?"*

Once a week a gardener named Pancho came to work on the Hapless grounds. Pancho was getting old and somewhat childish. All his life he had wanted to be a mason, so now in his old age he had bought himself a fifteen-cent spirit level, and he used it on everything in sight. If he moved a brick he put the level on it, and when he cut the grass he used the level to make certain it was evenly sheared, and Mrs. Hapless often told about the time she saw him take off one of his battered huaraches, turn it over and take a level on the sole.

In the center of her garden Mrs. Hapless had a lime tree, and one season it produced a huge crop of fruit — she could scarcely see the leaves for the limes. She told all her friends about it, and promised each of them a basket of fruit from the tree. The more she talked about it, the more pride she took in that tree and she waited impatiently for harvest time. When the day came she carried her baskets out to the tree and then discovered there was not a single lime on it. She was greatly perplexed, and unhappy. Later in the day she went down to the plaza, for it was Holy Thursday and there were big doings around the church. She saw one large crowd pressing in toward a central point, and she worked her way through and saw a man sitting on a makeshift throne. It took her a few moments to recognize her Pancho, for he had on new overalls and a new straw sombrero. He had become a sort of hero and he was being honored by the populace for a beautiful thing he had created, which Mrs. Hapless now saw: a head of Jesus Christ fashioned entirely of limes.

When Mrs. Hapless was a newcomer to Taxco she was sitting in the plaza and a Mexican man, passing by, spoke to her and lifted his hat. It took her a few seconds to place him, then she exclaimed, "The plumber!" He had been to her house recently and now she needed him again, something about a faucet, so she got up and scurried after him, and said to him, "Señor, could you do me the favor of coming to my house at six o'clock this evening?" He bowed and said he would be there. When he arrived at her house he had on his Sunday clothes and was carrying a small bouquet of flowers. Only then did Mrs. Hapless realize her error — he was *not* the plumber, he was the butcher she had patronized two or three times. She could not confess her mistake, so she invited him in and asked him to sit down. By now she was so flustered that she fixed him a highball. He stayed two hours, rolling his eyes at her once in a while but making no further moves. The next night he came back, bearing more flowers, and the scene was repeated. He kept coming back until she had to break it off by pleading other engagements.

There are two other women here, permanent residents, who fell in love with the Taxco cemetery. They had gone out to the *panteón*, which can be seen from the hilltops and which fairly sparkles and glows in the sunlight — the tombs are painted in bright colors and someone has described it as looking, from a distance, like a wedding cake. The two American women decided they wanted to be buried in this place, and even picked out the section of the cemetery they liked best. Downtown they found out that lots were available for fifty pesos. One of the women was so rattled that she asked if that price was "for a lifetime." To acquire title to the lots they had to go through a lot of paperwork with the Mayor and other municipal officials. At one point the Mayor picked up a chart of the cemetery, studied it, and then exclaimed, "But Señoras, you have chosen lots that are in the fourth class!" To which one of the women replied, "But we don't care what class we're in — we like the view from there." The Mayor protested: "But, alas, you won't be able to see the view." And the women replied, "We like it, and we want it." And they got it. I learned, in passing, that the old barber who cut my hair earlier today is the caretaker of the cemetery. After he trimmed my hair he probably went out and trimmed a few graves.

The American residents seem to be involved in a fresh uproar concerning the presence of pigs in the plaza. Apparently the constabulary is not consistent in its war against vagrant pigs. Pig dragnets are thrown only when the Anti-Pig faction is in the ascendancy. The Gringos in Taxco are the really civic-minded residents of the town and are forever campaigning for one thing or another. But they are split on pigs. One group holds that a pig wandering through Plaza Borda, especially if it should be a sizable sow with a litter of babies, is just as atmospheric in the eyes of the tourist as the Church of Santa Prisca. One of their number, in fact, got up at a meeting and said that if he were a tourist and came into the plaza for the first time and saw, on the one hand, the sow with her piglets, and, on the other, Santa Prisca, he would not hesitate. "My camera," he said, "would be turned to the sow. The pigs would make a better picture." This whole dispute was brought to mind today when we met Helen Hall in the plaza. She was once secretary to George Messersmith, noted American diplomat, and is now a permanent Taxco resident. She said: "I have been at home debating the matter of the pigs. And after much soul-searching, I've decided I'll cast my vote in their favor, and let them take over the whole town if they want to."

At dinner Vicenta got onto the subject of the depravity of modern young women. She used pantomime to demonstrate how the modern girl switches her behind as she walks along the street. Volleys of torrid *español* came from her lips as she described the modern dresses, Veed to the belly-button. It is the ancient complaint of the elderly — the manners and modes of the young are abominable.

Tonight we sat for a couple of hours on the Bar Paco balcony, Drinking in Atmosphere. There are two eyesores in the plaza, two soft drink stands, each with a juke box, and these machines are going full blast every evening, not with Pedro Vargas or Lara or *mariachis*, but with Frankie Laine and Nat King Cole and Sinatra and El Sideburns. We were the only customers in Bar Paco. One boy, a member of the Castillo family of silversmiths, would come up alongside me now and then and set off a skyrocket. The warheads of these rockets are attached to wheat stalks. The waiters and bartenders shoot them into the sky by holding the rocket head in the left hand, touching a cigarette to the fuse, and then letting go at the precise instant the rocket takes off. The procedure fascinates me, for I have become so conditioned against the dangers of fireworks that I run from a sparkler. I asked the Castillo boy if he ever held the rocket too long and got burned. He said never. He said it was just like a fish on a line. "You feel it pull," he said, "when it is ready to go, and so you loose the hand, and it goes." He thrust a rocket at me and suggested that I try one. I declined.

Taxco is famous for its fireworks, especially for the displays which go under the same name as that rocket-shooting boy: the *castillos,* or castles. These elaborate structures, sometimes bigger than the buildings around the plaza, are usually the work of one artisan. He is widely recognized as perhaps the greatest fireworks genius in the Republic, yet I was unable to find out his name — he is known simply as the Fireworks Man. Until recently he lived in a crowded section of town with many Americans for neighbors. He made the neighborhood lively with unpredictable explosions. It was his custom to conduct experiments on the roof of his house, testing bombs and rockets — sometimes in the middle of the night, for he was a genius and the rules don't apply to geniuses. About once a year someone would forget and drop a lighted cigarette butt in his house and the roof would blow off. He didn't seem to be upset by these disasters, but calmly replaced the roof and resumed his tests. His house became known to the Gringos as Casa Boom-Boom; and then one day, simply in the interests of self-preservation, Leslie Figueroa talked him into selling Casa Boom-Boom and he moved his operations to another part of town.

It may be that Taxco's Fireworks Man invented the device so popular here, the Torito, or little bull. This is an ungainly wooden frame representing the head of a bull which fits over a man's head and shoulders. He lights the fuse and then goes charging around the plaza, and fireballs shoot out of the bull's head. They are called *buscapies,* which means, "looking for your feet," and that is what they do. The Torito charges toward groups of people and the balls of fire go skittering and zigzagging along the ground, and the people shriek and leap to get out of the way, and some of them climb trees, and there is much laughter and fun and third-degree burns.

February 19

IN A book called *My House Is Yours,* by Elsa Larralde, I've just read an account of a Mexican servant girl who is explaining why she is not married to the father of her baby, even though she lives with him. His name is Liborio and it would seem that he has developed something special in the way of a line with the girls. This is how the servant girl puts it:

"Liborio says that married people always quarrel. He says that when Christ was on earth He favored couples who lived in *amasiato*

. . . My Señor said that one day Christ was taking a long walk near Jerusalem and He met a married couple who were quarreling and insulting one another, and our Lord passed by and shook His head sadly. Then a few paces further, He met two lovers who were living in sin and they were holding hands and talking happily, and Cristo passed by and smiled in approval. Liborio says it is written in a book because he read it, and it's true."

Both the women and men of the American colony here, and especially the women, make almost a fetish out of informality in dress and manners. It is emphasized in their talk and in their writings, if they happen to write. They say that each time a new family joins the colony, its members come down to the plaza or to the markets in stiffish attire — as if they were going downtown in San Francisco or Cleveland. They soon learn, however, that neckties are all but forbidden among the men, while the ladies forget about such things as gloves and hats and especially high-heeled shoes. Taxco is not a town for anything but flat heels, preferably sandals. One English lady who insisted on wearing her high heels downtown every day was known as *La Acróbata* from the way she caracoled over the cobblestones, and I was told that she spent a good part of her time laid up with sprained ankles.

While the ladies of Taxco and other colonial villages concern themselves with the type of heels they have on their shoes, many of the Indians of Mexico concern themselves with the type of heels they have on their feet. The heels I have seen in this country are the worst heels on earth. In Mexico City and in Taxco and elsewhere I have spent a good deal of time looking at Indian heels. Many of these people wear no footgear at all, and some go about in *huaraches,* and in both cases the heels are exposed. They are mottled and cracked, a purplish green as if they were gangrenous, eroded like the bed of a river gone dry. Why they should have this aspect baffles me, for I've watched their owners carefully, in city street and in rural cornpatch, and I can assure you that those people do not walk much on the backs of their heels. A chiropodist might be able to furnish an answer to the problem, if he could be lured within range; but I cannot imagine any self-respecting chiropodist who'd agree to ever get in the same room with one of those heels. My own guess is that the blotched and mottled heel is a mark of beauty and distinction among the Indians; a maid upon meeting a man will have a close look at his heels and if they are crusty enough and purple enough she'll give him the nod and they'll go away somewhere and flap tortillas at each other.

The American women here wear a sort of cape — a square piece of colorful fabric with a hole in the center. It is placed over the head and worn so that it hangs either squared across the front and back, or with the corners pointing downward. If a woman is married she wears it with the edges squared across. If she's a virgin, she turns it so the corners point down. Nelle has bought one of these capes and she cannot remember which position is which and most of the time she has been walking around Taxco, at her age, with this cape telegraphing word to the entire world that she is a virgin. I finally gave up trying to teach her the proper way to wear it. "You can just let your reputation go to hell, for all I'm concerned," I said.

Pat Pattridge, a winter resident of Taxco, was telling today about how he was recently invited to a christening in the home of a Mexican family. He showed up at the house with an appropriate gift and he was surprised to find the fiesta going full blast, even though the mother was still enormously pregnant. All was soon explained. There had been a miscalculation and the baby hadn't arrived on the date anticipated. The family, however, had ordered in a large supply of perishable food and as they had no refrigerator to preserve it, they decided to have the fiesta on schedule, and the christening could be held later when there was something to christen. Said the prospective father: "We will not tell the little one after he is born, and so he will think that everything was done properly and according to the rules."

(*Back home, as these pages on Taxco are being put together, we have had word that Natalie Scott is dead. She fell ill and was taken to a Mexico City hospital, where she died. Her body was brought back and by public demand her wake was held in the upstairs apartment of the Borda Palace, right in the midst of scenes she knew so intimately for so many years. Almost every servant in Taxco turned out, clamoring for the right to serve on the "guard of honor." There was one incident at the funeral that nobody in Taxco would have enjoyed better than Natalie Scott herself. The matron of the day nursery arrived with all her children, scrubbed and brushed and each carrying a little bunch of flowers. On orders from the matron the children ranged themselves around the coffin and then the matron said, in Spanish: "Now, all cry!" There followed an immense caterwauling as each child tried to outdo his neighbors, and then the matron commanded, "All stop!" And the wailing ceased as if a faucet had been turned off.*)

5

Noches de Mexico City

February 20

WHILE we were packing this morning for a reluctant departure from Taxco, a steady stream of servants came to the gate of Casa Clarita, bearing good-by notes, notwithstanding the fact that we said numberless good-bys yesterday and last night. One lady begs that when I write my book I make no mention of her lovely house. A guidebook once had a single paragraph about her house and tourists began seeking it out at all hours as if it were a public museum. One woman arrived and in peremptory manner demanded a quick tour of the premises.

"Madame," said the owner, "this happens to be a private home."

"I don't care about that," responded the lady tourist. "It's here in the guidebook and I want to see it, so let's get going — I'm in a hurry." She had a gate slammed in her face.

Vicenta walked with us down to the place where the car was parked. She was engaged in a long discourse about all the tenants of Casa Clarita in the past, and suddenly she said, quite distinctly, "*Muchos* peoples *Americanos*." That middle word is English of a sort, and is as near as she ever came to saying anything in our language, and I took it for a sort of farewell compliment. Vicenta described the antics of some of the previous tenants, and I judged, from her indignant tones as well as from her several eloquent gestures, that she was talking not only of their ferocious drinking habits, but of their sexual relationships. In this latter connection I thought I detected the word *conejo,* which means rabbit. And from the manner in which Vicenta was carrying on, I suppose I was better off for not being able to understand her.

We acquired our driver, Mike, at Bar Paco a couple of days ago. He is a local taxi driver, quite young, and his older brother came with him this morning to supervise the take-off. They stood off to one side and the older brother was giving Mike a stern lecture of some sort. It seemed obvious that he was telling Mike how to go about driving a car from Taxco to Mexico City and what to do upon arrival. I began to get a little nervous, for the mountain road out of Taxco is one that will make your hair stand on end just walking on it.

My apprehension increased just outside Taxco when Mike pressed a button and his automobile gave forth the sound of loud chimes. I pretended that this was most interesting and he smiled and pressed another button and a siren sounded. Next he yanked on a lever and a louder siren screamed at the mile-deep canyons. Then he did all three in rapid succession. I swallowed hard and for the first time became fully aware of the assorted decorations in and around the driver's seat. "Good Lord," I said to myself, "we're in the toils of a Mexican hipster, an Aztec hot-rodder. He's probably arranged with his pals for a few games of automobile *pollo,* or chicken, to be played along the way just to keep us amused." He had red-and-green plastic tape wound spirally around the steering wheel, the steering column and the gear-shift lever, and hanging from the end of the gear-shift was a tiny basket of plastic roses. Above the rear-view mirror was a ghastly head of Christ, carved from wood and wearing a crown of thorns and staring out at us through rivers of blood. Mike noticed my interest in the figure and reached up and tripped a tiny switch, which turned on a little blue light bulb. The bulb was inside a cup about the size of a shot glass, which focused the blue light on the face of Christ. Mike explained that he had carved the head himself, and done the delicate wiring, not being content with the dangling Virgins and medals affected by other taxi drivers. He said he is twenty years old, once worked as a silversmith, and that he wished we would stay in Taxco because he felt sure he could learn English from us.

Within a short time I realized that he was actually a good driver and knew his way around, and he delivered us safely at the door of the Hotel Reforma.

I tried to get H. L. Davis on the phone at the Instituto Nacional de Cardiologia. I said Day-viss. I said Dah-vees. No go. Nelle said, "Why don't you just give up trying to get anybody on the phone down here? You'll save time and wear and tear on your nerves by simply taking a taxi and forgetting the phone." So I took a taxi to the other side of town where there are blocks and blocks of huge concrete medical buildings. I found the one I wanted but had no luck at the desk with the name Davis, but I hammered away and finally the man said sixteen in Spanish. I can count only to twelve, so I had him write it down and then proceeded to the top floor and Room 16. H. L. Davis is a talented American writer and has been in the hospital for four months with two serious operations. I had met him many years ago and now I found him, minus his left leg, sitting in a wheelchair and banging away at his typewriter. We talked mostly about Oaxaca, where he now lives. I recalled that Oaxaca was one of the places D. H. Lawrence visited back in the 1920's, in the company of his wife and Dorothy Brett. Lawrence was a man of pronounced ascetic appearance, with a pale face and a red beard, and he had a lot of trouble with the Indians of Mexico because they thought he was Jesus. Everywhere he went the Indians would look at him and exclaim, "Cristo! Cristo!" and it would make him so furious that he would throw things at his wife and Dorothy. He was a queer one and I've never been able to understand a lot of things he did, but there is one thing I do understand. He did a thing in Oaxaca fully as great as the Conquest, or the Reform, or *Cinco de Mayo,* or the discovery of *mole poblano,* or the expropriation of oil. When Lawrence was invited to dinner in Oaxaca he responded as follows:

"I will come if the meal is at the time you mention — if I do not have to wait from seven until nine. If the dinner is at seven, I will come at seven; if at nine, I will come at nine." For the first time in Oaxaca history, nay, in the history of the whole civilized world, dinners were served at the precise time stipulated in the invitations. *Ole! Viva! Bravo!* Bully for D. H.!

This evening we had dinner with Maxine and the Wyatts, parents of Dixie Lee Crosby. The Wyatts are like a great many other Gringos — they can't adapt themselves to dinner at eight or nine or ten. They want to eat at six, and so they eat at six. I was happy to see, however, that they both ordered enchiladas and refried beans and they both cleaned their plates.

Later we met an advertising man who said he'd spent the last two hours trying to calm down a Gringo friend whose car had hit a Mexican in a dark street last night.

"The poor guy doesn't know whether he killed the Mexican or not," said the ad man. "Unfortunately, he knew that the only thing to do in such circumstances is to keep traveling, to get away from the scene and to get away fast. If you stop they throw you in jail, incommunicado, no lawyer; no phone calls. They'll throw you in jail even if you're only a witness to an auto accident. But if you're involved in the accident you may be held in jail for months. Especially if you give them any argument. Any time there is a traffic accident there is first the crash and then the pounding of footsteps as everybody runs away from the scene. Even bus drivers and railroad engineers leap to the ground and go racing off into the forests after accidents."

I said I was perplexed by such a state of affairs, and he said the *mordida,* or bite, is largely to blame. And the *mordida* exists everywhere because the salaries of cops and other public functionaries are ridiculously low. And it exists, also, because the people are indifferent.

I remember asking one educated Mexican if he thought all Presidents were thieves. "Of course," he said. "You can't blame them for it. They must provide for their security, because we have a law which says a man can only be President one time. What can he do all the rest of his years?" To which I replied, "He could cut bait." The expression didn't register with the Mexican.

Concerning the *mordida*, I've been told that everybody gives it, but nobody takes it. A *mordida* is a *mordida* only to the giver. He who accepts a *mordida* calls it by another name: a *gratificación*, something given in gratification for services rendered. That makes it all right.

February 21

NELLE made an important contribution to my notebooks this morning. She has discovered that Mexicans love popcorn and consume great quantities of it, and that most of it is imported from Indiana. They call it *palomitas de maíz*, meaning "little doves of corn," and therein, it seems to me, is summarized the difference between our two languages.

We were slightly startled, in the Reforma lobby, to come face to face with Dr. and Mrs. Heck from home. Dr. Heck has the exclusive concession for carving on both Nelle and me and has exercised it on several occasions. The Hecks are here for a surgeon's convention and they brought word that when they left home our road was so icy that the sand truck had to move over it in reverse, throwing sand under its own wheels in order to achieve any progress. *Bueno!*

I had lunch today with Bob Prescott, head of the United Press bureau here, and he reminded me that you miss a lot in Mexico if you don't read the Mexican newspapers. We went over to the UP office and I prowled through the file for the last few weeks to see what I had missed.

There had been a big riot in Cuernavaca and I hadn't heard a word of it. It started with an altercation between a motor cop and the step-son of a politician, over a parking violation. The cop shot the poli-tician's stepson. Several policemen were questioned before an arrest was made and, meanwhile, a mob of five thousand stoned the Gov-ernor in the Cortez Palace, this being their way of demanding that the entire traffic squad be fired. One cop had a curious alibi — he said he couldn't have done it because he had emptied his gun into the air on New Year's Eve and had never reloaded it. The cop who was arrested said, "I tell you, it was an accident — the gun went off when I was beating this fellow over the head with it." The Governor issued a statement declaring that the whole affair was Communist-inspired.

In the town of Banderilla, which we visited on our way to Vera-cruz, there have been serious riots. The citizens, by way of demand-ing that certain "vice centers" be closed and that law and order be restored, grabbed up rocks and machetes and tried to kill everybody in sight.

The weather report for Mexico City last week end, while we were in Taxco, said conditions were somewhat freakish. On Saturday there was a dust storm, this was followed by freezing cold on Sunday, plus a slight earthquake, followed by a hot spell with the temperature at 85, and then a hailstorm, a violent rainstorm, and another freezing night.

A new campaign against horn blowing has started. Mexican motor-ists used to be famous as horn blowers; they believed that the horn should be put in gear and left there. Then a law was passed forbid-ding all horn blowing, the penalty being fifty pesos. Taxi drivers, unable to function without making some kind of racket, developed the habit of expressing displeasure and annoyance by beating their hands against the outside of the car doors. But horn blowing stopped in the capital for a long time. Then it came back slowly — starting off with gentle peeps and beeps, then little toots, and now many motorists have reverted to the old ways.

An item from Jalapa. The Perez family couldn't decide on a name for the new baby. The argument was continued at the baptismal ceremony. Five persons were killed, seven wounded.

A man named Ruggiero has been charged with practicing medicine without a license. He promised another man he would grow a new hand on his "empty wrist."

La Prensa says that at least eighteen flying saucers whizzed over Mexico City in less than an hour on February 7. They were large, red-colored globes and they were heading south. The sky over Mexico is loaded with flying saucers all the time. They outnumber ours, and are much bigger, being known as *plativolos*, or flying plates. Mexican pickpockets don't have to jostle their victims in crowds. They stand on the street and look up into the sky; their victims stop and stare upward, figuring there are some *plativolos* going over, and the sheep are swiftly sheared. Not long ago one of the city's chiropractors advertised: "Stiff neck from looking at the *plativolos*? Come and see me for a massage."

The artist David Alfaro Siqueiros, just back from a world tour, held a press conference. A right-wing reporter began asking him about his Communist connections. A left-wing reporter screamed at the right-wing reporter, "You are paid with FBI dollars!" and tried to kill him with a chair. End of press conference.

My final item from the UP file tells of a tragedy that occurred a couple of days before we arrived in Mexico. A seventy-four-year-old Englishwoman, Margaret Augusta Honey, had been taking her annual vacation in Veracruz for years. This year her relatives wouldn't allow her to go, because of a heart condition. So Margaret Augusta Honey said to her maid, "If they won't let me go to Veracruz, then life is not worth living." With which she shot herself to death. I grieve for her, because I now feel much the same about Veracruz.

A horrible situation came to my attention in the UP news office. There were half a dozen Mexicans employed in the place, and all of them were whistling as they worked. In the United States the tradition that nobody should whistle around a newspaper office is stronger than the tradition of freedom of the press. A cub reporter can misspell every other word in his copy, libel the Mayor, sass the owner's wife on the phone, show up drooling drunk, and steal from petty cash, and he'll be forgiven — but let him whistle just one bar and he'll likely be beaten to death. I have heard several explanations for this tradition, but only one makes sense: nine-tenths of the people working in a newspaper city room are neurotics.

Tonight we had dinner with Paul Kennedy at Chalet Suizo. This is the restaurant of our friend Ernesto and it is one of the most popular eating houses in the city. I had wonderful Swiss sausage and Paul said his goulash was the best he ever tasted. Later Ernesto took us upstairs to his private apartment and served us champagne. And after that we strolled the Reforma, telling stories and laughing, until a car came whipping at us from around a corner, missing us by inches. Paul stood in the street, head tipped back, and roared with fury. "God-damn crazy Aztecs!" he howled into the wind. "They drag these illiterate toad-worshipers out of the hills and put them behind the wheel of the most dangerous weapon on earth! And then they tell these god-damned troglodyte bastards that when the seat begins to whirl, start guiding it!"

He spoke these words as if he believed them.

February 22

THIS morning around 4 o'clock our doorbell rang. It was a boy who said, "It is an urgent telegrafo." The telegram said:

HELP! IN HANDS EL BANDIDO! HELP HELP!

F. C. HOFFMAN

It was addressed to me all right and datelined Durango and it looked urgent enough, yet it had me stalled. Then I remembered.

This Hoffman was a man Carlos was taking on a trip through the mountains, and I had written a note to him warning him that Carlos was a bandit at heart and had been stealing me blind.

I met two interesting women today in the Bar Jardín. One was a Mexican lady, described to me as being pure Yaqui Indian. The Yaquis have been called the fiercest fighters in the whole history of Mexico. This Yaqui, however, proved to be attractive and charming and spoke good English. She told how Díaz, unable to subdue the Yaquis in their own Sonoran land, had them deported to the opposite end of the country, to Yucatán, where they became slaves alongside the enslaved Mayas. Many of them died of the heat and misery, but many more got away and *walked all the way back to their homes.* This is a walk of about two thousand miles, none of it on sidewalks or in shady lanes, and it demonstrates the home-loving qualities of the Yaquis. Love of fighting, in fact, is the only thing that will get them away from their native villages. The Yaqui lady said there was once a Gringo missionary, a plump, bald little man who announced that he was going in and convert them from their heathen beliefs. Everyone told him that he'd better not but he was a man of zeal and faith, and he went in. He managed to speak one sentence, uttering the purpose of his visit. They stripped him bare and whipped him out of camp with cactus thorns, and he was a sorry sight when he arrived back in Cajeme.

The second lady I met was a girl from Texas, who works for an oil corporation here. She said that normally she doesn't go for romantic verse, but she had read a poem today that simply slew her. She wrote it out for me as follows:

> *An Aztec*
> *Has tech-*
> *Nique.*
> *I was with a tall one*
> *All one*
> *Week.*

Nelle came in this afternoon from a walk on the Paseo and dragged me around the corner to meet Bob Peck, a tall young Californian who is assistant manager of the big new Woolworth's. The store is not precisely a five-and-ten. There are many thousands of different items in the establishment and among them expensive articles of sterling silver, imported French perfumes, and many articles of genuine native craftsmanship, such as pottery, silver, serapes, rebozos, and so on.

Bob Peck said that dealing with wholesalers in this store is often an unusual experience. The Indians come in from their villages, bearing their wares, just as they have been traveling to market for centuries; but when they arrive on the wide sidewalk in front of this splendid and glittering store, they turn bashful. They stand around, pretending that they have no business in the vicinity, glancing up at the sky, or out at the traffic flow. Bob has to go out and haul them into the store. They won't go much beyond the main entrance so their merchandise is spread out on the floor, in one of the aisles, and they get down on their knees and conduct their bargaining as if they were in the public market at Toluca.

Bob took us on a tour of the store. Ninety-seven per cent of all the articles sold in the place are made in Mexico, mostly from patterns out of the United States. Techniques in fancy packaging, never known before in this country, are gaining general acceptance largely through the efforts of Woolworth's. (One item that struck my eye was a shelf containing cans of Tres-en-Uno Oil). I mentioned to Bob Peck that I am stubbornly set against indiscriminate shopping in foreign lands. I recalled the remark made by — I think it was — Joseph Wood Krutch, upon seeing his neighbors unloading their car after a vacation in Mexico. "It's astonishing," he said, "the things that a woman would rather have than money." I said that my prejudice against foreign shopping is based mainly on my desire to travel homeward with the same amount of luggage I had on the outward journey. I also spoke of my belief that anything that can be bought in a foreign country can be bought in New York City.

"All except one thing, maybe," said Bob, "and I think this is an item that might interest you. It doesn't take up much space."

He got out a box about the size of a cigarette package and inside it were a lot of other boxes — the smallest paper boxes imaginable. He removed one of these and then, exercising great care, managed to slide the outer cover off and reveal the contents. Inside, so small that a magnifying glass is needed to detect the detail, were a bride and groom, richly dressed, standing as if for the wedding photographer. The paper box they occupy is five-eighths of an inch wide and one-fourth of an inch high. Bob explained that the tiny figures were actually dead fleas and that their costumes were just as wonderfully wrought as any prayer ever engraved on the head of a pin. He said that years ago the production of these items was quite brisk among certain Indian communities but now the demand for flea-boxes is so slight that only one man in Mexico is doing this kind of work.

"How much are they?" I asked.

"Five pesos."

"Five eights are forty," I murmured — you always say this sort of thing before laying out your money in Mexico — and then, "I'll take one." We concluded the transaction and I handed the tiny box to Nelle, advising her that if she had to buy things in Mexico, this was the type of thing she should buy.

There are two Woolworth stores in Mexico City, but this one, being located as it is, has become a big attraction to tourists as well as to Mexicans. The main idea is to sell to Mexicans, and there are only two or three English-speaking salesgirls in the whole establishment. The leading people of Mexico are regular customers. Among them are members of the Miguel Alemán family, and soon after the formal opening Señora Ruiz Cortines arrived to inspect the store. Bob Peck showed her around and she expressed delight with everything and then said that it was not polite to go into a store without buying something — and so she bought a paper-back murder mystery.

It seems strange that Woolworth's should attract tourists, but it does. Lady trippers come down the Paseo and see the familiar red-

and-gold façade and gasp with pleasure. Here, for sure, is a real touch of home, and into the store they go. Bob has to deal with most of them and they sometimes present difficulties. One of the most common complaints from them is, "But why don't you price your things in American money instead of these crazy pee-sos?"

"Occasionally," said Bob, "a tourist lady will come along and for some reason decide that I am a Mexican, an unusually bright Mexican able to speak good English and dress like an American. Quite a few ladies think I'm a Mexican and two or three times they have come in and asked me to throw on a *serape* and come out on the sidewalk and pose for pictures."

He said that earlier today a birdlike tourist lady came in and went flitting from counter to counter. He kept an eye on her and was just approaching her to offer his help when she let out a cry of relief. Bob hurried up to her and found her exclaiming over a tray of rubber tips for crutches.

"I've been searching all over town for these things," she said, "and I thought I'd never find 'em."

She picked out two crutch-tips and while Bob was having them wrapped for her she explained that she didn't want them to put on crutches.

"I'm just scared to death," she said, "that I'm going to forget myself and drink some of this tap water and get The Disease. So I figured out if I could find some crutch-tips and stick them on the faucets in the different hotel rooms, then I'd be certain not to drink any of the water."

The vigor with which companies like Woolworth's and Sears, Roebuck have gone into Mexico is producing one of the most important social revolutions in the nation's experience. Many years ago German mercantile leaders made a determined effort to crack the Mexican market. They tried everything in the book, but they failed because of a condition which they called *Verdammte Bedürfnislosigkeit,* which means "damned wantlessness." The phrase has been used again and again by other businessmen, down through the years, to describe the Mexican's lack of acquisitiveness. In years gone by when a poor Mexican discovered gold or silver or precious stones on his property, he was quite happy about it, and called in his neighbors and told them to help themselves. This philosophy is so alien to our own economic system that it makes some Gringoes sputter with rage. But the thing that is going on in Woolworth's is certain to bring a change — the Mexican girl is already demonstrating that she likes the bright, neat packaging of cosmetics and all the other items, and even the Mexican boy will prefer an attractive tube or bottle of pomade to the messy axle grease scooped from the five-gallon can on the floor of the barber shop.

Mexican business methods remain, however, somewhat baffling to the high-powered operators from the north. One United States firm (it may have been Woolworth's) became interested in a certain kind of straw mat produced by the craftsmen in a single Indian village. A representative of the company went out and talked to the head man of the village and said his firm would like to order several thousand of these mats. The Indian nodded, but said that the price per mat would be higher under such a mass production deal. His statement was confusing to the Gringo. The precise opposite should be true, according to all known laws of economics. But he didn't know about the special law of economics governing the Mexican Indian. "Why," he asked, "should the price be higher if we order thousands of the mats?" Said the Head Indian: "Because it is very tiresome to make the same article over and over."

Someone recently gave me a back copy of the *Mexican-American Review*, a magazine published by the American Chamber of Commerce of Mexico, containing an article titled, "Selling — Mexican Style," by Anne Dunham. It is a lecture directed at American businessmen, telling them that their own time-honored techniques are not worth a verdammte in Mexico, that in order to do any business in this country, they've got to learn something of the psychology of the Mexican people. They must learn, of course, that time is not as important to a Mexican as it is to an American. They must learn the difference between a Mexican's sense of courtesy, and an American's.

The Latin American businessman, says the article, "usually has a broader cultural background than the average American executive. He is vitally interested in literature, music, drama, and other forms of art, not just because he thinks he should be, but because that, too, is a part of living. And when he is taken to lunch by an American businessman, he does not expect to confine his entire conversation to shop talk, but rather is accustomed to interspersing business observations with his opinion of the last symphony concert at Bellas Artes, or the philosophical basis of a book he is now reading. He also possesses an extraordinary sensitivity toward human emotions, and is seldom guilty of bad taste in any situation. In particular, his jokes are always subtle, never raw, nor is he likely to appreciate outright crudity in a joke told over the lunch table."

I'm not sure I agree with that last part. The Mexicans I've met so far can joke me crude joke for crude joke, and outpoint me every time in matters of taste.

From another source I learn that the total enlightenment of the Mexican businessman is at hand. I have a newspaper account of a conference of Sales Executives in Mexico City in which various Mexican business leaders spoke on such topics as, "The Field of Advertising," "The Market Outlook for 1967," "New Concepts of Distribution," "The Future of Credit Selling," "The Salesmen — Ambassador of Your Company," and "The Importance of Improving Salesmen's Prestige." Reading about this conference, I had a feeling that I was right in the lobby of the Hotel Statler.

Sandwiched between our hotel and Woolworth's is an office building in which *Time-Life* have their quarters, and this afternoon I stopped in to visit with Dick Oulahan and his Mexican confrère, the very remarkable Rafael Delgado Lozano. I've been hearing about Rafael for years around New York and more recently here in Mexico. He is a chunky man who wears a Texas-style hat and a sad countenance. He was once a guide, stationed at the Reforma Hotel, and he had a canny way with tourists. The moment he got a party of Americans into his car he'd ask their names and their home towns and then, quite casually, he'd say, "Are you lovely people Democrats or Republicans?" If they said Republicans he'd wait a few minutes, maybe a half hour, and then he'd say with some fervor, "That Meester Roosevelt is a real sawn-of-a-beech for sure, is he not?" If, on the other hand, they were Democrats, he would speak harshly of Willkie or Taft or Dewey. He always seemed to get good tips.

In those days the "March of Time" people were shooting a Mexican film and Rafael approached them and offered to be their guide. They gave him the brush, saying *they* didn't need a guide, that *they* knew their way around. They didn't, and after spending a few days in difficulties they hired Rafael. They immediately fell in love with him because, in addition to being good company, he knew almost everything that needs to be known. Other *Time-Life* people heard of him and began using him, and eventually he was permanently hired. He has turned out to be a valuable man, a first-class reporter and a hard worker. His family was Spanish and quite wealthy at one time but everything was taken away from them in the Revolution. They became poor and hungry; the father died, and then the mother. "She died of cancer," said Rafael, "but in those days we called it rheumatism, but what she really died of was sadness because her children were hungry."

Rafael told the story of how, during the depression of the 1930's, he became stranded in Detroit with another Mexican, a gentle scholar and former college professor. They lived in a cheap rooming house, and in the adjoining room were two American girls. One girl, named Lola, had six goldfish which she adored the way an ordinary woman adores her children. None of the four had jobs and the two Mexicans couldn't get any relief money. The girls were virtuous, yet when they really got hungry and sat down to talk things over, Rafael would try to correct that fault, lecturing them in a most serious way. "Prostitution," he would tell them in his sweet and gentle manner, "is not really a bad thing. After all, it is the world's oldest profession, so there must be something decent about it, don't you think? Many millions of nice, pleasant, intelligent women have engaged in it. There are some really nice points to it and, *quién sabe?*, there might be a little fun." The girls, however, insisted that they'd prefer starving.

One day someone in the group came into possession of a half-dollar. Lola was out looking for a job. Rafael decided that the best course would be to buy a beef heart. He sent the kindly professor to the store with instructions to get one beef heart and one package of lard. The professor misunderstood the order and came home with two packages of lard. There was great despair in the house, for the two Mexicans didn't know of the system whereby purchases may be exchanged. Finally Rafael, hunger gnawing at him, placed himself in front of Lola's fish bowl and began staring at its plump occupants. The professor read his thoughts and said, "But she would be very upset." Rafael said yes, he knew that. "But," he argued, "is it worse that the goldfish die or that we die?" So they slaughtered the goldfish and fried them in lard and fell to and Rafael, being a fair-minded man, insisted that one fish be saved for Lola. He put a cloth over the fish bowl because he wanted to break the news to Lola gently.

"When she came home," he said, "we were all very nervous. In about half an hour we heard her scream. We had to tell her the truth, and she was hysterical, so I got the plate with the nice fried fish and held it out to her. But she wouldn't take it and knocked it on the floor and screamed and screamed and called us Mexican bastards and even worse than that, and started yelling for the cops. But I reasoned with her and when she calmed down I took the goldfish off the floor and went outside in the deep snow and ate him. But she was never the same after that, this Lola. Never very friendly."

As seems to be the course in any gathering, we got to talking about the horrors of Mexican traffic. Dick Oulahan told of how a Mexican newspaper reported that a motorcycle had crashed on the Puebla highway "and all eleven riders were killed." He investigated and found it to be true — a long plank had somehow been fastened across the machine and the passengers were sitting on it.

We have been introduced to the members of a film crew who are staying at the Reforma and who are shooting some kind of travel picture about Mexico. This afternoon the producer approached us in the lobby and said they would be shooting scenes in the Club Chanteclair at six o'clock if we wanted to stop in and watch it. This turned out to be a trick to get actors and we spent three hours in the club, playing the part of tourists. The other actors were mostly hotel employees. All the secretaries had been rounded up and put into evening gowns and were playing the part of international glamour girls, while two waiter captains from downstairs were cast as wealthy young men-about-town.

In Hollywood when they are filming a night club scene such as this the actors are customarily served cold tea, but the real stuff was being passed around tonight as a sort of reward to all the unpaid actors. There were many retakes, and script conferences, and pauses for light changes, and along toward the end things began to get a mite gay, and a few items of French pastry were flying through the air and people were talking at each other in loud tones. When we were finished with the filming some of the crew joined us and we stayed on to eat and listen to Denise Darcel, and later she joined the party. I met a couple from Great Neck and introduced them to another couple from Los Angeles. It turned out that the two men were in related businesses; one produces a certain kind of glass fibers, the other uses those fibers in his product. There was a long and heated discussion about the way the glass fibers are slanted, the Los Angeles man saying that he had never seen such poorly slanted glass fibers in his entire life. It was as lively as any discussion on art or books or music or ballet.

I was beginning to feel that I had experienced a full and complete day — the Bandido telegram, the Yaqui lady, the girl with the poem, Woolworth's (crutch tips and flea boxes and all), the *Time-Life* boys, three hours of movie acting, and then the wonderfully-fleshed Denise again. But there was one more sweet and tender and unexpected occurrence to come before I finally hit the sack.

To sum it up, I met two of the most beautiful of all Mexican girls tonight, in the ladies' room.

I left Club Chanteclair in search of a necessary and ran into Maxine and asked her where it was and she said she'd show me. We walked around the mezzanine deck until we came to the door marked *Caballeros*. The attendant was standing in the open doorway. Maxine suddenly got an offbeat inspiration. "I've always," she said, "wanted to see the inside of one of these things." She spoke to the boy in Spanish, asking if any customers were inside. No, Señorita. So in we went. She took a quick look around, went hmmmmmm a couple of times, and then we went out, and Maxine said, "Very interesting, but now you've got to see the ladies' room on the other side." I said, Oh no. She insisted. When Maxine insists, rocks wilt. I waited near the door while she went inside to check. She finally popped out, grabbed me by the arm, and in we went. Imagine my astonishment to find, sitting there in big comfortable chairs, smiling at me, these two ravishingly beautiful Mexican ladies! I let out a cry of distress, and made a move to escape, but Maxine held me prisoner. "These girls," she said, "have never seen a man in a ladies' room and they said they'd like to see it once in their lives." So I gulped and turned and bowed to them and said, Buenas noches, Señoritas, and they smiled and said, Buenas noches, Señor, and I took a quick look around, and saw little that interested me, and thought that this was as daffy as the time the pig came into the barber shop, and then out we went. One additional fact: I forgot the reason I went in the first place.

February 23

IF THEY wanted to, the people in the dining room at the Reforma could tell when I arrive without looking up from their Chihuahua steaks. Near the entrance is a piano player named Miguel Ríos Mena, and whenever Miguel observes my approach he *segues* into the lovely strains of Agustin Lara's "Noche Criolla." This has been going on for quite a while now as a result of the many times I have asked him to play the number, and other Lara songs.

Miguel himself is quite a personality. He is a prosperous accountant, head of his own firm, yet he spends six or seven hours a day, seven days a week, playing piano music here at the hotel. He is a big, soft-spoken man, wearing glasses, and he has the look of a United Nations delegate rather than a musician. He loves to play the piano and says that if he weren't doing it at the hotel, he would probably leave his accounting office every day and go home and play for six or seven hours. He is still mildly astonished over the fact that people like Charlie Bowers are willing to pay him money for doing something that is so much pleasure.

I've gone back to my notebooks of the Veracruz trip and found what Carlos had to say about the composer of "Noche Criolla," Agustin Lara. "To be such a fine good man," said Carlos, "he was almost the worse. He was always injecting himself with crocaine and heroines. He is married once to María Felix and if you don't know who is María Felix then you are a dumb Jonkee. He is married to María Felix although he is disfigured from the knife on his face . . ."

"What knife on his face?" I demanded.

"When Lara is much younger," said Carlos, "he is playing the piano in what you call a whirr house in Mexico City and this is where he writes his first songs, specially to this girl Rosa. She is one of the whirrs and nobody knows why but she cut his face from his ear down to his chin and if you see him you see what a terrible cut it was — is still there a big scar. The reason Rosa cuts him like this is probably because he is fooling around some more women so he can write some more songs, but anyway he writes this one called 'Rosa' which is beautiful and goes like this . . ." Carlos sang a few bars of "Rosa" and then resumed, "Why is this? Why does María Felix marry this man all cut on the face and skinny and injected full of crocaine? We all know why. He is for prosterity and María Felix knew this, and she wants prosterity also and so she married him and it only lasted one ycar and he wrotc a bcautiful song about her that we call 'Maria Bonita,' and it goes like this . . ." He sang some "Maria Bonita." "He has written one thousand songs for prosterity and he is the greatest writer of songs in this country and he is also the greatest writer of songs in your country because all the songs anybody in your crazy country ever wrote was . . ." Carlos now went into a whiny version of "Three O'Clock in the Morning." The important thing," he said, "is that Lara wrote one thousands songs for prosterity and every song is about a woman, and maybe a different woman for all I know, and then he ran out of women so he sat down and wrote 'Moo-hair.' "

"Moo-what?"

" 'Moo-hair.' That is Espanish word for woman. I think 'Moo-hair' is the best song Lara made but also I like 'Noche de Ronda' and maybe five hundred others, but not 'Noche Criolla' because you think it is good, you chip baster."

That is a slightly unorthodox version of the story of Agustin Lara but in its main points it appears to be true. Lara was born in a town called Tlacotalpan, in the region of the great Papaloápan River project (I keep wanting to call it the Fallopian River). That area, a sort of Mexican TVA, has lately been opened up; but in 1900, when Lara was born, it was so far back in the jungle that it's a wonder he didn't turn out to be a soloist on the armadillo guitar. The record says that when he was sixteen he fought with Villa. . . . I'm sorry I mentioned it. Everybody I meet down here fought with Villa at the age of sixteen, except those who did it at the age of fifteen.

Somehow Lara became a piano player in a Mexico City whirr house, as Carlos said, and wrote "Rosa" and got slashed and wrote "Mujer," which is pronounced Moo-hair, and means Woman. In popular esteem he is indisputably one of the greatest living Mexicans. He has not written a thousand songs, but maybe seven hundred, and he's still turning them out, and the Mexican people seize upon every one of them eagerly. His songs are beautiful. In them he says, "How come ya do me like ya do, do, do?" but he says it much purtier. Still he is relatively unknown in the United States. Only two of his songs have ever achieved any popularity among the Gringos — "Grenada" and "Solamente una vez," which we know as "You Belong to My Heart." Another that has been coming along is "Noche de Ronda," which both Carlos and I like; it is known back home as "Be Mine Tonight."

I have learned to recognize and enjoy perhaps a dozen of his songs so far, but my favorite remains "Noche Criolla." It remains my favorite in spite of a translation I had made of the lyrics, as follows:

> Verse:
> *Veracruz night — warm and quiet,*
> *Tale of fishermen that lullabies the sea —*
> *Vibration of fireflies that, with their light,*
> *Embroider the darkness with sequins.*
>
> Chorus:
> *Tropical night —*
> *Languid and sensual,*
> *Night that faints upon the sand,*
> *While the beach sings its futile pain.*
> *Tropical night — sky of tissue —*
> *You are the shadow of a Creole glance,*
> *Night of Veracruz.*

I have never known a night that faints upon the sand, or a beach that sings its futile pain, or even any fishermen that lullabies the sea. I think maybe this is a bad translation of Lara's phrases, because I've been told his lyrics are usually quite poetic. I hope we get to see him before we leave Mexico. He performs frequently at the Club Capri in the Hotel Regis. He has been described as a thin, gaunt, hollow-cheeked man with one side of his face slightly twisted by Rosa's knife scar. He sits at a piano, a soft spot playing over him, singing his songs or leading his own wonderful orchestra, and people tell me it is one of the great and moving sights to be seen in Mexico — ranking with the pyramids, the Monument to the Revolution, and the Alameda statue of the woman trying to give a man an enema.

Lara has often been called the Irving Berlin of Mexico, but he is also the Cole Porter and the Hammerstein-Rodgers and the Jerome Kern and the Harold Arlen. So far as his sins are concerned, I'm inclined to remember Lincoln's attitude toward Grant's drinking and to suggest that more and more people ought to be injecting themselves with crocaine and heroines.

Today I heard about Señor Rosado Verde. His true name is Pinky Green and he is a Texan engaged in the restaurant business here. When the Mexicans finally accept a Gringo into their community they often translate his name into Spanish. Joe Green becomes Pepe Verde. James Fields is known as Jaime Campos. Smith becomes Forjador, although a *forjador* can be either a blacksmith or a forger.

This Pinky Green has a standing bet of one hundred pesos that he can furnish the punchline to any dirty story he hears. For several months people have been rushing to find him whenever they've heard a new story. They tell him the story, up to the point of the punchline. Then Pinky either furnishes the last line, or he misses. Some say he's ahead of the game; others say he's slowly growing broke.

Tonight Virginia Woodcock took us to a night club called El Paseo because they wanted us to meet the proprietor, Bill Shelburne, and hear his story. El Paseo is a small restaurant about midway between the Reforma and the Hilton. Its main feature is a grand piano which is used by ten or twelve customers as a cocktail table while it is being played by Bill Shelburne. We got settled at a table in the rear and Shelburne came around and we arranged to get together at a later date. After a while Virginia reported to me that there was a very famous girl sitting on one of the stools at the piano.

"You remember the Jelke case," said Virginia. "Well, this is the

Golden Girl of the Jelke case. Real beautiful and a real interesting personality. You remember her?"

I thought back to the Jelke case in New York, and the Golden Girl, who was one of the principal figures at the trial. Her name was Diana something and I remembered that one journalist said she gave rich men the impression that they had red corpuscles as big as tomatoes. The newspapers were full of her pictures and she was a beauty — a sort of Marilyn Monroe constrained within reasonable bounds. She was, as I recalled, a sort of intercontinental product, costing about as much as a medium-sized ballistics missile, with warhead.

"Would you like to meet her?" asked Virginia.

"Certainly," I said. We proceeded to the piano where Virginia introduced me to the Golden Girl. She in turn introduced me to some cluck from Texas who was her escort.

"I'm so happy to meet you, Mr. Allen," said the Golden Girl, displaying as much poise and charm as any debutante who ever set foot in the Hotel Pierre. "I understand you're a writer."

"Yes, ma'am," I said. (Get me! Keep in mind that this is one of the most famous whores in all Christendom.)

"What an interesting thing to be doing!" she exclaimed.

"What?" I said. "Doing what?" I hadn't been doing anything but talking to her.

"Writing," she said. "I mean just writing. Do you write with a pencil or a pen, Mr. Crimmins?"

"Well, sometimes both, and a typewriter."

Maybe I was a little confused.

"I'll bet," she said, "that you've had some amusing experiences in Mexico. I mean with the Mexican people."

"Well," I said, "most of my amusing experiences have been with tourists."

"Ha, ha," she said. "I understand what you mean."

The Texas cluck at this point must have decided that our conversation was getting noplace, or someplace, for he interrupted and said that speaking of Mexicans, he knew a funny story about a Mexican. He started telling it.

"This Mexican," he said, "worked for me in one of my warehouses and . . ."

"One of your WHAT?" I broke in, being a wit.

"*Ware*houses," he said. There was much laughter all around, for we were all of the International Set and quite blasé, and the Texan never did get to finish his story.

"Miss . . . uh, Miss . . . Golden Girl," I said, not knowing her Christian name, "Uh . . . what are you doing in Mexico?"

"Oh," she said, "I'm just on a sort of vacation. I travel a lot, you know. Do you enjoy traveling, Mr. Oliver?"

"Oh, yes," I said. "Do you . . . enjoy . . . traveling?"

"Simply adore it," she assured me.

I once interviewed Franklin D. Roosevelt and I've talked to Lindbergh and Henry Ford and Jack Dempsey and Anthony Eden and Babe Ruth and H. G. Wells and Gary Cooper and Bertrand Russell and many others without getting overly nervous and tongue-tied. But with this girl I just couldn't seem to function properly and so I gave up.

I said, "Well, Miss . . . uh . . . well, it's been a great pleasure meeting you."

"My house," she said, "is your house."

Later on, back at the hotel, I said to Nelle: "You know something? We ought to do more night-clubbing. It's a good way to meet interesting people." To which she responded with some astringency, "Think of dust, and go to sleep."

February 24

I'VE about given up on the Cantinflas deal. Santiago Reachi has not acknowledged any of my telephone calls. It's too bad that I fouled things up, for I would have enjoyed that trip to Acapulco with the famous comedian. And I do think it's time the people of the United States learned something about the man. I have an idea that they'll be hearing a lot about him before very long. They already know something of his talents from the picture *Around the World in 80 Days.* It's quite obvious that there are big plans afoot to have him make more pictures in English.

He is probably the most popular person in Mexico today. I've just received Abel Green's essays on Mexico and in one of them he describes Cantinflas as being "like Maurice Chevalier to the French, Gracie Fields to the British, Sir Harry Lauder to the Scots, but more so." Charlie Chaplin once called him "the world's greatest clown."

The details of the man's life are confused, because he's the type who gives tricky and unorthodox answers to interviewers. He is now about forty-four years old and in his time has been a medical student, a singer, dancer, acrobat, prize fighter and clown. He wanted to become a bullfighter and some people say he could have been a great one, but he chose comedy, and so it is that his comic bullfight act is today the most popular piece of entertainment in the whole of Latin America. I have heard that in Mexico City the public is so wild about this act that when it is announced the government takes the precaution of closing down the National Pawnshop for two days before the show; otherwise the people would pawn their furniture and fixtures in order to buy tickets.

The masses worship Cantinflas because the character he portrays on the screen is the eternal underdog. That characterization has been nicely described by Don Ross in the *New York Herald Tribune* as follows:

> In his pictures Cantinflas wears patched pants that hang down precariously around his hips and always seem about to fall down. He is a sort of ragamuffin, a *pelado.* This is a word applied to the poor people in Mexico. They apparently see in him the apotheosis of the *pelado,* for in his

bumbling, daft way he surmounts adversity, solves problems, makes his betters look silly and makes it seem fun
to be a *pelado*.

The people love him for an additional reason — that of his phi-
lanthropies. I've been told that he gives more than half of his money
to the poor people of Mexico in one way or another. He once maintained an office where the *pelados* came at certain hours and told
him of their troubles and got money from him. Now he channels his
money into organized charities; in 1952 he pledged himself to raise
at least two and a half million dollars a year to improve housing and
build hospitals and clinics for the poor. He has kept the pledge.

His English is not too good, so that his remarks are often uninten-
tionally funny. Once he was given a press luncheon in Washington
and at the end of it he said farewell to the crowd in this fashion:
"Believe it or not, I never saw you before, but I feel like I knew you
a long time ago."

Here in Mexico an interviewer once approached him on the subject of Moo-hair.

"What age do you prefer in women?" asked the reporter.

"All age," said Cantinflas.

"Long skirts are coming back," said the interviewer. "Do you prefer women in long skirts or short skirts?"

"In no skirt," the comedian responded.

Though he is now a wealthy man with all the responsibilities that
a wealthy man accumulates, he continues to entertain the public
with his comic bullfight and the question has arisen whether or not
he is actually in danger in the ring. The truth appears to be that he
is in as much danger as a matador, perhaps more. "The bool," he
says, "does not know that I am suppose to be fonny."

We had lunch today at the home of Anita Brenner in one of the
outlying residential areas. We ate on the terrace with Anita and her
daughter Susie, feeding on Anita's own version of *paella*, a spec-

tacular casserole dish of chicken, rice, saffron, strips of pimento, little shrimps and bits of sausage.

Anita has done many things in her life but surely one of her most important achievements is her famous book, *Idols Behind Altars*. She wrote it thirty years ago, yet I remember that when I asked for it last year at the Chappaqua Public Library I was put on a waiting list and didn't get it for a couple of weeks. Another of her books that has become almost a classic is *The Wind That Swept Mexico*, an illustrated story of the Revolution.

Anita was born in Aguascalientes of American parents. As a young girl she saw the Revolution at first hand, and suffered under it; in those times a foreigner was kicked around by Villistas and then by Zapatistas and after that by Carranzistas and so on. She came out of it, however, admiring the Revolution and most of its leaders.

We talked of many serious matters, including her friend Cárdenas, and of many matters not so serious. She told about the time she had house guests from the United States and how a call came from an elegant and wealthy woman member of the American colony. The rich woman said: "We are having a silly party for people who are silly and we want you to dress up in silly clothes and come on over and do silly things." Anita begged off, explaining about her guests. "Bring your silly guests with you," the woman insisted.

Anita and her friends sat around and talked and agreed that people who do such things ought to be given their lumps. They debated what they should do. One idea they had was to stage a Mexican funeral procession and march it straight into the middle of the silly party. They finally settled on a picnic. They quickly acquired sandwiches and hard-boiled eggs and Flit guns and thermos jugs full of coffee and lemonade and a charcoal brazier. Arriving at the rich lady's mansion they took over the main room on the ground floor, spread their *petates,* laid out the food and equipment, built a fire in the brazier, and kept up loud and jolly conversation. When other guests came along Anita and her friends would not talk to them, but said to each other, "Rude tourists! For shame!" The smoke from the

brazier drifted upstairs, permeating the entire house. At last they
departed, leaving eggshells, wads of crumpled wax paper, smears of
mustard and other debris scattered over the room. They left without
notifying anybody, without speaking a good-by. The rich lady
wanted it silly; she got it silly.

Before we left Anita's she took us into her garden and showed
us a *palo bobo,* or "boob stick." It has also been called the idiot tree.
It is a tree lacking in beauty and it is considered to be tetched because it grows in unlikely places — it comes up through lava rock
or even out of concrete, disregarding all rational laws of botany. I
am not very good at describing plant life, but I *will* say that the
boob stick looks real crazylike.

From Anita's home we went to the residence of the Staffords, to
whom we had been recommended by Nic Adams of Chapel Hill.
Mr. Stafford is retired from the United States consular service, while
his wife is dean of the graduate school at Mexico City College. They
have a fine house in the Los Palmas district and it is well-staffed
with servants. They have four full-time servants and three part-time
and the total wages for all seven come to about eighty dollars a
month. For this sum they are able to have a chauffeur, a cook, a gardener, a cleaning woman, a sewing woman, and two maids. Mr. Stafford said that living in Mexico City is good for two major reasons:
the climate, and the availability of servants. He said that many members of the American colony are nervous over the prospect of a coming servant problem. In the first place the rapid industrialization of
Mexico is opening up better-paying jobs in the factories; in the second, there are disturbing reports that somebody has been whispering
in the ear of domestic workers, telling them about unions, and how
they can get their wages raised tremendously through organization.
"Some people," said Mr. Stafford, "are actually shuddering over this
possibility."

Mrs. Stafford said that many American students, when they finish
their studies here, could go home and get good jobs; by the time,

however, that they are ready to go home, they don't want to — they have fallen in love with Mexico and want to stay here and work, even at greatly reduced salaries.

Tonight in the Reforma lobby we ran into the film crew again. They had been to the bullfights this afternoon and they said the fights were exciting. The fans rioted because they thought the bulls were no good, filled the arena with seat cushions and built bonfires all over the place. At one point a boy got into the ring and was trying to kick a bull to death when he was rescued. He will probably grow up to be *Presidente*.

There are certain characters to be met with regularly in the Bar Jardín, and one of them is Sims McGowan. He is a blond, ruggedly handsome man in his middle thirties, and he is involved in some kind of mysterious business in Guatemala and British Honduras. He never talks about his business, and for all I know he may be a white slaver.

Sims McGowan is good company over and above the cloak-and-dagger atmosphere that seems to trail him about. Tonight he and I got to talking about the myth of Mexican laziness, and how it probably originated with American cartoonists, who got into the habit of always depicting a Mexican asleep in the street with his sombrero tipped down over his face. A cartoon about Mexico wouldn't be a cartoon about Mexico without that fellow. It is one of the worst of all libels on the Mexican people. McGowan and I agreed that we had never seen a more energetic and industrious people than the Mexicans. No waiters or waitresses on earth hustle like those in this country. Nobody could look at a Mexican *cargador* shuffling along with an office desk or a piano on his back and say that he held membership in a lazy race. Out in the rural areas we have often noted the industry of the Mexican farmers, working in the fields with oxen and wooden plow, their women walking four or five miles to tote water in five-gallon pottery jars, everybody toting and toting all day long. We have also noted that the Mexican taxi driver doesn't loll around in his cab between calls, the way it is back home. He busies himself scouring and scrubbing and polishing his car until it glistens.

We talked about the *mordida* in low places and high, and I remembered having read a sober report estimating that the politicians get about eight million out of every ten million spent on public works. McGowan said there is a Mexican proverb which goes, "Only the Cross does not steal, because it cannot move its arms." Then I recalled a story passed along to me by Carleton Beals, about the Palace of Fine Arts. When it was being built Porfirio Díaz appointed a Mexican gentleman to serve as director of its museum. This man immediately stole all the priceless works of art from the museum and substituted fakes and forgeries. Then he wrote an indignant book about the fraud and the fakes and the forgeries, and the book was very popular and made him a lot of money. "The book," said Beals, "was very authentic."

We discussed the public's seeming indifference to thievery and how easily the public is fooled, recalling the classic statement of Maximino Avila Camacho: "If you build a road for seventy-five thousand pesos and pocket one thousand, everybody will howl. But if you build a road for seventy-five million pesos and knock back a million, nobody will notice." The one-armed Obregón once told Blasco Ibañez: "All of us are thieves more or less, down here. However, I have only one hand, while the others have two. That's why the people prefer me."

I ventured the opinion that someday the people are going to smarten up and then there will be hell to pay — assassinations and maybe even bloody revolution.

"Oh, no," protested McGowan. "That day is past. There'll be no more revolutions, no more political assassinations, in Mexico."

I begged him to hold still for a few moments while I gave him one of my favorite recitations. Back home I sometimes speak of the coming day when The Bomb falls. People almost invariably say to me, "You must be insane. Nobody is going to drop The Bomb. Nobody could be so foolish as to drop it." And I respond, "Somebody *did* drop it. Somebody dropped it *twice*. Dropped it on people, including women and children, killing at least a hundred and fifty thousand of them."

McGowan is not the first person to scoff at the notion of another revolution or of further political assassinations in Mexico. Granted that this is the most advanced of the Latin-American countries, it is still a Latin-American country, and its own history of revolt and assassination is quite impressive. As late as 1944 an assassin's bullet pierced the jacket and vest of a Mexican president, and Latin-American gunners have been bringing down an average of one president per year in the last three or four years.

I was saying all this publicly, there in the Bar Jardín, when a colorful thought crossed my mind. I am prejudiced against having my head shaved and then painted red, white and blue. I decided to shut up and go to bed.

February 25

TODAY I finally got around to a talk with Bill Shelburne. We had lunch with him at El Paseo. Also present was Martha Davis, a prominent member of the American colony.

Bill is a tall, slender man who provokes arguments among the women as to whether he resembles Rex Harrison most, or Mel Ferrer. He grew up in a New England household under two major restrictions. He enjoyed fussing around the kitchen but he was always driven out and forbidden the place. And he wanted to play the piano, but his sister was a sort of musical genius and the piano was reserved for her, and Bill was told to stay away from it. Consequently he grew to manhood with two great passions: kitchens and pianos. He studied chemistry in college, served in the Navy, and then joined the Monsanto Chemical Company. Monsanto sent him to Europe and then to Mexico. Eventually the company decided Bill was needed back in St. Louis, but by this time he had been deeply afflicted by *virus mexicano.* He left Monsanto and then set about the business of satisfying those two primal urges of his youth. He had always had a secret ambition to play the piano and sing in a night club. He knew that he couldn't sing well enough to be hired by any other restaurant, so he went out and bought one for himself — El Paseo. He organized the kitchen for the production of first-rate food. Then he installed the big piano and began playing and singing two or three hours every night. All of his customers agreed that his singing was somewhat less than adequate, and kidded him about his voice, but still they flocked in and filled the establishment. Bill is a hoarse-type singer who usually sounds as if he had swallowed a couple of incompatible maracas, yet there are some songs that he makes sound pretty good, such as "September Song," in which he comes close to the Walter Huston version. Almost all his customers are Gringos, with few tourists, and they all have great affection for the reformed chemist. They applaud his singing and they applaud the excellence of his food.

During lunch Martha Davis was talking about some aspect of Mexican art and she concluded a sentence with ". . . that is, if you look at it folklorically." For some reason I repeated the word "folklorically" but got it twisted. She laughed, and tried to say it again, and *she* got it twisted, and we tried it half a dozen different ways, such as flocklyrically and florlickery and flickflorcally and forkflickerly. I just know it's one of those things that will keep me awake nights.

After lunch I stopped in the offices of the Committee of North Americans for Mexico and picked up a copy of the booklet, *In Mexico It's the Custom, Señor!* which is supposed to teach Gringos how they should behave down here. It is a good little book even though it contains this statement: "Bribery is no more — and probably no less — an accepted part of the economic system in Mexico than it is anywhere else." On the other hand it contains, in one paragraph, one of the most perceptive things ever written about the people of this country, as follows:

A Mexican thinks of himself primarily as a man — and only secondarily as a waiter, a cab driver or hotel clerk. Mexicans find it hard to grasp the North American habit of thinking of people in terms of their function first. For a Mexican, work exists for man, not man for work.

Back in the hotel Maxine Smith made a telephone call in my behalf, to a Mexican, and it was interesting to hear her spell out my name: "Essay . . . Emmay . . . Eee . . . Tay . . . Ah-chay." And a bit later I heard some talk between a couple of men in an adjoining office which made me happy that I don't have to deal in big money. The sounds of large sums, as uttered in Spanish, are almost frightening. To specify the sum, $14,678.83 it is necessary to say, "*Catorce mil, sesientos setenta y ocho pesos, ochenta y tres centavos.*" And $28,976.55 comes out, "*Vientiocho mil, novacientos setenta y seis pesos y cincuenta y cinco centavos.*"

Still, the more I hear of it the better I like this language. Before I came to Mexico I had pretty much the same attitude as the English maiden lady, described by Cyril Ritchard as saying, during a visit to one of the Latin countries: "I don't see why, if one speaks slowly and distinctly, English should not be understood by everybody."

Day by day I pick up new words even though they are not always proper words. Occasionally I've heard an expletive, "*Fuchi!*" and wondered about it. A day or so ago I asked the elevator boy what it means. "*Eet steenks!*" he told me, grasping his nose to emphasize the thought. A very handy word to know.

Many women in the American colony are said to be contemptuous of Spanish, refusing to take it up in a serious way and learning no more than a simple variety known as "kitchen Spanish." This is just enough to get along with the servants. In Tepoztlán I met a retired Boston politician, now resident in Mexico City, who told me about kitchen Spanish and gave me an example of it. He said a woman of his acquaintance gave a dinner party and after she had consumed four or five cocktails, went to the kitchen door and yelled, "Put th' goddam *carne* on the *estufa!*" That's kitchen Spanish. There was another man at Tepoztlán who addressed me one evening with a phrase which could very well serve as an all-purpose greeting. He passed me on the terrace and said, *"Buenos ditches."* Seems to cover both night and day.

In Taxco, Leslie Figueroa told of how a tourist lady in a Mexican restaurant saw the phrase HAY SANDWICHES, meaning "There are sandwiches." The woman said, "What on earth is a hay sandwich?" And even such an old hand as Natalie Scott once flubbed badly. At a local dinner she was called on for a few remarks, without having been forewarned, and the first thing she said when she got to her feet was, "I am very *embarazada."* This means, "I am very pregnant."

The language struggle, of course, is equally amusing in the other direction. The Mexican trying to learn English often has a rough time of it. Fidel Figueroa once greeted a dignified lady who was Leslie's house guest with, "What's the matter you no smell good today?" He meant smile. Fidel's father owned a mare and in trying to explain it, he said, "When I was a very child, my father had a woman's horse." Fidel's sister, Margarita, also had her difficulties learning English. She couldn't master the word "her" and would say, "I am going to she's house." Leslie drilled her and drilled her and finally, one day, the beautiful Margarita appeared at a party and told everyone, "I am going to hor house." Fidel was once ill for several days and when he returned to his work he was greeted by a Gringo who had made an effort to learn the phrase, *"Sienta mejor?"* meaning, "Do you feel better?" The Gringo said, instead, *"Sienta mujer?"* which means, "Did you ever feel a woman?"

Alma Reed recently gave me an essay about Felipe Carrillo, which had been translated from the Spanish by a Mexican girl who is one of Alma's friends. Some of the things in the translation follow:

Don't you feel emotioned when listening to it?

Then highing his voice a little, he said . . .

My generous friend rose his eyes and fixed them in a deep crack of the wall and began his tale.

They had climbed up these steps of the City of Art and before descending, this time, they found out how far they still were of excelsitude, but it didn't discouraged them.

He was shooted together with his brothers. That way ended his glorious life, and his mortal body was annulled.

I have one of those little phrasebooks in which the questions are given phonetically, such as, "KWAHN-toh TYEM-po tay-NAY-mohss kay esspay-RAHR?" which means, "How long must we wait?" Carlos has looked through this little book several times and on each occasion he has grinned and chuckled and laughed aloud. He is amused by the comical aspect of his own langauge in phonetic form. Well, it works both ways. For some years I have preserved a literary curiosity published by *Time* in 1943. It was sent to the magazine by Belle Flegelman of Helena, Montana. She said that in Mexico City she had seen a professorial-looking man drop a paper just before he boarded a bus. The bus drove off with him, but she retrieved the paper and found that it was a phonetic version of the Star Spangled Banner, as follows:

TRADUCCION FIGURADA DE LA LETRA DEL HIMNO AMERICANO
(*Translation figurative of the words of the American Hymn*)
STAR-SPANGLED BANNER
> *oh sai ken yu sai bai di dons er li lait,*
> *juat so proud li ui jeld at di tuai lais last glimming,*
> *jus estraips end brait estars tru da per il us fait,*
> *or di ram parts ui uach uer so ga lant li strimming —*
> *and di ra quets red gler, bams berst ting in er,*
> *gev pruf tru da nait dat aour flag uas estil der,*

Coro
> *oh sai dos dat estar espang gald ba ner yat ueif,*
> *or da land of di fri end di jom of di breiv?*

February 26

AT THE beginning of this journal I spoke of Mexico as being a land of contradictions. The evidence accumulates. This morning I undertook some research on two minor subjects. The first of these was the matter of the Grito. The Grito was the "Cry of Dolores" as uttered by Father Hidalgo to start the revolt against Spain in 1810. It is the "Give me liberty or give me death!" of Mexico. The words of the Grito are surely the most important words in the life of the Mexican nation. So, I wish to God someone would decide just what those words were!

I can't find any two people agreeing on the wording of the Grito as it was gritoed by Father Hidalgo. And I'm not at all sure about the wording as it is gritoed each year by the President, standing on a little balcony of the National Palace. I have searched through all the books I can find and I am able to testify that there are more versions of the Grito than there are verses to "Frankie and Johnnie."

Frances Toor said it went this way: "Long live the Virgin of Guadalupe and down with the bad government!"

Ernest Gruening quotes a Mexican historian, Nicolás León, with this version: "Long Live Independence. Long Live America. Down with the Bad Government."

Erna Fergusson has it: "Long live Our Lady of Guadalupe! Long Live Independence! Death to the Spaniards!"

Byron Steel's version: "Down with the tyrant's yoke; long live the Republic of Mexico!" This is the only version I've seen with a semicolon in it.

One authority says that the words cried out by Hidalgo are unprintable. I have had fun speculating about this.

As for the cry uttered by the President on the big night of September 15, someone has simply got to haul a tape-recorder down to the Zócalo and get it as it is gritoed. It has been set down as ranging all the way from a simple, "Long live Mexico — Long live Independ-

ence!" to "Mexicans! Long live our heroes! Long live our Independence! Long live Mexico!"

One thing is certain — it's all full of *vivas* no matter how they
may be strung together. A Mexican knows how to *viva* if he knows
nothing else. Sometimes when a crowd gets into a real patriotic mood
there are cries of *"Viva Mexico!"* and *"Viva el Presidente!"* and *Viva*
this and *Viva* that and *Viva* some more, and then, during a quiet
moment, there is always the cry from some Mexican wit: *"Viva todo
el mundo!"* Meaning, "Long live everybody in the world!"

The Aztecs had a law which prescribed death for any person who
falsified history. If modern Mexico had half as much concern with
historical accuracy, someone would get Father Hidalgo's grito
straightened out and then go to the President and say, "This is the
way it ought to go. Grito it this way or don't grito it at all." Otherwise, I don't think the people should attach a bit of importance to
the Yelp from Dolores.

My second investigation concerns the expression "Rosario de Amozoc." A free-for-all fight is called a "Rosario de Amozoc," and a nice
little story lies back of the expression. Amozoc is a town east of
Puebla on the way to Jalapa and Veracruz. The first time we drove
through it Carlos said, "This a-village is famous all over Mexico for
making silver spurs and stirrups." And I said, "Don't try to cover up
the sins of your people. This town is more famous for a big fight."
The story goes that one evening, many years ago, the villagers of
Amozoc gathered to say the rosary. One woman stepped on another
woman's rebozo. A quarrel started, then a fight, and soon everybody
in town had joined in the battle. They fought for two days and two
nights and they'd still be fighting if the federal troops hadn't arrived.
And so a lively expression, similar to our own Donnybrook, passed
into the language.

Now I discover that there may not have been any fight at all,
that nobody stepped on a rebozo. Gruening quotes the Mexican historian Fernández del Castillo concerning an old Amozoc custom. In
the old days each Indian of the area had his own personal Christ,

and believed that his Christ was a better and more powerful Christ than those possessed by other Indians. Each year in Amozoc there was a grand fiesta, and the Indians came from all around, each carrying the crude statue of his own Christ. After the playful part of the fiesta was over, custom decreed that the Indians begin fussing and arguing over the relative merits of their individual Christs. Then they all began clubbing each other with their images, trying to beat each other senseless, "to prove which is the most miraculous." I suppose that the statue which brought down the most people was the most miraculous. In any event, according to the historian, the custom installed a phrase in the language, the saying, "It ended like the vespers of Amozoc." Thus has one of my favorite Mexican stories been shot to hell, to be supplanted by one even better. I find myself wishing that I had a graven image of Henry Steele Commager, wherewith to beat a few Mexicans historians on the head.

So it goes — one contradiction follows another, and nothing is true. It is commonly said in Mexico that the big meal is eaten at midday because of the altitude. The digestive process is slow at high altitudes and so, if a big meal were taken at night, people wouldn't be able to go to sleep. Just yesterday a man told us that this is a lot of hogwash. Dinner in the middle of the day, he said, is an old Spanish custom; all Spaniards, no matter what the altitude, eat their big meal at midday.

Henry Fink came up from Cuernavaca at noontime and the two of us set out for the Hipódromo de las Américas. Henry is so close to being a character out of Damon Runyon that I automatically thought of a horse track when we made our engagement. He is a small, trim, dapper, good-looking fellow and he will live in the memory of man, almost forever, because he wrote the song, "The Curse of an Aching Heart" (subtitle: "You Made Me What I am Today, I Hope You're Satisfied").

Henry Fink came out of Milwaukee, worked around race tracks, was a boxer for a while and then got into vaudeville. Eventually he played in musical comedy and in motion pictures, and then owned a series of restaurants and night clubs. Early in World War II he was running the Club Samoa in New York. He was a great fan of the New York Giants and knew everyone on the team and the Club Samoa was a meeting place for the players.

"One day," said Henry, "I saw some handwriting on a wall and so I sold out." The handwriting he saw on a wall involved a few "sort of gangsters" who were pressing him to sell his club. He now found himself with a lot of money, a beautiful young wife, and nothing to do. He decided on a two-year vacation in some place where it is always warm, because his great passion is golf, and he wanted to play golf every day. Finally he settled on Phoenix because the Giants trained there. He headed south into the worst winter Dixie had experienced in many years. "Down in this place called Pensacola," Henry said, "it was snowing and I bought some goo-lashes, it was so cold." . . .

"In this place called El Paso," he went on, "I wanted to cross over into Mexico, but my wife she was afraid of Mexico because she had it mixed up with smoke signals and bows-and-arrows and scalping off scalps. But I said we would just go across for one hour so's she could say she'd been in a foreign country, and we went over there, and the idea was to buy some postcards and send 'em back to the lugs on Broadway."

They went into a novelty store in Juárez, and Henry, confused by all the Mexican talk around him, suddenly seized his wife's arm and said, "My God, I just heard some character talking Yiddish!" They traced it down and found that the Yiddish came from the proprietor. Henry had a dozen postcards in his hand, and his version of the ensuing colloquy goes this way:

PROPRIETOR: Where you goink to?
HENRY: Phoenix.
PROPRIETOR: Phoenix Schmoenix! Vats in Phoenix? Go to Mexi-cuh.
HENRY: How much the postal cards?

PROPRIETOR: Nodding in Phoenix, planty in Mexicuh.
HENRY: How much the postal cards?
PROPRIETOR: Acks-spansive in Phoenix. Much chipper in Mexi-cuh.
HENRY: How much the postal cards?
PROPRIETOR: In Mexicuh is alvays varm, alvays son shine.

At this point Henry turned to his wife and said, "Why fight it?" And so they headed south, knowing not a word of Spanish, knowing nothing at all about the country, believing, as Henry put it, "that everybody lived in big hossiendas and danced on their hats and slat each other's throats."

In Valles his pocket was picked. "All my life," he said, "I am around the worst hoods on earth, and never once did I lose a penny to them, and then I lose my wallet to a Mexican." He went into a restaurant and approached a group of American tourists and asked for a ten-dollar loan, explaining how he needed that much to get to Mexico City, and explaining also that he had bushels of money in the trunk of his car. The tourists insulted him, called him a bum, and told him to hit the road. A young man overheard the talk, however, and called Henry to one side and offered him ten dollars. "I got a fortune in traveler's checks in the trunk of the car," Henry assured him. "Well," said the young man, "why don't you get them out?" Henry explained that the trunk had been sealed by the customs people at the border. The young man laughed and said, "You can open it now — you're in Mexico." So they opened it and got out the checks. Henry cashed one for a hundred dollars in one dollar bills, walked over to the party of tourists who had insulted him, flung the money on the table and said, "Buy yourselfs a drink of poison, you bastards."

In Mexico City he rented an apartment and then made connections with a Mexican banker. He had enough money to command the attention of the head of a bank, rather than an assistant cashier. During his conversations with the banker the subject of golf was mentioned and Henry said he had been playing for many years and mentioned his score. They began playing together once a week and then one day the banker said, "Have you ever tried Cuernavaca?" Henry said, "No, I'm not much of a hand to drink." The banker took him down to a beautiful golf course in Cuernavaca and as they came up to the first tee they encountered a foursome. The banker introduced Henry to the other golfers. One of them was Miguel Alemán, President of Mexico. Another was the Governor of Morelos. "My God," said Henry, "just think of it. One minute I'm being in-sulted over a lousy ten bucks and the next minute I'm shaking hands with the President of the country. They told us to go ahead of them, and I had to drive off that tee in front of the President, and I tell you I was shook. But I talked to myself a little, and reminded myself that I once played opposite Blossom Seeley and I used to be pals with Jolson and why should I be so nervous and then I hit that ball. One of the best drives I ever had in my life. The President and the others all let go with a lot of Mexican cheers and the President hopped over and gave me a hug and banged me on the back. My God! Imagine it! Me, Henry Fink! So I says to my friend the banker that I liked this place and wanted a house here, right on the golf course if I could get it, and he got it for me."

About a week after that first game the Governor of Morelos came to Henry and said he'd be willing to teach him some Spanish if Henry would let him, the Governor, play golf with him three times a week. "I'll buy that!" Henry told the Governor. President Alemán heard of this arrangement and *he* came to Henry and asked if they might play nine holes together once a week. "God yes, President!" Henry replied. So his house became a sort of nineteenth hole, with huge buffets and plenty to drink and card games. "We played a lot of poker," Henry said, "and I must say these Mexicans do not play the same brand of poker that us Broadway lugs play, but these Mexicans throw money around like it was sand, and this made me very happy as I am quite a good poker player." Eventually he opened Henry Fink's Shangri-La, which is the most felicitous name a motel ever had. It is a regular stopping place for Bill O'Dwyer, who is an old friend of Henry's. O'Dwyer is a man of vast sentiment and loves to recall the good old days through the good old songs. He and Henry and sometimes some others spend hours harmonizing, and they even sing "The Curse of an Aching Heart."

At the racetrack we occupied the box of Charles A. Pickard, a big auto dealer in Mexico City. I did all the betting. Henry said: "I quit betting when the tote boards come in. I used to enjoy betting with bookies because a bookie is someone you can talk to, and argue with, and a tote board you can't talk to. But I still know how to figure them."

I had been trying to make out the distance of the next race from the program, and from the phrase *"De cuatro años, 53 K"* arrived at the conclusion that it was 53 kilometers and said so to Henry. "Good God!" he said. "That's half way to El Paso!"

He said he wrote his famous song in 1912 "between shows in a theater in Bayonne, New Jersey." He wrote it on the back of a laundry slip and later, at the end of his act, he told the audience, "My act is over, but I've got a new song that I just wrote and the title of it is 'The Curse of an Aching Heart.' " They laughed. He sang it, and they cheered. (Sigmund Spaeth has suggested that the song was written as a joke, but I feel certain that Henry was serious about it, and is still serious about it, and is proud of it).

"I was the first man," he said, "to put 'God bless you' in a song. Nobody had the guts to put it in a song till I did it, and then everybody started putting it in. They even put it in 'Mother Machree.' "

He spoke about some of the other songs he has written, among them being "If I Had My Life to Live Over," "Since Becky Became a Conductor," "You're Just a Little Pansy but You're Sweeter Than a Rose," and "Write Something Sweet to Me, Dear." He reached in his pocket and brought out a slip of paper and studied it a moment. "Oh," he said, "here's something I thought might interest you. On the register at my hotel I always look for funny names, especially combinations of Spanish and Jewish names, and I've had some sweethearts. Here are three of them you might want to put in your book: Santiago José Rabinowitz, Jesús Goldberg and Family, Señorita Guadalupe Schwartz."

Henry has written two songs recently. One of these, which he feels certain will be a hit, is titled "If You Love Me in Oaxaca Like You Did in Cuernavaca, Adiós! Adiós! Adiós!" Another was written in his car, while his wife was driving, and was inspired by Mexican highway signs. The title: "Un Momento, por Favor, Despacio." He said it means, "Take your time, don't rush me," and he sang it for me.

All this while Henry Fink, the reformed horse-player, had been giving me the benefit of his knowledge and I had been betting his choices and now I was, as the track people say, empty. We were joined by a couple of businessmen, Henry Uhthoff and Mike Kestler, friends of Henry's. Before we left there was one horse-racing question I wanted to ask. At the start of each race the man on the loud-speaker doesn't yell "They're off!" He cries out something that sounds like, *"Arrrrrrrrrrranca!"* I asked Henry Uhthoff about it and he said it is an expression which means, "They tear themselves off."

Tonight Henry Fink took us to the home of a young friend, Andy Leone, a former Chicagoan who is practicing law with one of the biggest firms in Mexico City. Andy is a member of the famous Leone Restaurant family and his mother, of course, knows her spaghetti. A year or so ago she came down from Chicago and spent six weeks visiting her son. She was not satisfied with the things turned out by Andy's cook, a brisk and efficient Mexican girl named Rosa Esquivel Salazar, and so she taught Rosa how to cook Italian spaghetti. That was what we had tonight, and it was superb, and later I asked Andy to call Rosa out of the kitchen and ask her if she ate spaghetti herself. She came in and they jabbered Spanish and Andy said that she said she loved spaghetti. Then Rosa let go with a long and excited burst of Spanish, much as if she were reciting the Constitution of 1917, and when she was finished Andy turned to me and said, "She says it tastes much better on the second day."

February 27

ANDY LEONE telephoned this morning and said that last night after we had gone he happened upon a copy of the *Reader's Digest*, the Spanish version which is known far and wide in Mexico as *Seleccíones,* and in it was a translation of an article of mine. He had read it aloud in Spanish, for the edification of two leftover guests, and while he was reading Rosa, the cook, stood in the doorway listening. When he had finished Rosa exclaimed: "My! Mr. Smith writes good Castilian, doesn't he!"

At breakfast Nelle said, "What's a what-chin-chinga?"

"What the hell kind of a question is that?" I countered, being a person who is always in a good mood early in the morning.

"You were saying it in your sleep last night," she said. "I heard you say it, what-chin-chinga, three or four times."

I gave it some thought, trying several things, and finally got it. I had been saying *huachinango,* or red snapper — the fish we enjoyed so much in Veracruz. It sounds something like what-chin-chinga, but not much. I was happy to learn, however, that apparently I have started dreaming in Spanish. Bilingual people place a lot of importance in the language they "think in." Pepe Romero speaks good English, yet he says he thinks in Spanish. I consider it even more significant if you dream in Spanish, if only about a red snapper.

There was once a Spanish writer of some genius named Angel Ganivet, who produced a sagacious description of his fellow countrymen: "Each Spaniard carries a passport which says, 'This Spaniard is entitled to do whatever comes into his head.'" The trait applies equally well to the Mexicans. It is unlikely that anyone will ever figure out the mysterious reasoning processes of man but even if they do, they'll have to give up on the Mexican. I have been collecting "shaggy Mexican stories" to illustrate this point.

Among the most famous is the one about the telegraph company. It was once proposed that the company inaugurate all-night service. The company issued a statement: "This is impossible because our offices are closed at night."

The same idea lies back of Charles Flandrau's experience in a Puebla hotel. He had to leave on a journey at six in the morning so he asked the boy to have breakfast ready at 5:30. The boy said it could not be done "because the cook does not light the brazier until half-past six."

Another famous anecdote tells of the Mexican who was run over by a train and badly cut up. At the hospital he explained that he had been sleeping on the track "because it is well known that a snake will never cross a railroad track."

Many writers have found out that it is useless to expect sensible answers from most Mexicans. Flandrau once asked a Mexican lady, "Does it rain here in summer as much as it does in winter?" To which she promptly replied, *"No hay reglas fijas, Señor."* (There are no fixed rules).

One noontime in Tepoztlán, Stuart Chase asked a Mexican what time the fiesta was to begin. "It will take place right now at about three or five o'clock," was the answer. And Sydney A. Clark once said to a plane pilot, "Will you make connections at Torreón?" To which the pilot replied, "Sure I will, maybe."

Margaret Cousins came out of her hotel in Mexico City one morning and saw a peddler with a tray loaded with gardenias. "When I found out they were about five cents each," she said, "I decided that for once in my life I was going to have all the gardenias I wanted." She told the man she would take them all. He cringed, and began to whine. "Oh, please no, Señorita," he begged. "Do not take them all! What would I do the rest of the day?"

Mexicans often have a delightful way of explaining their odd behavior. In 1947 Diego Rivera was crossing a street when a bus came within a few inches of hitting him. He shouted an insult at the driver, who stopped and spoke feelingly of Señor Rivera's mother, at which point Señor Rivera removed a revolver from his pocket and fired one shot at the driver, missing him. Word of this incident got out and reporters called on Señor Rivera. "I do not see," he said, "why you are making such a to-do about this matter; it is one of those common, ordinary things we see daily on the streets, arising out of difficulties in transit."

Last year three Mexicans were caught burglarizing a church in Mexico City. The cops lectured the prisoners on the enormity of their deed, asking them if they did not fear the hand of Providence. They replied: "God is too occupied with affairs in Europe to pay any attention to us."

A man named José Ramón García read in a newspaper that he was dead. He wrote an indignant letter to the paper, saying, "If I am dead, why is my employer paying me for working?" And one Rafael Duenas, of Mexico City, tried to kill himself with an icepick earlier this year. He had written a note saying, "I killed myself to see what it felt like."

Mexicans sometimes have difficulty adjusting to progress. Back in the time of Father Hidalgo's Revolution, his peasant soldiers, seeing cannon for the first time, rushed forward and clapped their sombreros over the mouths of the guns.

During the period when people all over the world were concerned about "Asiatic flu," the Mexicans talked about it in terms of mild indignation. "There is no reason," they said, "why we should get the Asiatic flu. Our own flu is just as good as anybody's."

When wheelbarrows were first introduced during the building of railroad lines, the Indians tried them and found them unsatisfactory; they removed the wheels, and carried the loaded barrows on their backs. (There is a fine thread of wheelbarrow running through the grim and tragic tapestry that is the Spanish character. Salvador Dali once planned to produce a movie with Anna Magnani playing the part of a woman in love with a wheelbarrow. I don't think the picture was ever made, for which I'm sorry — I'd like to know how it came out).

February 28

AMONG the habitués of the Bar Jardín are several who, on occasion, groan and sigh and even whinny as a consequence of overindulgence. I have discovered a piece of literary balm and consolation for them. It concerns Guadalupe Posada, one of the important names in Mexican art. Posada was an illustrator whose work influenced both Rivera and Orozco. He worked for a publisher in Mexico City and most of the time was industrious and conscientious and abstemious. His employer once told Anita Brenner about Posada's singular drinking schedule. All year he put aside fifty centavos a day, keeping his savings in a little box. On the 20th of December he sent all his money to his family in León, and they bought as many barrels of tequila as the funds would allow. The tequila was shipped to Posada in Mexico City and on New Year's Eve he cracked the first barrel. He drank and he drank and he drank until he had finished all the barrels, which usually took him from a month to a month and a half. For a fortnight afterward, said his employer, Posada could not work because his hands shook.

Amateur economists speak frequently of the "new middle class" that has arisen in Mexico. There is no middle class, they say, in any of the other Latin-American countries, where society is divided into the two extremes of the very rich and the very poor. They say that the hope and future of Mexico lies in its middle class, which is growing rapidly.

At lunch today there was talk of this middle group and how its members behave upon first achieving their new economic and social status. Almost invariably they want, first, an electric refrigerator; once they get it they wouldn't dream of putting it in the kitchen, where nobody would see it. The gleaming refrigerator goes right into the living room or, if not that, at least into the dining room. It is decorated with doilies and flowers and candelabra and sometimes even a small shrine to the Virgin of Guadalupe is installed on top of it. The home refrigerator is an extremely important acquisition among the Mexican people. The masses don't even have iceboxes and they must spend hours each day shopping; that is the reason that all the markets are constantly crowded.

Somebody brought up the subject of Mexican servants and how most of the girls who work for American residents love to brag about the habits and possessions of their employers. The big brag among the Mexican maids at the moment is the Waring mixer. Maids from three or four different households in, say, the San Angel neighborhood, will get together and begin talking, and one of them will speak of her master. "He has," she will say proudly, "two drawers full of shirts; he changes to a fresh shirt every day, sometimes even *twice* a day." Another girl brags that her people have *two* electric razors, one for the Señora's legs. Another tells about the rubber separators in the ice-cube trays at her house. Meanwhile the girl with the ace in the hole keeps mum, letting the others talk, and then at last she says, simply but devastatingly, "My people have a Waring meexer." That is the living end. That shuts the rest of them up. They go home to their houses full of shirts and electric razors and rubber separators and they begin sulking and fretting, and they scorch things, until finally someone asks them why they have become so ill-tempered, whereupon they blurt out their complaint: "We have no Waring meexer!"

In the Reforma barber shop this afternoon I saw a man having his hair sandpapered. The barber took a sheet of sandpaper and gave the man's hair a brisk going over, preliminary to a shampoo. While I sat getting a simple trim, this same man was later tilted back in the chair and the barber gave him a leg massage, right through his pants.

Soon thereafter I overheard a conversation between the customer in the next chair and his barber. The customer was an American, who might have been a professor. He was asking the barber about certain localities in the Zócalo and the Alameda which were associated with the Inquisition — sites where the victims were tortured and executed.

"This is all much exaggerated," said the barber. "Is lay-yend." (Mexicans call a legend a lay-yend, when speaking folklorically).

"But," said the customer, "there was always much torture and cruelty in those times."

"May *be*," said the barber, "but is only lay-yend."

"You know, of course," said the customer, "that Cortez was basically a cruel man — that he tortured Cuauhtémoc unmercifully."

"I know," said the barber. "It is lay-yend."

The customer let matters rest for a few moments. There was a slight smile on his lips. Finally he spoke. "The Aztecs," he said, "before the coming of Cortez, used to rip out the hearts of their victims by the thousands. Right?"

The barber paused in his barbering. "Right!" he agreed. "Is the truth!"

Bob Peck called for us this afternoon and we headed for the Pedregal and the residence of Juan O'Gorman, who might rightfully be called a Mexican huevo-head. O'Gorman is the painter and architect responsible for one of the most spectacular structures in the world — the Central Library building at the nearby University of Mexico. This is the ten-story building, windowless, whose four exterior walls are covered with mosaic murals, designed and executed by O'Gorman, using natural colored stones brought from different sections of the country.

The O'Gorman house, known to his friends as The Cave, has some of the same mosaics in the ceilings and walls. The place was chopped and chiseled and dynamited out of the Pedregal lava and appears to be on half a dozen different levels. Sitting in the living room was much the same as sitting in a well-furnished cavern. O'Gorman is a slender, dark-haired man, half Irish and half Spanish, and he doesn't look like an artist — he could pass for a clerk in a brokerage house. His wife, Helen, is an American who is famous locally for her gardening and for her paintings of flowers and other vegetation.

She has painted virtually every plant that grows in Mexico and she hopes someday to have this work incorporated into a single big book.

O'Gorman has known and admired Lázaro Cárdenas for many years and told some stories about him. When Cárdenas was President, the representative of an American firm manufacturing expensive automobiles came to him and said that the company was giving free cars to all the heads of state in Latin America. The President replied that he could not accept such a gift — he said he liked the automobile, but that if he took one he would insist upon paying for it. "Please quote me a price," he said to the man, and the man smiled knowingly, and said, "One hundred pesos." Now Cárdenas smiled, and took out his wallet, and extracted from it four hundred pesos and handed them to the man. "But," the Gringo protested, "I said *one* hundred pesos." "Yes, I know," said Cárdenas, "but at that price I'll take four of them."

"And," said O'Gorman, "he got them."

From O'Gorman's we proceeded to Fonda El Refugio restaurant, where we enjoyed the best Mexican food we've had yet.

March 1

CARLOS returned today from his long trip and brought his "people" around for a drink. His people are the Hoffmans (he's the one who sent the telegram from Durango), and in introducing them Carlos said, "You have heard of him, he is the one, Hoffman, kidnap the Limberg baby."

Nelle is quite handy with the English language until it comes to the names of drinks, and then for some reason she flies all to bits. There is a tequila drink she favors which, I believe, is called a tequila sunrise. I have heard her order it as a tequila sunset, a tequila moonrise, a tequila stardust, a tequila surprise, and a tequila sunflower. In her "vodka period" I remember the time in the Beverly

Hills Hotel, in the company of some important movie people, when she wanted a drink called a screwdriver. "I'll take a corkscrew," she said to the waiter, and he fetched her one. Apparently he thought she had brought her own bottle.

She and Maxine went to look at the National Pawnshop today and Maxine bought an Aztec idol — an ugly little man fashioned from some kind of stone that is as heavy as lead. The little man is in a squatting position, has a painful, strained look on his face, and has both hands clasped across his belly. We have christened him Señor Tourist Trot.

Save for occasional command appearances in the lobby, I have been working in our room today, trying to assemble notes on all the different types of Mexican humor we have encountered up to now.

Some distance back I quoted from an American publication in which the Mexican businessman was represented as telling jokes that are always subtle, never raw, never crude. *Salchicha grande!* (Bologna!)

In 1923 Wallace Smith wrote a good book about Mexico called *The Little Tigress,* and in it he said: "The Mexican joke, like Mexican food, is highly spiced. And never so peppered as when it plays with the relations of men and women."

When we were in Veracruz, Carlos and I stopped one day to look in the window of a bookstore. We saw a collection of paper-back joke books and went in and bought five or six of them and took them back to the hotel. I put Carlos to work, reading them to me, in translation, and I can report that most of them were crude and vulgar and far from subtle.

One of the most popular joke forms in Mexico is the Pepito story. Everybody knows and tells Pepito stories. He is a small boy, frighteningly precocious, who is always getting into trouble because of his knowledge of worldly things and his frank manner of expressing himself on such matters. Nobody needs to tell Pepito about the birds and the bees. There is no such thing as a "clean" Pepito joke that I've ever heard about. I have one that I think will serve to illustrate, in a mild way, what they are like.

The teacher (often Pepito's victim) was sitting on the platform when she noticed little Juan staring at her in a peculiar way.

"Juan!" She spoke sharply. "What are you doing?"

"I am only admiring your beautiful ankles," said Juan.

Pointing a finger toward the cloakroom the teacher commanded: "Out! Thirty minutes!"

Soon the teacher noticed that little Pablo was staring at her.

"What are you doing, Pablo?" she asked.

"I am only admiring your beautiful knees," he replied.

"Out!" she cried. "One hour."

Pepito, meanwhile, was doing a real job of staring, twisting his head to one side, lowering it, bending far over.

"Pepito!" exclaimed the teacher. "What are you doing?"

Pepito rose to his feet and said loudly, "Out! Two years!" — and left the room.

In our roamings around Mexico I have heard many jokes and anecdotes and a major portion of them are of the earth earthy. For an example, there is a tale about a pig wallowing in the mud, and a cow happens along. Says the cow, "You should be ashamed, a big grown-up pig and all filthy dirty like that." The pig gives the cow a searching, overall inspection and then replies, "You are the one to be ashamed. All grown-up and wearing no brassière."

Carleton Beals says that he knows of no people on earth who have "a more profound sense of humor, both mordant and outright funny, be it Indian, mestizo or Spanish."

In Tepoztlán Larry Brookwell said that the local humor usually dealt with violence and was never subtle. A joke in Tepoztlán has to end with a character getting his head sliced off in order to fetch a real laugh. The humor of the Tepoztecans also hinges, quite often, on dumbness and stupidity, and many jokes start off, "This dumb Indian came in to town to vote and . . ." And the natives all over the land have jokes about the Gringos. One that is popular among the Tepoztecans concerns a woman tourist who went into a restaurant, wanting milk. She asked for *leche* and got goat's milk, which she couldn't drink. She fetched out her little phrasebook and with great determination fell to work. She wasn't able to locate the word for cow, but she kept trying and finally came up with, "I want some milk of the wife of the bull." This joke simply slays a Tepoztecan.

There are Mexican jokes that are jokes only to Americans. The most famous of these is the story of the American tourist who stopped a fat Mexican riding on a burro, his wife walking ten paces behind.

"Why," demanded the tourist, "do you, a big strong man, sit on the burro and permit your poor barefooted wife to walk all the way to town?"

The fat Mexican's eyes widened in hurt astonishment, and he spread his arms and said, "Is my burro!"

There is also a story I have met with in two or three different books. When people build a new house, or an addition to a house, the various workmen involved usually celebrate its completion with a small fiesta. One American woman had a bathroom added onto her house and when the workmen assembled for the party, they told her it was customary that she should go in and take the first bath. She did go in, and the workmen waited outside, and soon she came flying out with cries of alarm. No hot water came through the faucets at the tub, none came through at the basin, but there was hot water aplenty when she flushed the toilet.

The Mexicans themselves joke about anything and everything. They are forever poking fun at their political leaders. One of these, President Obregón, was himself something of a wit. Blasco Ibañez once asked him for a true account of how he lost his arm in battle. Obregón told him that after the arm had been shot off and first aid administered, he sent some of his officers out to look for the arm. They returned without it. Then Obregón's personal aide said that he knew how to find it. He took out a ten-dollar gold piece and held it above his head, and instantly from the bushes came "a bird with five flapping wings" — the missing hand flying toward the money.

When General Guadalupe Victoria was President he was not noted, in the popular esteem, for being overly bright. The story was told that a Spanish envoy arrived with a dispatch from the King. The seal on the dispatch showed an eagle with two heads. The President studied it a few moments and then told the envoy, "I have often heard of this two-headed eagle, and now I understand we have located some specimens of our own down in the hot country, and I have sent to have a few brought here. I think they are a great improvement over the one-headed eagle."

A popular story about Cárdenas concerned the time he, with a couple of aides, arrived on the steps of the National Palace. A blind old soldier was sitting on the steps with his hat in his lap. Cárdenas stopped and dropped in a few coins and the old soldier said, "Thank you, my General." Cárdenas took a few steps and then stopped and said to his aides, "How did he know who I was? He must have served under me in the army. He must have recognized my voice, or my footsteps." His aides said that they doubted that the old man could recognize either the President's voice or his footsteps. But Cárdenas was sure of it, and he returned to the old man and asked him how he had known he was speaking to a General. "Because," said the old man, "every damn fool you meet nowadays is a General."

No man ever becomes President without acquiring a nickname — usually one that is not quite complimentary. One recent President was called El Trompudo, or "The Big Mouth." Another was named "The Snail," "because he is both slow and slimy." Ruiz Cortines, because of his cadaverous appearance, was known as Skullface, and there was a popular story about how the Egyptian government broke off diplomatic relations with Mexico, claiming the Mexicans had stolen one of their chief mummies and installed it in the National Palace. When he was campaigning for the Presidency, Ruiz Cortines arrived one day in Guadalajara. He habitually wore a bow tie, which is unusual among Mexicans. Just as his car arrived in the central part of Guadalajara, the opposition turned loose a hundred stray dogs, each wearing a bow tie. It is recorded that Ruiz Cortines, ordinarily a solemn man, laughed out loud.

The only joke I can remember hearing about Miguel Alemán, one that had wide circulation after he left the Presidency, was this: "Do you know who is the three richest men in the world? Aga Khan, Aly Khan, Aly-mahn!"

One of the best of all the political jokes was circulated in the time of President Calles. He came from Sonora and was surrounded by men from the same state. During his administration it was decided to build an additional story onto the National Palace and to do this it was necessary to surround the entire building with scaffolding. Passing the Palace, one Mexican would say to another, "They are crating it up to ship it to Sonora."

The Mexicans know how to use ridicule, especially against their own heroes when those heroes fall into disfavor. The most famous of their horsemen, General Mariles, is well known in the United States. After he and his horse, Arete, had taken high honors in the Olympic games, he came home a great hero and was made a General by Presidential decree. He and Arete went on to win other honors, at home and abroad. One day Arete and another horse got into a fight in a corral and Arete was so badly injured he had to be destroyed. Throughout the following season General Mariles made a poor showing; the younger Mexican riders were winning, but not the General. And so the disgusted fans turned on him. They began referring to his old mount, Arete, as "General" Arete, and as for Mariles — they called him "Horse" Mariles.

Artists are important people in Mexico, so jokes are made about them: "He was so expert that once he painted the north pole so real that everybody had to wear overcoats when they looked at it; and he painted the President so real that every two days he had to shave him."

One rather singular aspect of Mexican humor is the monument joke. Mexicans have always loved to put up monuments and statues, and then to make jokes about them. All the big monuments at the *glorietas* along Reforma have their jokes. The simplest and most telling is that concerning the famous equestrian statue of Charles IV, which stands at the downtown end of the Paseo. This Spanish monarch was "a handsome, ignorant, good-natured imbecile" as well as one of history's outstanding cuckolds. The Mexican people, of course, have never had any use for him. The statue, however, is said to be one of the two greatest equestrian executions in the world, and so it is retained, but the name of the man on the horse is never mentioned. The statue is known as El Caballito, or The Little Horse.

In walking distance of the Hotel Reforma, on Sullivan (!) Street, is a monument to The Mother. It consists of wide and massive stone walls and pillars and steps, and in the center is the figure of a mother and child. The Mexicans say of it, "Too much es-stone, not enough Mother."

The statue of Christopher Columbus on the Paseo shows him standing with one hand extended, as if he were beckoning, while the figures of several men are at his feet. He is saying, according to the Mexicans, "Bring me some women, I got plenty of men."

There is even a common joke about The Angel which surmounts the 150-foot column of the Monument to Independence at the fourth *glorieta* on the Paseo. (This is the same Angel knocked from its perch by the 1957 earthquake). The Mexican people venerate The Angel and it is not unusual to see women murmuring their prayers in front of the monument. Some of the men, however, must have their joke. They stand below the monument and look up at The Angel, and then suddenly clap a hand over an eye, and cry out, "Hey! Listen, Mister Angel, if you have to do that, come down and do it in the bushes, *por favor!*"

In Veracruz on the waterfront stands a huge statue of Carranza, wearing a *guayabera* shirt and, of course, his long bushy whiskers. The first time we drove by this statue Carlos said that the local people have a joke about it. They say that the Gillette company is trying to buy the statue and use it for an advertisement; they want to put a sign on it saying, "Do you want to look like this?"

The Mexicans make jokes about the people of certain provinces, just the way we sometimes make jokes about Texans or Ozarkians or Brooklynites. The chief victims in Mexico are the people of Monterrey and Yucatán.

Monterrey is a bustling, thriving, industrious city of the North and some Mexicans say it is more like a Gringo city than a Mexican city. Perhaps because of their sharp business sense and their concern for money, the people of Monterrey have achieved a reputation for frugality. The very name "Monterrey" is almost a synonym for parsimony. Mexicans employ dozens of gestures in their sign language (many of them are quite vulgar) and among the most common is the one indicating stinginess. It means, at the same time, "He is from Monterrey." To say that a person is stingy (or that he is from Monterrey) it is only necessary to pat the left elbow with the right hand or, if sitting down, to hit the right elbow on the table or on the arm of the chair.

They tell of the Monterrey man who wanted to commit suicide. He hung from a rafter by his left hand and choked himself with his right to save the expense of buying rope.

Near Monterrey is a mountain formation — two peaks with a "saddle" depression between them. It is said that this was once a single peak, but one day an Armenian peddler lost a peso up there and the whole populace of Monterrey turned out to search for it, and they searched so assiduously that they wore the mountain down.

A young Monterrey couple got married and the bridegroom went alone to Mexico City for the honeymoon, because the bride had already visited the capital.

A Monterrey boy was being fitted for glasses and his father said to him, "Remember, son, don't wear them when you're not looking at anything."

One Monterrey story that is more elaborate than most concerns two wives who were having tea. One of them was wearing expensive furs and jewels and the other asked her how she managed to get them. "One morning," she said, "I just walked into my husband's bedroom without any clothes on and with a market basket on my arm. He asked me where I was going and I said I was going shopping, and he wanted to know why I had no clothes on. I told him that he never gave me any money for clothes, so I was forced to go naked. So he handed me five thousand pesos and told me to go buy anything I wanted." The second wife decided to try this stratagem on her husband. The next morning she walked into his bedroom, naked, with a market basket on her arm. "Where are you going?" demanded the husband. "I'm going shopping," she said. "Well," said her husband, "you might at least shave." And he turned over and went back to sleep.

The Yucatecans are the people who really get the jokes thrown at them in wholesale lots. They are a wonderful race, certainly undeserving of ridicule. They have always been a very proud people and many of them do not regard themselves as Mexicans at all — and they say so, with great frankness. Back in the time of Abraham Lincoln, Yucatán sent a delegation to Washington asking that their country be admitted to the United States. It may be that this aloofness and insularity is the reason the rest of Mexico enjoys poking fun at the Yucatecans. In any event, the Yucatecan joke is never very flattering. It is related to the "moron jokes" which were a fad for a while in the United States, with overtones of the hillbilly joke. The Yucatecan, in these stories, usually emerges as a rube of the dumbest ray serene, yet in many of the jokes his observations, seemingly stupid, contain a germ of genuine wisdom. Also the stories are sometimes shaggy-doggish. Just a few days ago I saw a Ripley cartoon in the local *News* with a Yucatecan-type joke in it. The cartoon was about Karl Friedrich Cerf, who was general manager of the Royal Opera in Berlin but who never learned to read or write. "Cerf's secretary," it was said, "read the manager's confidential mail to him, but was required to wear ear plugs so he would not hear what he was reading."

A Yucatecan once went into a store to buy a mirror. He looked in the first one and frowned. He tried another, and frowned. He looked at a third and scowled. Then he said to the storekeeper, "You should be ashamed. I am going to tell all my friends that this store sells the worst mirrors in the whole world."

A Yucatecan from Mérida went to Progreso to visit his cousin and saw the sea for the first time. The two men stood on a dock and the rube peered and sighted and exclaimed, "What a big amount of water!" His cousin said, "Yes, is a lot, but let me tell you something you don't know — *underneath is even more!*"

A Yucatecan answered the telephone for the first time. The party on the other end asked, "Who is this?" The Yucatecan pointed to himself and said, "Me."

A Yucatecan boy met an American girl and they spent an evening together. Neither knew the other's language, so they used signs, and got along quite well. They had cocktails, and then dinner, and then went to the movies, and after that the girl took paper and pencil and drew a picture of a bed. Whereupon the Yucatecan boy exclaimed: "Gee, I wonder how she found out I'm in the furniture business!"

A Yucatecan went to an optometrist for an eye test. He was asked to read letters and words on a chart. The optometrist held the sign up and the customer said, "I cannot read it." He moved it a few feet closer. "I cannot read it," said the customer. Five feet closer. "I still cannot read it." Once again closer, and the same answer. The optometrist exclaimed over the customer's condition, saying, "If you cannot read it at this distance, then you are almost totally blind." The customer replied, "Oh, no, it is not that. I cannot read it because I do not know how to read."

(Jokes about eye-doctors are quite common in Mexico. There is even one about the Monterrey optometrists who always include, on their eye-charts, a line saying "fifty pesos" just to make certain the customer knows the fee that is expected.)

Many Yucatecan jokes are concerned with the rube's experiences in Mexico City. One young man from Mérida came to the city and got a job and was told to show up at 7 A.M. He sauntered in twenty minutes late. His boss was indignant, and pointing to the watch on his wrist said, "Look — 7:20!" "My goodness," said the Yucatecan, looking at the watch, "I would have thought it cost much more than that."

In the Alameda a stranger fell asleep on one of the benches, and when he awoke he found a visiting Yucatecan sitting next to him. The stranger rubbed his eyes, glanced at the sky, and then said to the Yucatecan: "Pardon me, but I have been asleep — is that the sun up there, or the moon?" The Yucatecan looked at the sky and then replied, "I am very sorry, I cannot tell you, as I am a stranger in this town myself." The same Yucatecan heard a clock in a nearby tower strike two. He observed, "That clock must be running good, it has just struck one o'clock twice."

A Yucatecan was standing at a bar in Mexico City when a big, loud *charro* from the north came in. The *charro* was in a belligerent mood, jostled the Yucatecan, and then said, "Listen, my friend, where I come from there are nothing but men — real men. See?" The Yucatecan took a sip of his drink and then responded, "Well, in my country we are half of us men and half of us women and we like it that way."

March 2

THIS afternoon we went to Martha Davis's house for a barbecue. There were fifteen or twenty people scattered over the lawn, some of them stretched out on *petates* or blankets. Bill Shelburne arrived in a taxi, bringing the cake and the fixings for Bloody Marys. A young chemist of Spanish extraction, described as being a talented cook, did the steaks over charcoal with great skill and authority. Also present were a geological explorer for a big oil company, a professor of dramatics who helps stage and direct local amateur theatricals, a woman pediatrician with her doctor husband, and a heavy-set, pleasant, talkative man with a black mustache who seemed to be somebody important. Most of those present were Gringos and there was much talk about how American customs are being inflicted on Mexico. One woman said she heard a prominent Mexican complain that his country was being "Coca-Colonized."

I noted that there was no off-color talk of any kind, no suggestion of vulgarity in any of the conversation, in contrast to the same type of gathering back home. Martha Davis said that there was one delightful couple she had wanted us to meet but when she phoned yesterday the wife said, "Oh, we couldn't! Haven't you heard? We're divorcing."

"Happens all the time," said Martha.

"Happens at home quite frequently, too," I said.

People seemed to be hanging on every word uttered by the man with the black mustache, and I whispered to the wife of the geological explorer, "Who is that?" She said, "Why, that's Pedro Armendariz." I said, "And who the hell is Pedro Armendariz?" Pedro Armendariz heard me say it, and instead of coming over and punching my head, he just smiled in an amiable way. I was sorry, but I didn't know that he is one of Mexico's top movie actors, and that he has appeared in many important films in Hollywood as well as in Europe. I don't even know the identity of our own movie actors unless they happen to be either Joan Crawford or James Cagney.

I overheard one guest say, "Morelia is perfectly charming — a wonderful city." Another replied, "Morelia is the most hideous town I was ever in." One of the men said that Mexican movies are no good. Another spoke up and said that Mexican movies are better than

Hollywood movies. Pedro Armendariz said that he would stay neutral. A woman said that So-and-so drinks too much. Another woman said, "I know her well, and she doesn't drink much at all." It's the same old story — there's something about the Mexican climate that causes people to become contentious and cantankerous. During all the time we've been in Mexico local people have been kind enough to lend us their books about the country. And all of these books have one thing in common, in addition to being about Mexico. They are annotated. Their margins contain penciled notes, and these notes refer to statements in the text, and most of them say such things as: "Wrong!" "Good God!" *"Estúpido!"* "Crap-*Crap*-CRAP!"

During the party Bill Shelburne revealed that all of the drinking he does each night in his restaurant is not drinking at all. "I have so much responsibility," he said, "with the kitchen full of insane people and the waiters and bartenders candidates for commitment, that I've had to give up drinking. But while I'm playing the piano and singing, people expect me to be drinking so I'll keep on the steadily rising beam with them. So I fool them — I drink consommé on the rocks." He said that it is troublesome because when the consommé gets cold, little blobs of fat appear in it and he doesn't like that. The chemist-cook told him how to rectify this condition by mixing up a lot of different things and stirring the mixture into the consommé. Nelle had a more sensible suggestion for him: bouillon cubes.

Bill told about how he went back to New York a couple of years ago and got the tourist complaint three times in two weeks. "I found myself shying away from the water taps," he said. "In the homes of my friends I was always searching around for the big water bottle and, not finding it, looking in the refrigerator for the smaller one. Some of my friends got insulted because they thought I was suggesting that their drinking water had been poisoned."

Pedro Armendariz finally came over and sat down with me and didn't mention my rude remark. He said that he became an actor "because the altitude got me." He was once a tourist guide, just the same as Carlos or Don Quixote, with no idea in the world of ever becoming an actor. He enjoyed his work but he was annoyed by the fact that tourists were always more interested in the altitude than in anything else. The tourists would say, "What altitude are we now?" and not "What is the story of this village?" or "Who lives here and what do they do?" Pedro wanted to tell them about people and history, but all they wanted to know was how high they were at a given moment. He recalled one of his last trips as a guide. He was with two elderly ladies, traveling all over Central Mexico, and they kept hammering him with questions concerned solely with the altitude. At length they arrived in Acapulco and got into their bathing suits and went to one of the beaches. They were lying on the sand near the water's edge when one of the ladies, in all gravity, asked, "What altitude are we now?" Pedro got to his knees, laid his face against the sand, sighted over it, and then said, "The altitude here is one and one half inches." Soon after that he gave up guiding and drifted into the movies. "Maybe," he said, "I should be happy that those ladies were so interested in the altitude."

6

West to Pátzcuaro

March 3

WE ARRIVED in Querétaro this afternoon but this time the city
had a different aspect, and one we hadn't anticipated. The whole
town was swarming with people, and the plaza, which we got to know
during our last visit, was mobbed up like Coney Island on a hot
Sunday in August. All the excitement stems from the fact that *el
Presidente* is in Querétaro — his first visit here since taking office.
Farmers and their families from many miles around are here and
one of the first disillusioning things I learned is that they are paid for
coming in and demonstrating enthusiasm for the President.

Weeks ahead of time, government agents went through the countryside contracting for people at five pesos per head, the money to be
paid over at the conclusion of the welcoming ceremonies in Querétaro. Later today we saw one such agent on the south side of the
plaza, surrounded by a clot of peons to whom he was doling out the
pesos. In times past, I've been told, this same system was employed
in Mexico City in order to get the people to demonstrate on behalf
of certain politicians. It may still be done and it would seem to indicate that the Mexican people are more than a little cynical about their
political leaders. By coincidence I have just been reading Bertita
Harding's fine book about Maximilian and Carlota, *Phantom Empire*.
She says that no European monach ever depended on spontaneous

applause when appearing in public, and that professional cheerleaders were always kept on the payroll to whoop it up and get the crowds started whooping. Life is real, life is earnest, polly-wolly-doodle all the day.

We had quite a battle, struggling through the crowds to get to our hotel, and then we found that once again our room had been usurped. In his phone call, Carlos had specified the big front room which we had occupied on the previous visit, and they had said all right; but now they told us that someone else had taken it, and they wouldn't say who. So we had to take a lesser room, which was quite crummy.

Querétaro is a good place to visit not only for its importance in Mexican history but because it has a certain, indefinable atmosphere unlike that of any other Mexican town. Few tourists come here, even to see the little chapel on the spot where Maximilian was executed. I understand that before long one of the new highways will begin bringing hordes of tourists to Querétaro; up to now it has been a little out of the way. The reason for the President's being here is to dedicate a section of the new highway. The Maximilian chapel is at a grubby spot called the Hill of the Bells on the outskirts of town and we expect to visit it a second time when we head out for San Miguel. The place where a famous man died is much more interesting to me than the place where he was born. At birth he is nothing but a blob of noisy meat; at death he's often in surroundings he has known for a long time and loved. I've never had an urge to visit Florida, Missouri, where Mark Twain was born; but I have been to Stormfield in Connecticut, where he lived the final years and died, and I thought I could feel his presence there. I'm not suggesting that Maximilian had any overwhelming affection for Querétaro. He was not a great man, but he seems to have had heroic qualities, and these he demonstrated at the Hill of the Bells and elsewhere in Querétaro. He begged that his generals and aides be forgiven and that he alone be shot, and he asked that his servants in Mexico be allowed to return to Europe. Bertita Harding says that his great virtue was honor, for which the

Hapsburgs were famous. Personally I think that kind of honor can be overdone. A little of it goes a long way with me.

Around our hotel lobby the State and National politicians are as thick as *moscas* and the *abrazos* fill the place with constant thumping noises. The hotel and the town are swarming with men in uniform. Some are soldiers but there are five or six different kinds of cops present — Local, State, Highway, National, Secret, and probably some others.

Late this afternoon Nelle and I decided to walk to the second plaza, just a few blocks from the hotel. It's a lovely spot and we strolled around there for a while and then circled back toward the hotel. We were coming down a street toward the monument to La Corregidora when we saw some men running. They were headed in the direction of the monument and I figured that something was doing with *el Presidente*, so we started running and arrived just in time to get in the front row at the monument, with the crowd surging up behind us. In a moment the President and his party arrived, toting big wreaths which they placed at the base of the monument. La Corregidora was a Querétaro woman, wife of the Mayor, who sent the word to Allende and Father Hidalgo that their plot had been discovered, thus starting the Revolution. La Corregidora couldn't get out of the house, but she whispered the warning word through a keyhole to a courier, and he lit out for San Miguel. The monument itself has a huge keyhole on it, and now the President and a dozen other men took their places at the base of the column. Their assignment now was to pose for pictures, and the tableau that followed is repeated a thousand times a year in Mexico. The Mexican President and all the other officials stand perfectly still, speaking not a word, cracking no smiles, scarcely moving a muscle, for almost ten minutes. This is the traditional way it is done. The crowd, too, remained silent and the only sound was the whirring of the movie cameras. Then, the instant the President moved, turning to speak to the Governor, the crowd began shouting, *"Viva el Presidente!"* and *"Viva la Corregi-*

dora!" and some other yells I couldn't understand — perhaps they were also crying, *"Viva the Keyhole!"*

It seems worth remark that I was standing less than twenty feet from the President during all that time. The town was crawling with police and army officers, yet I could have assassinated the President with a good-sized rock. At one point, in fact, I could have fetched him with a ball bat.

After dinner this evening we went into the street to see the Aztec dancers, and someone told us that there were more people in Querétaro today than ever before in the town's history. Soon the Presidential bus came slowly through the crowd — he travels from point to point in a big silvery bus — and he got out and made his way toward the door of the hotel. I was standing on the curb in front of the hotel entrance and two well-dressed Mexican men, both sloppy drunk, were next to me. Suddenly the crowd parted and the President came walking straight at us. The two drunks staggered forward, hands extended and uttering hoarse Vivas, and the President shook hands with them. Then he gave me a glance and apparently recognized the fact that I couldn't vote so he passed me by. He disappeared into the hotel and I followed after him, wanting to find out why he had come. Carlos talked to several of the hotel employees and then told me, "Well, it is this way — the President was just passing by and then he got a slight attack of the tourist disease and he had to stop." After ten or fifteen minutes, the President came down the stairs and through the lobby, passing within inches of us; and this time as he came even with me he looked me straight in the eye and gave me a big, friendly smile. I tell you, he's a *great* President, a *great* leader. He did the same for Nelle, who immediately yipped, *"Viva Mexico!"* which is not what she intended to yip — she had planned on giving a Viva to September Fifteenth because it is her birthday and Mexico's Independence Day although celebrated on September Sixteenth, sometimes I wonder if I know what I'm saying.

At the doorway, standing in all the bustle and confusion, were some tourists from Nebraska. They had been in town all afternoon and now one of the ladies said to Nelle, "Isn't this exciting? Who is he, the President of the town or the President of the State?"

"He's the President of Mexico," said Nelle.

"Oh, my God!" cried the woman. "And I didn't even look at him good!"

Just then a big Mexican in elegant *charro* costume pushed past her. "Oh, I *like* that!" she cried, reaching out to touch the silver decorations on his costume. *"Muy benetto!"* she said. He gave her a Villista glare and passed on, though I wouldn't have blamed him if he'd whacked her in the teeth with his spurs.

Soon the fireworks began, and they put on a real show for the President. We Gringos have developed a pretty substantial prejudice against fireworks but when I saw the *castillos* and the other things going tonight, I had to admire the artistry and mechanical skill and sheer genius that goes into their construction. As a windup, a streak of fire crawled up the façade of the big church and then a fiery portrait of the President burst into view, and rockets that seemed to be as big as jet planes began crisscrossing low over the plaza. *Zisssss! Zisssss! Zissssss!* As I watched them go, I thought of Madame Calderón's story of the time a prominent Mexican was visiting King Ferdinand in Spain. The King had a great curiosity about the nature of the faraway people he ruled.

"What do you suppose the Mexicans will be doing now?" he asked.

"Letting off rockets, Your Majesty," said the visitor.

That afternoon the King said, "Well, I wonder what they are doing now in Mexico."

"Letting off rockets, Your Majesty," he was told.

That evening: "Well, what will your countrymen be doing now?"

"The same, Your Majesty, letting off rockets."

After all the Querétaro rockets had been let off, Carlos and I adjourned to the hotel bar for a drink, and I recalled for him a bit of local history which he didn't know (I sometimes tell him that I'm going to dismiss him and hire a burro to guide me around the country). On July 25, 1531, the greatest fist fight in history took place right where we were standing. The town at that time belonged to the Otomi Indians. An army of mail-clad Spanish soldiers was closing in and the Otomi chief called for a powwow. He told the Spanish commander that the way things were shaping up, the fight would not be a fair one, that the Indian arrows were worthless against the armored Spaniards. He suggested that both sides put down their weapons and fight with their fists. And so, thousands of Spaniards and hordes of furious Indians fought all day and at sundown it was agreed that the Spaniards had won. Just to show that they were good sportsmen the Indians — those who could get up off the ground — put on a fiesta that same night in honor of Charles V.

"I have never heard of this," said Carlos, "so it is not true. It is from some no-good Jonkee history book that is made up of lies."

The bar was lined with dressed-up Mexicans who were having a good time, with much loud laughter, and it was apparent that they were telling stories. There was one word that seemed to recur in their talk and after I'd heard it several times I asked Carlos what it meant. The word was *camote,* and Carlos laughed and said: "It is the word that means in English sweet potato. It is what the Mexican men in this town . . . well, it is what they say of themselves."

March 4

THIS morning we walked over to the Teatro de la República where, in 1867, Maximilian and his generals were tried, and where the Constitution of 1917 was signed, and we found the place full of workmen giving it a complete overhauling. We drove on out to the Hill of the Bells for another visit to the site of Maximilian's execution, and after that we moved on to one of our favorite Mexican towns, San Miguel de Allende.

Early this afternoon I left the hotel and crossed the street to the newspaper store, where I fell into conversation with an elderly man from my native Illinois. He was a trifle on the shabby side, and a little dirty, but he was not reticent.

"I was in the fedrull guvment," he said, "and got retard, and I kin live here on my pension and my social security. I got the ony goddam penthouse in town and it ony sets me back twenny bucks a month and that includes gas and lectricity and a ole cleanin' woman and toilet paper is furnished. I woosh you'd walk up there with me and see it — I woosh you'd walk along with me — I like to be with my own kind."

We went up past the plaza, toward the market, and he kept talking.

"They's a buncha homosexials live here," he said. "What we call queers back home, goddamndest buncha no-good bums, I don't never feel comfable around queers and these queers is worse than any others because they're writers and artists and stand around with one hand on their hip. I don't feel comfable around them and so I quit goin' to these here saloons and I do my drinkin' in decent places. All these here goddam artists would drive a man start, starin' mad, all they ever paint is them churches and you can buy the goddam churches on penny postcards till yer hand gits tard reachin' in yer pocket. It's disgustin'. Me, I been here eighteen months and got me this penthouse and these here Mexican maids, down here we call 'em *moo-cha-chas*. That's what they like to be called. They come in and I make me a beef stew, they stand around and watch, and by god they can make a beef stew as good as you ever put in ycr mouth, on one watchin'. Mexican food? It ain't fit to eat. I wouldn't never eat no Mexican food 'less I furnished all the groceries and stood there and seen to it they didn't put nothin' else in, and even then I wouldn't eat it. These goddam Mexicans will put grasshoppers and worms and sand and dog — and Christ knows what else in their cookin' if you don't stand by and watch 'em. They's a butcher here I been learnin' to talk English because they don't know how to cut meat down here, they cut it all wrong, and I'm learnin' him how to cut meat and talk English at the same time. He's learnin' me to talk

Spanish, but I already know all I need to know to git along with these *moo-cha-chas*. I hope some of them comes in when we git up there. Man, you'd oughta see the tiddies on them girls and they don't mind you coppin' a little feel, ordinary. This is a rotten country and they got rotten food and they all carry guns er knives and they ain't got no more morals than a hawg, but you cain't beat the prices. I hope you ain't got nothin' to do for a while, so we can visit. I like to be with my own kind."

He showed me his penthouse, which smelled like a goat pen, and none of the *moo-cha-chas* turned up for feel-coppin', and then he took me to a "decent" saloon, which smelled like two goat pens, and we had a couple of drinks, and then I left him. People who have reached the golden, twilight years are so sweet and wonderful, and there is nothing I enjoy more than to sit at their feet and listen to them talk and absorb the wisdom they have accumulated down through the long years. I do hope that I'll be able to grow old gracefully.

Later in the plaza a different type of elderly man sat down on the bench beside me. He was handsomely dressed and carried himself in a dignified manner. He said he was a retired businessman from Texas and that he had been traveling around Mexico for more than forty years and he asked the nature of my business. When I told him the purpose of my trip he sang an old familiar refrain: "Good God! Writin' a book about Mexico after only four or five months down here! Some of you guys oughta be bored for the simples!" I refrained from reminding him that the most famous book in English on the subject of Mexico was the work of a man named Prescott who never once set foot in the country. A bit later he mentioned the city of Celaya in a familiar way, so I asked him if he knew what famous historical event took place there (Obregón defeated Villa, but lost his arm). He tried to change the subject to pipelines but I kept at him, and asked if he knew what famous Mexican was born in Celaya (the architect-poet-painter Tresguerras). He pretended he didn't hear me, and began talking about natural gas. The old son of a bitch had me sore, and I didn't let up.

"Who was the first Emperor of Mexico?" I asked him, and he thought for a moment and then said, "Maxmillen, anybody knows that." And I said only Texans know it — that the first Emperor of Mexico was Agustín de Iturbide.

He asked where I came from and I told him I was from New York. "Good God!" he exclaimed. "Everybody I meet down here is from New York!" And I said, "That's because we've got more money than you people in Texas." I could have said worse, but he was an old man, and there's a Bulgarian proverb which says, "Respect for the aged is respect for God." I have Bulgarian blood in me.

There was a Mardi Gras thing in the plaza tonight so we went over to have a look. The plaza was jammed with people, walking around and around, but now there was a big difference in the *serenata*. At various points in the plaza were women with huge baskets filled with colored eggs. They had been preparing these eggs for months in advance. The end of each shell had been removed; the shell was then stuffed with confetti, and tissue paper was glued over the opening. Thus the eggs became *cascarones* (toy bombs). The young people buy them and as they promenade around the plaza, they whop one another with them, usually on the head. If a boy keeps whopping a girl with colored eggs all evening, it means he has a special place for her in his heart. They really swing hard, jarring the neck joints, and the shells disintegrate into a colored dust which gives a weird appearance to the hair. Nelle and Carlos and I were sitting on a bench when a young Mexican in overalls spotted Nelle's white hair. He came up to us with a big grin and said, *"Con su permiso,"* and then gave her a gentle whop with an egg which left a large green spot in her hair. Meanwhile Carlos was in conversation with some younger boys and I saw him, the dirty *puerco,* slipping them some money. We got up to join the promenade and the kids came along behind us, whopping me in the back of the head, one whop after another, steadily like a trip-hammer, until my head began to ache and the egg shells were dribbling down inside my clothes and giving me a Mardi Gras itch. And so at last we returned to the Posada to spend the next hour or so shampooing and scrubbing. Nelle's hair was mostly green — the kids apparently decided that green suited her — but she also had two spots, one red and one black, which were most attractive and gave her the look of an Aztec sacrificial victim.

March 5

THIS morning I sat on the wall of the elevated plaza and watched one of San Miguel's many *cargadores*. He came along the cobblestones just below me with six cases of beer on his back, held on by the usual tumpline stretched round his forehead. He had to hold the back of his head with both hands in order to keep it from snapping off; this left him with the problem of what to do with his sombrero. He held it gripped between his teeth. The whole thing looked poorly organized, a ridiculous way to tote, and I said as much to Carlos. I said I thought it would be more sensible for the man to use his shoulders to support the weight, rather than his forehead. Carlos said no, that it had been done this way for centuries, that it had been proved that the neck muscles can support twice as much as the shoulder muscles. Some of these *cargadores* have necks no bigger than size 13½, and I said I still think it's an inefficient way to tote. My Texas friend of yesterday was seated nearby and heard our talk and gave us the benefit of his sere and yellow wisdom.

"The answer," he said, "is that the Mexicans are stupid in everything they do. Anybody with any gumption knows that you can lift more with your shoulders than you can with your neck. But the Mexicans don't know it because they're the dumbest bastards in this hemisphere. You ever notice the way they hitch their oxen? Over the horns. We do it the sensible way and hitch 'em at the shoulders. But these idiots down here, they hook the plow up to their horns just because the horns happen to be handy and an easy thing to hook onto. They've been doing it that way since the Aztecs and all hell wouldn't change 'em. You've gotta go some to find the match for a Mexican when it comes to pure ignorance."

Grow old along with me, the best is yet to be!

An amiable, convivial guide named Hernando, who insists that he be called Herb, is here with a party of tourists. Around noon today Carlos was walking past La Cucaracha bar when he heard Herb's voice. He went in and found that his friend had been having extensive traffic with a bottle of mescal. Carlos got him out of the place and walked him up the street past the police station and into a small restaurant where they took a back table and ordered coffee. They were just leaving the place when a police officer in an elegant uniform entered the restaurant. Herb gave the cop a sweeping bow and said, "*Buenas tardes, mi capitán!*" The cop frowned and said, "*Buenas tardes.*" For some reason Herb resented the tone of the response, and uttered The Awful Obscenity. The cop whirled around and demanded, "What was that you said?" Herb now repeated it, with venom and with decoration, "C----- -- ----, you son of a bitch!" he said, slowly and distinctly. It was a remarkable bit of name-calling, done in two languages and with an economy of words: eight of them, put together to combine the major insults of two nations. The cop seized Herb by the collar and jounced him out the door and down the sidewalk and into the jail. Carlos had to spend most of the afternoon getting him out. He had to "see certain people" to swing it, but finally Herb got his freedom and was put to bed.

While Carlos was working on the liberation of Herb, I strolled around town and on a back street saw a cantina named "The Emotions." And this reminded me that I have been collecting names of *pulquerías* and cantinas, as well as the legends and mottoes that are painted on Mexican cars and trucks.

In the United States we are sorely lacking in imagination when it comes to naming our saloons. There is one in Mexico City called "The Underwear of Pancho Villa" and another, discovered by Gertrude Diament, called "I Feel Like an Aviator." Among the many famous names of *pulquerías* is the often-quoted, "Memories of the

Future," as well as "Your Office," "Among the Violets," "The Loves of Cupid," "I Am Laughing," and "Wise Men Without Education." I have seen a cantina with a name which translates as "The City Dump." Anita Brenner once collected a few *pulquería* names, among them "The Glories of Obregón," "The Lady Lion Tamer," "Why Do I Laugh?," "The Spirit of St. Louis," "The Celebrating Monkeys," "My Consulting Room," "The Mysteries of Commerce," and "Let's See What Happens." Frances Toor found a saloon with a sign, "Have Another One." And I find in my notes the names of two additional *pulquerías*, "Here I Wait for You," and "The Fan of Madame Pompadour."

There is a famous story concerning the naming of saloons. Once the proprietor of a dirty *pulquería* in Mexico City named it "The Knights of Columbus." Members of the Knights of Columbus saw the sign and sent a delegation to protest against it. The proprietor finally submitted to pressure and the next time the Knights passed by they saw a new sign which said, "The Mules of Columbus."

The legends and mottoes on cars and trucks may be seen on all the highways of Mexico. Some are religious, some have to do with love, some are frankly comical and some are even ribald. Weldon F. Heald has written of the time he encountered a wild-riding truck in the mountains and as it careened past he noted the motto on the rear bumper, "God Is My Co-Pilot." Some of the others Mr. Heald has spotted include "The Disobedient Son," "Look Mama — He's Flown the Coop!" "The Holy Terror," "The Absent One Has Returned," "Beloved How Cruel You Are," "Don't Insist — I'm Married," and "Almost an Angel."

Among the truck mottoes I like best are *Aburrido me voy* (I Go On But I'm Bored) and *No creas, se sufre!* (Believe It or Not, One Suffers!) And in the city markets quite often even the pushcarts have mottoes. Two of these, which need no translation, are *Los Amores de Romeo y Juliet,* and *Las Desgracias de Perl Jarbor.*

Today Nelle met a well-to-do American widow who lives here. She has a nice house, plenty of servants, and, for want of something to do, she enrolled in Stirling Dickinson's Instituto Allende, the big art school here. "God knows I'm not arty," she said, "but all my life I've enjoyed fooling around with paints — painting on cloth and on shawls and skirts — but I simply can't be arty. So the teacher out at the Institute puts a record on the machine and gives us some paper and ink and a brush and says, 'Now, paint what you feel.' I thought, my God, what kind of crazy business is this! There it is, the music going, and we're supposed to paint what we feel! You know what I did? I painted a fiddle."

Charles Allen Smart and his wife came down the hill this evening to have cocktails with us. Years ago he wrote a fine book called *RFD* and now he makes his home in San Miguel and has just finished a book about what it's like to live in Mexico (*At Home in Mexico*). He told us about some of the people we might run into, and I told him about our previous visit to San Miguel. I had fallen in with three or four guys in La Cucaracha bar and they had told me they were writers, but it turned out that they were writers who never wrote anything — apparently they just drank and wenched and were in and out of the local jail. Smart said he knew about these boys and that two of them got into a quarrel and one killed the other with a portable radio.

Later we met James Norman Schmidt, who writes under the name of James Norman, and whose current novel, *Father Juniper and the General,* is a delightful tale of a "miracle" in a town that is San Miguel thinly disguised. The novel reflects life as it really is in almost any Mexican town of this size; it is filled with authentic little touches, such as a description of the town's telephone service. The community has one phone which, after the first rain of the season, always rings steadily for three days and three nights. Another phone was good only for incoming calls, and then only if the subscriber managed to snatch it up before the second ring. When Father Juniper tried to call his bishop in the state capital, the operator finally informed him that the line was down. "Someone has stolen one of the poles," she said. "They are looking for it. Do you wish to wait, padre?"

March 6

BEFORE we left home our neighbor Eduardo Cárdenas, editor of international editions for *Reader's Digest,* told us he was building a house in San Miguel and that we could have it for the winter if we wanted. We had to decline, but today we went to look at it, and felt sad that we were unable to accept his invitation, for it is a beautiful house. Standing on the roof and looking across the garden to the mountains, I got to thinking about the big Cárdenas mixup of 1940.

In that year Lázaro Cárdenas left the Presidency of Mexico and Eduardo Cárdenas, who came to New York from his native Colombia, joined the *Reader's Digest* in an executive capacity. Soon after Eduardo's connection with the *Digest* was announced, Norman Cousins, famous liberal editor of the *Saturday Review,* encountered Charles W. Ferguson, a senior editor of the *Digest,* on Park Avenue.

"Tell me," said Cousins, "is it really true that Cárdenas has joined the *Digest?"*

"It's true," said Ferguson.

"I'd certainly love to meet him," said Cousins.

"Well," said Ferguson, "that should be easy. Give him a ring and tell him so."

"You mean," said Cousins, "just call him up on the telephone?"

"Sure," said Ferguson.

"Do you suppose," said Cousins, "that if I asked him, he would let me give a small luncheon in his honor? I have a number of important friends who would love to meet him."

"I'm sure he'd be flattered no end," said Ferguson. "Call him up and ask him."

Cousins did call up and Señor Cárdenas said he would be most happy to attend a luncheon at a certain Manhattan hotel on a certain day the following week.

At the appointed hour Eduardo entered the hotel lobby and found Norman Cousins waiting for him. Cousins seemed a bit taken aback at first; Lázaro Cárdenas habitually wears a mustache and Eduardo had none, but Cousins simply assumed that it had been shaved off. In actuality there is a vague physical resemblance between Lázaro and Eduardo, save for the mustache. Cousins now escorted Eduardo into a private dining room where the other guests were waiting in eager anticipation of meeting the famous liberal Mexican. There were eight or ten prominent Americans in the room, including William Allen White.

Eduardo said that he first began to suspect that something was out of kilter when, upon entering the dining room, the waiter bowed to him and addressed him as "Your Excellency." He was still in a sort of daze, however, from all the attention he was getting and from the celebrity of the other guests. He thought: "My goodness! It is really a big and important thing to work for the *Reader's Digest!*"

The luncheon began and a string quartet came in and began playing. Norman Cousins promptly leaped to his feet and went to the musicians and protested in loud whispers — he had wanted them to play the Mexican National Anthem and, instead, they were playing "Estrellita."

Eduardo sat next to William Allen White, who, by common consent, had been chosen as the person to question him while the other guests leaned forward, listening intently to every word that was spoken. Mr. White began asking Eduardo certain things about Mexico. Eduardo felt that he had to make a good showing if possible, that he could not act as if he were uninformed — that would be a reflection on the *Digest* — so he did the best he could, bluffing the answers. Fortunately most of the questions were of such a general nature that he was able to handle them. Then, when dessert and coffee had arrived, Mr. White hit Eduardo with a question which required a close knowledge of the Mexican government. Eduardo considered for a moment and then turned to Mr. White and said, "I am sorry I cannot answer that. You see I have never been in Mexico in my life."

For a minute the table froze. Then the guests began talking to

one another in an embarrassed sort of way. Mr. White spoke to
Eduardo of the weather, and the fascinations of New York. And then
Norman Cousins announced that the luncheon was over. There were
expressions of thanks, and good-bys, and Eduardo walked out into
the sunshine. He knew, now, what had happened.

March 7

THIS morning we left for Guanajuato, by way of Salamanca,
which is one of the nation's big oil centers. Carlos said he wanted to
show us this place as an example of Mexican "how-know." He said
there is a need to refute the argument that Mexicans are incapable
of managing their own affairs. That is the argument often put forward by Americans in their attacks against the expropriation. The
Mexicans, according to this argument, are too dumb, too lacking in
technical skills, to operate their own oil industry; they *need* the help
of foreigners, and since the foreigners are good enough to come in
and do the job, then the foreigners are entitled to most of the oil. It
is the same as if I went into my neighbor's orchard and began har-
vesting his apple crop for myself on the grounds that he had stupidly
been using the wrong kind of spray on his trees.

Carlos drove us through many acres of trim little houses occupied
by the Salamanca oil workers, who formerly lived in adobe huts.
Many of these cottages had television antennae; all were neatly
painted and most had garages. "Very pretty sight," said Carlos
proudly, "and by night all the oil wells are litted."

Although he often professes a strong distaste for Cárdenas, Carlos
now gave us his version of expropriation.

"The English," he said, "the Dutch and the Gringos was running
the Mexican oil business, and Lázaro Cárdenas said, 'You must make
working conditions better and raise the wage.' And the English and
Dutch and Gringos said, 'Who says?' Then the Court said they must
do what Cárdenas ordered because they had agreed to do it. So they

said, 'You keep talking this way and we close down everything and you will have no oil and no money.' Cárdenas, he said, 'You do that and by Jesus we expropriate." And they did and he did. It took much courage to do. It was a dangerous thing because it might have been war. But it is now coming out that Roosevelt agreed with Cárdenas about the oil; it is now coming out that Roosevelt believed the oil belonged to Mexico and nobody else; Cárdenas could not have done it if Roosevelt had not whispered in his ears, 'Go ahead, Cárdenas.' "

It has occurred to me that part of the hard feeling engendered by Cárdenas is traceable to the word "expropriate." It is an unfortunate word for the thing involved. In the popular mind "to expropriate" means to take something away from its rightful owner. The word suggests grabbing, it almost suggests piracy. What happened in Mexico was, to my nontechnical mind, a simple affair. Suppose several big corporations from England and Holland and Mexico came into the United States and quietly leased a lot of desert land, discovered oil in great quantities, and started taking it home with them. What would happen? Hay — sooooos!

And so we arrived in Guanajuato and found it to be nothing less than a dream town. After two hours of cruising around, we decided that *this* is the place, that if we ever live in Mexico this will be our home. (We've decided the same thing about a dozen other towns.) We went up into the hills and looked down on it, and we drove through the clean, narrow streets of the downtown area, and through a famous winding thoroughfare which passes between walls and beneath stone buildings, the whole thing giving a person the feeling that he has suddenly been transported into a medieval setting. "It is like," said Carlos, "when the knighthoods rode their horses and shot the sideways bow-and-arrow." All the streets are clean and so are the people, who seem to radiate friendliness. The main plaza is very small but beautiful, the sidewalks being a checkerboard of green-and-black tile and the Indian laurel trees trimmed and squared off. Our hotel, fronting on this plaza, was surprisingly good. For the first time in several weeks I got out the movie camera, went to the roof, and shot two rolls of film.

Tonight we loafed in the plaza and would have enjoyed it more if Carlos and I hadn't got into a discussion about Porfirio Díaz. "He did some things wrong," said Carlos, "but he did many good things also." There, in one simple sentence, is the national attitude toward political bastards. A man can tyrannize and steal and otherwise betray the people, but so long as he patches up the railroads or builds a few high-ways or sticks up some pretty monuments, then we shouldn't be too harsh with him. I insisted that Díaz was a tyrant and a crook and told Carlos about the things Blasco Ibañez wrote on the subject. He said that the Díaz gang got rich slowly, taking thirty years to accumulate their fortunes, because they knew they would be in power a long time and so, alongside the fast-grabbers of later administrations, they had the look of honesty. Carlos grinned and gave me a sidewise look and said, "Well, that's the way I do — I always prefer to steal slow."

March 8

TODAY we visited the Granaditis, which played such an important part in Hidalgo's revolution, and looked at Diego Rivera's birthplace, and inspected the ancient Teatro Juárez across the plaza from us, and then went to the cemetery. Compared with our own, Mexican ceme-teries have a gay and giddy look from the use of brightly colored paints on tombstone and vault. This one is real special, occupying a site on a high hill overlooking the city. Long ago it reached capacity and a wall was built with compartments like the lock-box section in the lobbies of our postoffices, and these compartments were filled with coffins. Then it was discovered that something in the soil caused the underground corpses to turn to mummies. Somebody got the idea of establishing catacombs and storing the mummies in them — thus making room for more people in the graves. The cemetery itself is somewhat shabby and littered and up near the wall tourists are allowed to enter a hole in the ground, climb down a narrow stairway, enter a damp and gloomy corridor and look at the mummies. At one end of the dismal hall, skulls and bones have been stacked as if by a master mason, creating a wall that is fifteen feet deep, with a mummified body or two slung carelessly across the top. At the other end of the corridor are mummies in standing postures, crowded side by side along each wall, male and female, as may be discerned. One mummy near the door is that of a woman said to have been buried alive, one arm drawn up across her brow, a seeming look of agony on the skull face; some of the mummies still have their pubic hair — a fact I mention because it is mentioned frankly and loudly by tourists in the catacombs. One woman mummy has a tiny mummy foetus attached. The whole thing is most distasteful, even disgusting, and yet it is the favorite spot of almost all tourists who come to Guanajuato. From Carlos and from the man in charge I learned that most men take one look and then want to leave, but most women insist upon staying down in that ghastly hole and staring at those unsightly creatures. What this signifies I do not know, but I know that my own wife had to be dragged out of the place, and I know that grown men make a living and support their families by selling postcards to tourists up above — cards with closeup pictures of the mummies.

Back in the plaza a little boy smiled at me and said, " 'Ello, Gringo!" I smiled at him and said, "Hola, Greaser!" We sat on a bench for a while and Nelle said that of all the wonderful things in Mexico, the one she would most like to transport back to the United States is the zócalo, or plaza. It would be wonderful, she thought, if Mount Kisco and Chappaqua and every town in the country had its plaza and it was put to the same use as down here — all the people gathering there of an evening, the band playing, the young folks promenading and doing their flirting in the presence of their elders. I said it was a nice thought but that it wouldn't work in our country. Our young people would be goosing one another, and letting go with zip-guns, and indulging in rumbles with switchblade knives, and mugging their elders. I said that the Mexican institution I'd like to take home is the fender-slapper. This works with trucks and buses as well as automobiles. Whenever a car is backing up, in tight quarters, somebody will stand by the back fenders and slap on them — two slaps mean that the driver should keep coming back, one slap means stop.

In the hotel tonight we met a man from California, one of the few tourists we've seen here, and he said that Guanajuato's chief item of export is birdseed. He said that a small amount of hemp seed, which is marijuana, is mixed in with the ordinary seed, and this is what makes the birds sing. "Or maybe," he said, "it is what keeps them from singing — I'm not sure which." He said that about twenty-five years ago the officials of San Quentin prison were baffled by the fact that so many convicts were displaying an interest in keeping canaries. What they were really after was the birdseed with the marijuana in it.

We had a drink in the hotel bar and I noticed a group of university students at a nearby table, drinking beer and arguing heatedly. I could tell from their gestures and their facial expressions that they were deep in some subject such as physics or logic or literature. I imagined that they were talking about *Don Quixote* or *The Itching Parrot* or *The Underdogs*. I called Carlos's attention to the students and he bent an ear in their direction, and listened for a few minutes, and then said, "They are talking about a girl who lives on the other side of town and has a beautiful bottom which she has on sale this week for only twenty pesos."

Later tonight Carlos and I decided on a game of pool and found a nearby parlor. We were assigned to the rear table and I was a bit startled to find a black coffin on trestles, standing against the wall, and next to it an open urinal. Pool-shooting became a trying sport here, for when I undertook certain shots the butt of the cue would bang against that coffin; and university students, standing at the urinal, would wrench their heads around and stare at me, never in all likelihood ever having seen a Gringo pool-shooter before. It was all pretty grim and gruesome, and I remembered that my mother told me, long years ago, always to stay out of poolrooms. A bit later I found out that the coffin was a prop, used in a recent fiesta. The students were soon standing three deep around the table, watching us shoot straight pool Gringo-style, which they had never seen before. With the natural curiosity of young scholars, they asked many questions of Carlos and he explained the game to them. They play a crazy form of straight pool which I have observed and which I am unable to understand. But now they were really interested in our version of the game, and after a while Carlos and I finished and started to leave, and he called my attention to the fact that the boys at two of the tables were already shooting our game. "Listen," said Carlos and I listened and heard one boy call out, *"El cinco en la buchaca del centro!"* Which means, "The five ball in the pocket of the center!"

March 9

OFF today for Pátzcuaro, and Nelle was taken with a sickness so when we arrived we decided not to take the boat trip out to the Island of Janitzio. She went to bed and Carlos and I had a look at the big UNESCO place near the hotel, occupying the building which was once Lázaro Cárdenas's home and which he gave to the United Nations. I had read that when he lived here Cárdenas often walked from his house in to the center of town, to the Hotel Ocampo, where he enjoyed two of his favorite dishes — *chicharrones* and *chilaquiles*. In spite of all hell I remain an admirer of Cárdenas, so I told Carlos I wanted to go to the Hotel Ocampo and eat *chicharrones* and *chilaquiles* the way Cárdenas used to do it. We ran into another guide, a young man named Ernesto, and asked him to come along. Downtown on the main plaza we found the Hotel Ocampo, a small place, and went in. A man was mopping the tiled floor inside and Carlos asked him if Cárdenas ever came there. "Who?" said the man. Carlos explained about Cárdenas and the man said that maybe he came there; he wouldn't know, because personally he had never heard of anybody named Cárdenas. This brought roars of laughter from both

Carlos and Ernesto, who are anti-Cárdenas, and then Carlos asked the man with the mop if we might get some *chicharrones* and some *chilaquiles*. The man said the hotel didn't serve them, and so we left; I was downcast and suggested that we find a saloon and have a drink or two.

We entered a saloon on the plaza and stepped into an experience I shall never forget. Carlos stood at the bar on my left, Ernesto on my right, and I was vaguely aware of a loud man wearing a big white sombrero who was standing next to Carlos. I was speaking of the person who wrote the bit about Cárdenas and the Hotel Ocampo and I used an old American expression, namely, son of a bitch. At once Paracutín erupted — exploded all over the place. The white sombrero swung around and revealed the most evil-looking face in all of Mexico. The man was short, dark, muscular, with a hawk nose and bloodshot eyes; he was as drunk as three goats and he let out a yell of fury. "I been Unite' State' eighteen year!" he yelled. "I know *sawn of beech*. YOU sawn of beech Gringo, you sawn of beech, I feex you!" He was so ferocious-looking that I quietly resigned myself to mummyhood; it seemed a sure thing that he was going to leap upon me, bite my nose off and then shatter my skull. I'm certain he would have done it but for the bartender, a huge Mexican weighing around three hundred pounds, who reached across the bar, seized the brigand by the shirt front, and gave him a short but compelling lecture in Spanish.

Carlos now tried to explain to the villain that Gringos often say son of a bitch when they don't mean that anybody is a son of a bitch. He explained carefully that a Gringo will sometimes say son of a bitch when he hits his finger with a hammer, or when his lottery ticket loses. Gradually White Sombrero calmed down, and now he grew friendly — too friendly. He came over to me with his hand extended, saying over and over, "Jake! Jake! Jake!" I jook his hand and then he insisted on buying all of us a drink. There was a younger man, a boy, on the other side of him, and now he demanded of this boy what he wanted to drink. The boy made a mistake by saying,

"*Nada*. Nothing." In some circles (drunk circles) this response is considered rude, and there is a penalty made and provided. White Sombrero roared at the big bartender, "*Nada! Un vaso de nada!* One glass of nothing!" The bartender got out a glass about a foot high and then went along the length of the back bar, putting in a little from each bottle — wines, whiskies, rums, tequila, brandy, mescal, and finally a couple of jiggers of beer. White Sombrero took this awful concoction and thrust it at the younger man and roared, "Drink!" For such is the punishment ordained for anyone who orders a glass of nothing. He had to drink it, or that *bandido* would have bitten *his* nose off.

I wanted to get out of there before something of a similar nature — some other savage barroom custom — might come in my direction, but Carlos and Ernesto were nervous about this guy, and indicated they wanted to humor him. Meanwhile he had been buying rounds of drinks so fast that we couldn't keep up. The drinks were piling up on the bar, and we were trying to conceal from him the fact that we were not drinking all of them. At length White Sombrero went to the back of the room for something and we quickly made our escape and hopped in the car and scurried back to the hotel as fast as our little tires would carry us. I never did get to see how the young man fared after drinking that glass of *nada*. I assume that it killed him.

The three of us went to call on the ailing Nelle to tell her about our adventure. "Oh, Nelle," said Carlos, "you should have been there to see your coward hosbon', how he shivered and shook and crawled on the floor to get under the table." And I told her, "You know very well that Carlos is lying to cover up for himself. Just as soon as this terrible man turned on me, Carlos said, '*Con so permiso* but I have to go to the bathroom,' and he went to the men's room and locked himself in. I just took hold of that mean Mexican and cocked my fist and said, 'Listen, you sawn of beech, one more word out of you and I'll whiten your features!" And Ernesto now offered his version of the affair. "Mrs. Smith," he said, "you should have seen them — they both unchickened, they ran out in the street yelling for the police and the army, and I stayed there and picked up a bottle and hit this man on the head with it, and after that he apologized, and said to me, 'My friend, if I had known you were here I would not have tried to make any trouble, as you are too tough for me.' That's the way it really happened."

March 10

NELLE has recovered, so this morning we did another tour of the main part of town, staying away from that saloon, and in one of the houses where the Tarascan Indians manufacture and sell their famous lacquerwork, I broke down and bought a saucer of exquisite beauty, done in lacquer and gold. We wandered through the Sunday market and I tried to listen to the talk of the Tarascans, because Anita Brenner said "they speak a rippling, twittering language" in the manner of birds. I didn't hear any of this bird-talk here or after we got on the road and stopped in the village of Tzintzuntzan, which means City of the Humming Birds.

In Morelia we checked in at the famous Hotel Virrey de Mendoza, once a bishop's palace, and then walked around another beautiful city, sparkling clean, full of well-dressed people, a lovely place from any point of view.

Once again the problem of a bottle-opener has arisen. The hotel people of Mexico hoard them as if they were solid silver. Tonight I had a bottle of beer in my room and couldn't find any place to get the cap off. Earlier I had asked the boy to leave an opener in the room, but he acted as if I had insulted him, and wouldn't do it. So now, pretty sore about the whole thing, I stepped into the corridor and saw a suit of armor standing in a corner. I walked over to it and began trying to clatter the cap off the bottle. An employee of the hotel arrived on the double. "Oh, no, Señor!" he cried, as if I were desecrating his father's grave. He pulled out an opener and took off the cap but he wouldn't give it to me, wouldn't even sell it to me.

This evening I had a short talk in the lobby with a man who has been a hotel manager nearly forty years, in all sections of the United States. I asked him what he felt was the most significant thing he had learned about people in all that time. He thought a while and then said, "The thing that has impressed me most is the number of married couples in the world who don't like each other. You can spot them in any hotel dining room — they sit and eat and they never say a word to each other through the whole meal."

March 11

A FEW steps from the hotel is the College of San Nicolás, which was established burro's years ago and which is perhaps the most famous school in Mexico though it doesn't appear to be much bigger than a supermarket. Father Hidalgo was educated in San Nicolás and then became a teacher there, and instructed Morelos. The name of Melchor Ocampo, who was right-hand man to Juárez, also is associated with the college (the State of Michoacán is a sort of anagram of his name).

I read in a guidebook that the heart of Father Hidalgo has been preserved and is on display at the college. I didn't care about seeing it, because I belong to the school which says a heart is nothing more than a muscle, and not the thing it is proclaimed to be in song and poem and story. Nelle, the mummy-looker, couldn't rest until she had a look at that heart. I walked over to the college with her and inspected the inner court while she went heart-looking. After a while I went back to the hotel and loafed around the lobby and when she failed to return within a reasonable period, I walked back to the college. I finally found her in a big room staring at a heart in a glass jar. "It's not the heart of Hidalgo," she told me, "but the heart of a man named Ocampo. The caretaker said he was as great a man as Hidalgo." I looked at the heart, which was pale gray and actually didn't look much like the kind of heart we bandy around on Valentine's Day. From its looks it could have been the kidney of a mud turtle instead of the heart of Ocampo. I finally got her away from the thing and she sallied forth into a more splendid adventure.

Carlos and I left her wandering in the public market and about two hours later she returned to the hotel, a faint smile on her face and a story to tell. At the market a well-dressed Mexican, somewhat drunk, had trailed her around for a while and then, approaching her, had said in halting English, "Would you like some enjoyment, Señorita?" She remembered my lecture about being polite in any and all circumstances and so she responded, *"No, gracias, Señor,"* and moved on. He followed at some distance behind her as she headed back toward the plaza. He caught up with her and again asked, "Would you like some enjoyment?" She said, *"No, muchas gracias, Señor."* He kept after her and finally she saw a church and remembered vaguely about the rule of sanctuary and went inside. She stayed there for about half an hour, looking at paintings and statues. When she went outside again she didn't see him but as she started down the steps a shadow moved in and a voice spoke, "Señorita, would you like to have some enjoyment?" She said, *"No, gracias, Señor,"* and lit out for the hotel. She told her story with a sort of glow, and finally admitted that the man's approaches were pleasing to her, except for the fact that he was drunk. I told her, "You should not leap to unwarranted conclusions. It is my opinion that the guy merely wanted to take you to the movies." And Carlos said, "Yes. Either that, or he wanted to buy you some frijoles."

Out in the plaza we saw a boy walking along ringing a little bell. He had no merchandise in view and apparently wasn't selling anything, so I asked Carlos about him. "It is a warning," said Carlos, "that means, 'Gringos in town, watch your things.'"

Our hotel room has a little balcony overlooking the plaza and the main street, and this evening I was sitting there when my ear picked up the sound of marimba music coming from the nearby *portales.* My *veracruzano* blood began to leap, and soon the three of us were on the street, bird-dogging that music down to its source. We found the marimba in a sidewalk café, and so we had an hour of "Noche Criolla" and "Peregrina" and, for Carlos, "Mujer." He insisted on explaining the song title again. "It means woman," he said. "Lara always made his songs about womans. So-so-womans, bad womans, good womans, all kinds of womans. And all very sad."

Carlos said that the hotel clerk had told him about an American family, recently settled in Morelia. There were two small children and the mother had a police whistle which she used to summon them in from play at mealtimes. Back home it had been her custom to blow five short blasts on the whistle, a signal which meant dinner was ready. She resumed the custom here, but soon there were dark looks and mutterings from her Mexican neighbors; to them the five short blasts represented The Awful Obscenity. When the thing was finally explained to her by one of her more amiable neighbors, she changed the dinner signal to three longs instead of five shorts.

On this night I learned an important thing. In Spanish beer is feminine and whisky is masculine. *Una cerveza. Un whisky.*

March 16

WE HAVE been, during the last five days, loafing at San José de Purúa, one of the famous resorts in Mexico. It is a big place tucked away in the mountains and it is patronized almost exclusively by American tourists. Most of them come straight to this hotel, looking neither to right nor left, caring nothing whatever about Mexico. They spend much of their time dunking themselves in pools of brown, stinking, dirty water — they might as well be in a mud puddle in Iowa.

Nelle and Carlos and I loafed and ate and drank and joked and I got to read several of the Mexican books I've been toting around. Also I managed to do some writing, copying an assortment of unrelated items out of my notebooks, little things I've picked up along the way. They are items mainly of interest to scholars, historians, social scientists, bricklayers and sprocket-manufacturers. I offer them to the world here, in one batch:

When Montezuma walked abroad, as he did when he went out to greet Cortez for the first time, his elbows were supported in the palms of the hands of two nobles, the Kings of Texcoco and Iztapalapan. I'm confused by this. Did he suffer from tired elbows?

If you have trouble pronouncing the vowels in Spanish, don't worry about it; just remember that back home we have plenty of people who can't handle the vowels in English, as witness the words either, neither, vase, aunt, etc.

Occasionally we hear people say, "You'll get Thirty-threed," or "I don't want to get Article Thirty-threed." This refers to a constitutional provision under which any foreigner, caught meddling in Mexican politics, can be thrown out of the country instanter. It happens to quite a few Americans, and to some who were not really meddling in politics. They just happened to say the wrong thing in the hearing of the wrong people.

Mexico City has a population of about four million. In recent years it has been expanding so fast that the nose-counters can't keep up with it. Responsible authorities say it is inevitable that, within about a decade, the city will be the largest metropolis in the world.

In some outlying Indian communities an oversexed woman is called a *caliente,* meaning a hot.

At least two dozen persons have told us, almost in the exact language, "In Mexico you never get anything done unless you know somebody." In our country we say, "It's better to know somebody," but it really means the same thing.

Americans sometimes consult Mexican *curanderas,* or witches. I've heard of an American lady, once resident in Taxco, who went to a witch to cure her grandchild of car-sickness. The witch told her to get a certain copper coin and plaster it over the child's navel. Grandma did it, and said that it worked. The trouble with such things is that they never stop where they should; before long Grandma will begin sprinkling powdered goose dung on the child's cereal to ward off athlete's foot.

In the early days of the labor movement in this country, the oil workers went on strike. Among other things they demanded polo ponies and polo fields and since they didn't know how to play the game, they demanded that the company engage an instructor to teach them.

When the Aztec rulers mounted the throne they swore they would make the sun to shine, the clouds to give rain, the rivers to flow, and the earth to bring forth fruits in abundance. It is the same with rulers in the United States, except that they promise these things before mounting the throne.

Mexico City is not a good place for visiting athletes because of the altitude; the exception, of course, is the football player whose job is to do the punting. A punt will carry about fifteen yards farther in Mexico City than in most United States cities.

It is said that Pancho Villa didn't smoke, didn't drink . . . but women! Witnesses report that the mere presence of a good-looking woman turned him to jelly, and a light froth appeared on his lips. Yet he wouldn't touch them without going through the sacrament of marriage; he married them, one after another after another after another.

Mexicans never seem to throw anything away, especially tin cans. The big ones are used for toting water, or for flower pots. The chambermaids in many hotels, including some of the big fancy ones, often carry their scouring powder and furniture wax in little cans that formerly held vegetables.

Observation: It almost seems as if, any time four or five persons came together at the same locality in Mexico, they dropped whatever else they were doing and built a cathedral.

Of all Mexican artists, I think I admire most the one named Xavier Gonzalez. He began as an artist for the railroad. Whenever a train broke down he would rush to the scene and make a sketch of the defective or broken part, and race back to the shops with it so that a replacement could be made. That took talent.

Conservation is a good thing, but it can be overdone. In Acapulco there have been complaints that the handbag and luggage manufacturers have all but exterminated the crocodiles from neighboring swamps and streams.

John Houston Allen, who once lived in Mexico, wrote an article in *Holiday* which included this line: "I have remembered every Mexican I ever knew." It's a strange thing — on reflection I find I am the same way. Normally I can't remember names or faces, but down here I remember every Mexican I've met, even if only for two minutes.

Flandrau wrote about a woman who refused to expose herself to the night air until her doctor explained, "Señora, during certain hours of every twenty-four, night air is the only air there is."

Quite a few tourists who lounge around hotel lobbies read paperback books. I sometimes saunter past them and try to detect what they are reading. Almost always the books are mystery novels. This is shocking, when you consider how many wonderful books are available on the subject of Mexico.

There is a plant down here called Mala Mujer — the Wicked Woman flower. I found out first that it is supposed to cure gonorrhea. Then I learned that if it is placed under the bed, it will kill bedbugs. Eventually I found out where it got its name. It is much worse than poison ivy — the slightest touch will produce painful blisters. The Indians rubbed it on their wives when the wives were unfaithful.

The toll highway from Mexico City to Acapulco doesn't make sense. An intelligent plan would have sent it in the other direction, to Veracruz, which is the nation's chief port. When they built it to Acapulco, they said it would be a great thing for the tourist trade. Nuts. It is no favor to the tourist; far better if the road to Acapulco were a winding trail, so the traveler could get a good look at the countryside. The whole picture is clear: the superhighway was built for the big-car Mexicans who have fancy homes in Acapulco.

The word for Evil Eye is *ojo*. If you are a person accustomed to saying "Oho!" better be careful. Don't stare at anybody when you say it, and keep your fingers in your pockets. Somebody might retaliate and give *you* the Evil Eye, in which event you'd have to be rubbed all over with pigeon grease, and wear a bag of deer's toenails at your neck. Might delay your trip some.

I heard a lady say, "It's got a tildy over it." I ran it down, and found out that a *tilde* is the little squiggle over a letter, as in *señor*.

In Guanajuato they have each year a tableau depicting the Last Supper. Much care goes into the casting and the staging, and the final result is said to be wonderfully impressive. Marie MacDonald, who is involved in Mexico City theatricals, told me that she saw the tableau once and thought it was beautiful, except for one glaring anachronism. On the table in front of Jesus and each of the apostles stood a bottle of Coca-Cola.

Someone has remarked that Mexican men wear hats all the time, yet a bald Mexican is a rare sight; this would seem to kill the theory that hat-wearing leads to baldness.

In the time of Díaz and even later, the people of quality who had darkish skins spent hours each day making themselves look white, usually through the employment of rice powder. Díaz himself entered office looking like the Indian he was; by the end of his reign he was as white as the Princess of Monaco. It is said that he retained a French expert to paint his lips and whiten his cheeks.

When Will Rogers came to Mexico thirty years ago he made a speech in which he said bluntly, "I didn't come down here to tell you that we look on you as brothers. That would be a lot of bunk. We look on you as a lot of bandits, and you look on us as one big bandit." Incidentally, Will Rogers did not say, "I never met a man I didn't like." He was once talking about a possible epitaph for himself, and he suggested it read, "I joked about every prominent man of my time, but I hardly ever met a man I didn't like." There's a big difference.

Every time I go down Avenida Juárez to call on Louis Zeh, and see his Wells Fargo sign, I get a swashbuckling sensation, a feeling that the stage is gonna be attacked by road agents and maybe I'd better ask Louis if I can ride shotgun on the next one out.

An American long resident in Mexico City told me that a Mexican will always try to respond to a question with the answer he thinks you want to hear. You take your car to the garage with a motor knock that Beethoven could have heard, and you ask the mechanic if he thinks there's a knock in it. He reasons that you don't want to have a knock in your motor, so he says, "No, Señor, I hear nothing."

Hammocks are very popular throughout Mexico, especially in the tropical areas. Many hotel rooms in spots like Acapulco and Veracruz have a hammock as well as beds. The most popular size hammock is called a *matrimoniale*, which seems to be an interesting fact; I have trouble making out in the things when I'm by myself.

We are always reading about how our movie stars and our heiresses are having affairs with bullfighters in Mexico. Where do they get enough bullfighters to go around? I'm beginning to understand. Any young man with a handsome countenance who has ever so much as stuck out his tongue at a bull is a *torero*. One of the waiter captains at the Reforma is a bullfighter and Bob Prescott told me that one of the office boys at the United Press is a matador.

The little street next to the House of Tiles (Sanborn's) is known as the Calle of the Two Countesses. In colonial times a carriage containing a countess entered at one end just as a carriage containing another countess entered at the other end. There was no room for the two to pass, but they proceeded slowly toward each other until the horses were almost touching noses. Pride would not permit either countess to order her coachman to back up. They sat there for three days and three nights and they would be there yet if the Viceroy hadn't come up with a Solomonic solution. He proposed that they both back up, one step at a time, and thus neither countess would lose face.

After tussling for weeks with difficult proper names in Spanish it was a pleasure, one recent morning, to pick up a newspaper and run across a good old American name — viz., Ethel Snowball.

An American correspondent told me of a method he has for getting rid of bothersome visiting firemen. He takes them to a restaurant called El Centro del Sureste and quietly orders the house specialties, which include octopus in its ink and unborn baby eels. This procedure usually causes the visiting fireman to sicken of the whole country, and he packs and goes home.

A hard-sell insurance agent would starve to death in Mexico. Mexicans simply don't go for insurance, possibly because the courts wouldn't tolerate the kind of damage suits we have back home — an action for a million dollars because of a broken toe. In this one respect, at least, Mexico is a sensible country and we are a ass.

An American lady of my acquaintance came to Mexico last year and, arriving in Taxco, noted all the signs saying, "Joyería." This means "jewelry store," but my friend thought it meant bawdyhouse and, until she learned better, had an idea she was in the most corrupt town on earth.

7

Señor Duck and Some Burros

March 17

OUR arrival at the Hotel Reforma today was much like coming home. By now we know almost everybody and even Denise Darcel rushed up to welcome us back.

This afternoon Nelle went out to do some research on Señor Duck. The newsstand lady who owns him gets ready to go home at about 2:30 each afternoon. She drags out a little wooden wagon, equipped with roller-skate wheels. Señor Duck is always pecking around in the little mudhole about fifty feet up the street. His ear is tuned to the sound of the little wagon and when he hears the wheels on the sidewalk, he sets up a quacking and comes waddle-trotting down to his Mama. She loads some old magazines and other junk on the little wagon and starts off for home, crossing in front of the hotel entrance. Señor Duck waddles along behind the wagon, his eyes fixed on it, guarding it, and if any pedestrian comes too close to it, he pecks viciously at them.

After Nelle had given me this report I went out and talked to Don Quixote. He was indignant because we call the bird "Señor."

"No *Señor* Dock!" he said. "Is *Señorita* Dock. This little dock the lady has brought since she is two inches big, every day until now she is a big dock. Yes, to go home they cross one street. The lady pulls the little wagon and behind comes the dock. Bosses, trocks, automobiles, all put on the brake and stop. The dock lives in the apartment with Papa and Mama. The lady is called by the guides La Perroquita, which mins The Parrot. Not because she talks, because she is quiet, but because her hosbon's name is Pedro. Dock no likes little children, packs at them. Cholly Bower no likes this dock to be here, tries to put him someplace else, but everybody saize 'No, Cholly Bower! Dock stays!' "

So I went upstairs and called on Charlie Bowers and spoke to him of Señor Duck. We have decided to continue calling the duck Señor Duck in spite of Don Quixote's objection. The error is no greater than the one made by Disney and accepted the world over — Donald Duck.

Charlie Bowers spoke feelingly about Señor Duck. He made it clear, however, that he is not prejudiced against the duck as a duck — he hates the bird because it is a symbol of the ramshackle newsstand and its proprietors. Charlie has always been proud of the Reforma's reputation as a quality hotel, and the newsstand is to him an eyesore. So one day he undertook a campaign to get rid of it. He went to the bank across the street and found out that they had no objection to the opening of a handsome newsstand on their corner. Then he went to Pedro and told him that he, Bowers, would build an elegant stand across the street and, in addition, he would give Pedro a large number of pesos if he would agree to move. Pedro did agree, and Charlie was happy, until a representative of the newsdealers' union walked into his office.

"This bum," said Charlie, "told me that the arrangement was all okay except for one minor point. He said I would have to give *him* five thousand pesos before, as he put it, he would permit Pedro to be 'kicked around.' I threw the bastard out of my office and that, of course, killed the entire deal. Now that damned newsstand will be there forever, and the quacking of that damned duck, drifting up here to my windows, reminds me of it all day long."

Charlie knows that I'm working on a book, so now I told him that I expect to write at some length about Señor Duck. He gave me a long stare (the same kind of stare I imagine he sometimes gives the duck).

"Why," he wanted to know, "would you want to write anything about a stupid damn duck? What kind of a writer are you, anyway?"

"Right now," I answered, "I'm a duck-writer."

"Well," he said, "if you've got to be ridiculous, get one thing straight. I *like* ducks — on a plate."

March 18

TODAY I called on Bob Peck again at Woolworth's and found that establishment has become a dangerous institution. A Yo-yo craze has seized Mexico City. We became aware of it yesterday on our return when, the moment the hotel elevator door closed, the boy whipped out a Yo-yo and began trying to operate it. Two or three of the guides at the entrance were playing with the things, including Don Quixote. Everywhere we looked we saw Yo-yos going, in the hands of both kids and adults. The fad is the result of a big promotional campaign put on by Coca-Cola in conjunction with Woolworth's and the Yo-yo manufacturers. I'm told that such fads are quite rare in Mexico, but this one has certainly taken hold in the capital.

Bob Peck took time out for coffee and we talked about the Yo-yos and other matters. I spoke of the uncomfortable chairs to be found all over Mexico, especially those in public dining rooms. The straight-back chair is uncomfortable here because its back is not straight: it tilts inward, digging into the ribs and spine. Since these crazy chairs were used in most restaurants, I suggested that they were deliberately made uncomfortable to keep the customers moving and to get a big turnover. Bob said he had given the matter some thought. His theory is simply that the Mexican is not built the same way as a Gringo, especially in the hip area. "He's fastened together differently," said

Bob. "If you don't believe it, buy a pair of Mexican shorts and try to wear them. They have a different type of butt."

He said he had gone over to the barber shop in the Reforma this morning for a haircut. These *peluqueros* are the aristocrats of the Mexican barbering world; the one who worked on Bob asked him if, instead of a tip, he could have a Yo-yo.

March 19

THE bellboys in the Reforma were not hustling as hard as usual today. I noticed them huddled around the corner, beyond the house phones and screened by the lobby foliage, playing with Yo-yos. I ran into Charlie Bowers and asked if he knew his employees were so engaged. He said he did. "I was just in the kitchen," he said, "and the chef is making one of the things go. He tried to hide it but I told him it was all right, as long as he didn't get it in the soup. I don't understand about these things. What is the purpose of them?"

I said I thought people played with Yo-yos just for fun. He said this made it more perplexing than ever.

"My wife has bought one of the things for the baby," he said, "but the baby is too young to do anything with it. I picked it up this morning and fooled around with it, but I couldn't make it go."

Tonight we hailed a taxi and headed for Fonda El Refugio again. The taxi driver had his girl friend riding on the front seat with him and the radio was tuned to a program which we judged to be a *jabón ópera*. The driver and the girl were holding hands, but only one each, and it didn't slow him down. They listened to the radio drama with rapt attention as he whipped the car through traffic at frightening speeds. The program was in Spanish, of course, and the part we heard was a long colloquy between a man and a woman, each speaking passionately, and the man was slapping the woman, or she was slapping him, or they were slapping each other. There would be a few lines of dialogue, then "Whap!" An exclamation of astonishment from the woman, as if she didn't believe what had just happened, then "Whap! Whap!" After that some more wild and weepy dialogue, and "Whap! Whap! Whap!" I hadn't heard such slapping since the last time I broke a tire chain on Millwood Road.

El Refugio again was almost deserted, which is a mystery to me, for the food is classical. Best *chiles rellenos* I've eaten to date.

March 20

TODAY we went to the American Embassy to investigate a subject that is dear to my heart, namely, the Mexican burro. I have been asking people all over Mexico about burros and while I've collected a good deal of burro lore, I haven't found many people who really appreciate the animal. Paul Kennedy told me about a Mrs. Gomez at the Embassy who, he thought, had made a study of burros, and she was the person we sought today. First, however, we observed protocol and called on the press attaché.

"What can we do for you?" he asked after I had identified myself as an American writer.

"I want to get some information about burros," I said.

"Well," he responded, "I think we might be able to fix you up. Just what type of information are you after?"

"Oh, how many there are, where they come from, the business of shipping them to the States, things like that."

A puzzled expression spread over his face. "I don't think I understand," he said.

Some people won't believe this, but it is pure truth — that man thought I was after information about the Burroughs Adding Machine people, who have a big branch here. We had a laugh over this and then I mentioned Mrs. Gomez and he sent me to the Agriculture offices on another floor.

We spoke to the man in charge of Agriculture and when I mentioned burros he chuckled, and then took us into Mrs. Gomez's office. When I spoke of burros, she smiled. It is the same everywhere — the burro is a lovable creature but he is also funny and the mere mention of his name brings on a smile or even laughter.

Mrs. Gomez said that all she knew about burros was the procedure by which they are shipped back to the States. She pondered for a while and then said she would phone the "small animal man" in the Mexican Department of Agriculture. She felt that he would likely know all about burros. She got him on the phone and talked to him in Spanish, with much smiling and laughing. When she got through she said that the small animal man was greatly amused, because nobody had ever asked him about burros before, and he really knew very little about them except that they carried things. He said there wasn't much *to* know about burros, but he gave Mrs. Gomez the name of another man in another Government department and she called him and asked, at my request, if anybody had ever written a book about burros, or even part of a book. This man said he had never heard of such a book, and he didn't know anything about burros except that they were important in getting things to market, and that most of them had fleas.

All over Mexico I have sorrowed and bled for the burro, seeing him loaded with burdens that, I felt certain, would shatter his frail legs within a very few minutes. I have looked at his masters, the grim and taciturn peons of the rural areas, and I have envisioned them beating the helpless little animals with clubs and straps, and underfeeding them.

In time I learned that my qualms were unwarranted. Ruth Nordhaus Pearson, a writer who knows about burros, informed me that it is all but impossible to overload a burro. In some sections of the country the natives believe that a burro is unhappy and dejected if he is not carrying a heavy load and so these people, on the journey home from the marketplace, load up their burros with heavy rocks just so the animals will be contented and comfortable during the trip.

Known elsewhere as an ass or a donkey, the burro dates back at least to the fourth century B. C., and in rabbinical literature it is clearly stated that he was created by God to bear burdens. Mrs. Pearson speaks of how the burro's small feet find their way around dangerous mountain trails as surely and as safely as the mountain goat, but he far surpasses the mountain goat in strength. Pound for pound the burro is a far better load-toter than the horse. Mrs. Pearson says that if a heavy draft horse could carry a load as big in proportion, he could walk off with a two-story house on his back.

A burro is only about two feet across at his widest point, and the streets and turnings in many Mexican villages were designed to accommodate him plus a reasonable load, just as the egg-sized cobblestones were put down to accommodate his feet. If the load is bigger than it should be, it has to be of some flexible substance, such as cornstalks or a lardy peon, else the burro won't be able to get around the corners. I have been told that the animal is instinctively polite, that when he meets you in a narrow street he will turn aside to make room for you to pass; his gentlemanly instinct, however, takes into account only the width of his own hind quarters, and not the load he is carrying, so that the pedestrian may be knocked down by a package of a hundred bricks or stacks of roof tile or firewood; the burro simply doesn't know how far out his load projects.

Historians have been harsh with Juan Zumárraga, first Bishop of Mexico and the man who accepted the miracle of Guadalupe, because he burned a great pile of Aztec manuscripts "of priceless historical and human importance." Stuart Chase has said that the world will always be the poorer for this act. But in my opinion Bishop Zumárraga at least partially redeemed himself, for he was the man who brought the burro to Mexico, fetching along a pair of the animals when he first arrived in the country. I'm sure that there are Mexicans today who, even though they worship no god greater than a bullfrog, would bow their heads in tribute to the Bishop if they knew he gave them the burro.

Considering that there are approximately three million burros in

Mexico by government count — meaning perhaps five million actually — I became curious about where they all came from. I thought there might be special ranches for the breeding of burros and, if so, I wanted to visit one of these places. I put the question to a droll little Spanish-born doctor, Julio Samper, who practiced in Mexico for a number of years. "Where do the burros come from?" I wanted to know. Dr. Samper held his hand, palm down, a couple of feet from the floor, then jerked it upward, repeating the gesture in various parts of the room, and saying, "They just pop up from here, from here, from there, from there, much like cabbages."

The burro usually has a deceptive look of sadness and melancholy, as if he didn't have a friend on earth. After I had looked at hundreds of them, observing their gloomy and dispirited state, thinking about their lifelong enslavement, their lack of voice in their own affairs, the way they were downtrodden by their tyrannical masters, I announced to Carlos one day in Veracruz that I was going to head up a Revolution of the Burros. Underneath their shaggy hides, I said, they are sweet and noble creatures, entitled to certain inalienable rights, entitled to a fair share of the world's goods. Carlos, who usually disapproves of Revolutions, said he would be happy to join with me in this one, and serve as Head General, drilling the burro troops, moulding them into an efficient fighting force, teaching them to advance backwards so they could kick the enemy to shreds.

There are, of course, some cases in which burros are whipped and otherwise abused, but as a general thing the Mexican considers his burro almost as a member of his family. Sometimes he regards his burro as a philosopher and will spend long periods talking to the animal, reciting his troubles and outlining all the things that are wrong with the world. An American businessman who has been in Mexico for a dozen years said that a Mexican considers his burro to be an individual with a distinct personality and usually will feed the animal before he feeds himself. In many cases, out in the country, the burro lives in the house with the rest of the family.

In one section of Mexico there is a criminal act for which a burro is punished quite brutally. Mary and Fred del Villar, who wrote a book about their travels in the rugged wilderness south of Lake Pátzcuaro, told of seeing an occasional burro without ears. They asked questions and found out that these burros had paid the penalty prescribed for having invaded the family cornpatch. Since corn is the basic food of the people, such an invasion by a burro is a grievous sin. Usually the animal is whipped the first time or two, but if he repeats the offense several times, then his master hones up his machete and with one expert slash, removes the burro's ears. This serves not only as punishment, but notifies the rest of the world that this is a burro who violates cornpatches.

There are superstitions about the burro, one being that his blood is a remedy for jaundice, and another that if a person is stung by a scorpion, he should climb on the back of a burro, facing the animal's tail, and he will be cured. There is also the story that the dark cross on the back of the donkey was communicated when Christ rode him into Jerusalem.

In San Miguel we were told about a woman from Ohio who came to visit friends living in the town. The Ohio woman was a very devout person and part of each day was devoted to reading the Scriptures. Her hosts noted one bit of peculiar behavior on her part — she was antagonistic toward all burros. In San Miguel a person is brushing against burros all day long, and the Ohio lady would slap at them, and say, "Get away from me, you mean thing!" Finally her hosts asked her why she had no use for burros, and she said, "In all the pictures I've ever seen of the Holy Family, the little sheep and the goats and the birds all have looks of angelic reverence; but the donkey always stands there with a look of dumb contempt on his face, not caring one bit about being in the presence of Jesus and Mary and Joseph. He's a creature of the devil and should be treated as such."

Mexicans tell many funny stories involving burros and one of the best I've heard is about a Yucatecan and his burro. It was his custom to make a daily trip from his home village to a town twenty kilometers away, with two bags of salt on the back of his burro. One day he got an assignment to carry two heavier bags of salt to a town forty kilometers distant. The Yucatecan talked sadly to his burro about the job, explaining however that they would get more money, which meant more for the burro to eat. The burro said nothing. So the Yucatecan loaded the heavy bags on the burro and they set out and finally came to the town which was their usual destination. Here the burro stopped and refused to move another step. His master pushed and shoved and pulled and pleaded, with no success. Finally he said, "All right, my friend, I will do the job myself if you refuse to do it." So he took the heavy bags of salt from the burro and strapped them on his own back, and having done that, he climbed onto the burro and said, "Now, you lazy one, let us proceed with the journey."

It is probably pure myth but one book says that a burro was responsible for the tremendous silver boom in Taxco during the time of Borda. In 1717, according to this story, a burro belonging to Don José de la Borda stuck a hoof through the ground, opening a hole which led to the discovery of the silver vein of San Ignacio. If the story is true, Borda's burro ranks with the one encountered in modern times in Cuernavaca by Hudson Strode.

Professor Strode writes of going to an American home in Cuernavaca where seventeen dogs served as reception committee. Then:

"In the drawing-room a donkey stood by the radio listening rapt and moist-eyed to a sentimental rendition of 'La Paloma,' a song that had been a favorite with the Empress Carlota three-quarters of a century ago. The mistress of the house was very proud of the she-ass's musical appreciation as well as her perfectly housebroken good manners. The donkey was named Blanche, after her mistress . . .

"When we went to the patio for cocktails, Blanche accompanied us. She took her stance politely by her mistress's long chair; the *mozo* trickled a cocktail into her wide-open mouth. As she closed her eyes and a tremor ran along her donkey ears, master and mistress led the laughter."

There really are people like that in Cuernavaca.

I believe the part about Blanche's drinking habits. When we were in Acapulco we somehow missed making a trip to the island of La Roqueta where they have the beer-drinking burro. The chief purpose of a tourist's visit to the island, I judged, is to feed beer to the burro. I'm told that after he has had several bottles, he becomes just like a human and wants to go on drinking indefinitely; he will sidle up to a table occupied by tourists, suddenly seize a bottle of beer in his teeth, throw his head back and drain it down. Then he does various little tricks, showing off, making a fool of himself, and if he had hands he'd put on a funny hat.

In recent years the business of shipping burros into the United States has been largely in the hands of Sears, Roebuck. Their current catalogue gives the burro prominent billing, offering him for $82.50. The catalogue listing says: "Burros have a gentle disposition that is 'made to order' for youngsters. Can be easily trained for riding or driving. Upkeep is small . . . they live comfortably on small quantities of grass, hay and grain. Mild-mannered burros have a soft bray not as loud as a dog's bark."

That last sentence is ambiguous. I take it to mean that if you are lucky enough to get a burro that is mild-mannered, it will have a soft bray. Most of the burros I listened to in Mexico had brays that were far from soft — they sound like trolley cars going around a curve.

The Sears burros are given all manner of dips and inoculations and other tests before they arrive at a "burro pool" in Illinois. Here they are given time to acquaint themselves with the peculiar behavior and language of Americans, and I assume their brays are checked, and the ones who bray louder than a dog's bark are sent home in disgrace. One problem Sears has had concerns the papers that must travel with each burro — in this respect they are much the same as people. The papers have to be fastened to the animal's body and in the past the burros have been eating them off each other. The latest word is that Sears has acquired a stock of Prince Albert tobacco tins to use as containers for the burros' passports, tourist cards, vaccination certificates, customs declarations, and so on.

Discussing burros with Charlie Bowers, I found out that there is a fine Italian sausage called *mortadella* which can be bought at a certain delicatessen on Insurgentes and which is made from the meat of Italian donkeys. Charlie said that it is one of the most flavorsome sausages in the world. I would like to suppress this information, rather than let the Mexican people find out about it, because I still think the burro has a hard enough time as it is — but Truth must be served.

Many complimentary things have been said about the Mexican burro but I found the greatest tribute to him in an old schoolbook once used by my daughter, called *Spanish Book One*. It says: "The burro comes perhaps nearer than any other creature to being a true and understanding friend of man." Certainly more so than man himself.

March 21

THIS is Juárez Day. All business is closed down and there are celebrations and ceremonies in various parts of town. Small parades have been coming down the Reforma all morning with drums and cornets and banners and with half the marchers swinging Yo-yos to the rhythm of the music.

Americans here have recommended that we stay away from Mexican gatherings of a patriotic character, not because Gringos are willfully mistreated at such affairs — it's just that the Mexicans tend to get exuberant. Bob Peck said he believes in trying everything once, and so he went down to the Zócalo on one Grito night, September 15th, and plunged into the crush determined to see it all. He came out with his clothes in tatters, fireworks burns on his neck and face, a wrenched arm and several minor cuts and abrasions.

Paul Kennedy told us of the time he attended a big patriotic shindig in the same Zócalo and after a while discovered that his wallet had been lifted. He yelled for the cops and they came and surrounded him, notebooks at the ready and ball-points poised. They asked him questions, slowly and carefully, and then they wrote and wrote with their ball-points, and Paul finally lost his patience and yelled at them to do something and quit writing. One of the cops then put his hand gently on Paul's arm and asked, "Are you a Catholic, Señor?" Paul responded with heat, "What the hell has that got to do with somebody stealing my wallet?" To which the cop replied softly, "Well, you could pray to Saint Anthony for its return."

Bob Prescott came by and explained to us why there are so many jokes about optometrists in Mexico. This is one department in which the Mexican shows his vanity. He will go around walking into trees and buildings before he will ever admit that he has a need for glasses. "This is also the reason," said Bob, "that so many Mexicans wear dark glasses. They can't see and they have to do something about it, so they have their prescriptions fitted in dark glasses, and then pretend that they are sun glasses." He said that he knows a Mexican doctor who is an altogether rational and enlightened man, but his wife wears dark glasses even at night. Bob encountered her one evening and decided to cross-examine her on the subject and maybe trick her into an admission that her eyesight was bad without glasses.

"Why do you wear those glasses?" he asked her.

"Because of the sun — it bothers my eyes."

"But there is no sun now, it is dark."

"Yes," she said, "but at night I wear them because it is bad to have the night air get into the eyes."

"But you are not keeping it out," argued Bob. "It comes in around the edges and gets into your eyes."

"Oh," she protested, "but you don't understand. It's the night air blowing straight into the eyes that does the harm."

Tonight we decided to try the suburban Fonda Santa Anita for dinner. We hailed a cab on the Paseo and this time we drew the world's champion *glorieta* jockey. It was easily the wildest ride we've ever had. He'd come up to a *glorieta,* turn it on full steam, and charge into the wild merry-go-round with the speed of sound. Several times Nelle and I clutched each other in a sort of farewell embrace and, in fact, once or twice I would have welcomed death. Yet he got us safely to the restaurant and after we had stopped shaking we ordered some enchiladas and frijoles. Soon a young man with bobbed hair hanging down to his shoulders came in and sat down at a Hammond organ and began playing "Three O'clock in the Morning" and "September Song." I got up nerve enough to approach him and tell him that I had a Hammond organ back in *estadosunidos* and I would like to see how sounds "Noche Criolla" and "Noche de Ronda." He said *"Con mucho gusto"* and lit into "Noche Criolla," softly at first, and then swelling, with the Latin beat, and it was great. He continued playing while we finished dinner and then on our way out I stopped by to thank him, and both he and the *capitán* insisted that I give it a whirl, saying in Spanish, "Oh, come on and *play!"* and I bridled and pawed the floor with my hoof and said aw, I wasn't good enough, and then finally I surrendered and mounted the bench and clawed out "Melancholy Baby." When I had finished Long-Hair clapped his hands together softly, and said, "Yoosta beginner. Yoosta beginner." I should have popped him one, but instead I said yoost play one more time "Noche Criolla" so I might watch his hands, which is the way I learn, and the way he did it was a marvel greater than the Aztec calendar stone.

We fought our way through the traffic to the other side of Insurgentes and this time our taxi was one left over from the First Battle of the Marne. It had an old-fashioned gearshift, growing up out of the floor; the floor in the back seat was split open so that carbon monoxide fumes drifted steadily into the car, and the gears made a heavy throbbing and grinding noise underfoot. The driver was a young man in a leather jacket, a great fellow for doing things with a flourish, even when shifting gears. Each time he shifted gears he did it as if the Moment of Truth had arrived in a bullfight, flinging his arms about in the manner that Isadora Duncan might have employed in driving a car. He did his best to keep up with the flow of traffic, but the ancient cab was too feeble, and we were compelled to chug along most of the time on the outskirts of the normal madness. In the end he delivered us safe and sound and slightly asphyxiated at the door of our hotel.

March 22

THIS morning I found Don Quixote playing with his Yo-yo near the hotel entrance. I asked him which was the toughest assignment for a guide in the immediate vicinity of Mexico City. He said it was the pyramids. "Is many history there," he said. "Is not so motch history as motch talking. Have to start talking ten tousan years ago. Is plenty toff." I said that if he could find time we would have him take us to the pyramids, as I would enjoy hearing him start talking ten tousan' years ago. "Is many good history," he assured me, "so better start early." I also told him I hoped we'd get to go with him to the Shrine of Guadalupe.

While we were talking a husky, well-dressed Mexican came up toward the Reforma entrance. He had a big blue paper bag of the type given out by local department stores, and it was full of purchases. The man was staggering slightly, with a happy alcoholic grin on his face. He stared up at the façade and wobbling his head around, called out, "Is Hotel Reforma? Is Go'damn Hotel Reforma? How get to boolfight? What is altitude thees Go'damn place?" There were roars of laughter from the other guides, for this was one of their number, putting on an impersonation of a Gringo tourist. I thought it was very funny, but as I walked into the hotel and crossed the lobby I was thinking that it was unfortunate that the Mexicans have such a low opinion of us — that we're really not that stupid. I crawled onto a stool at the bar and ordered *una cerveza*. Two men were on adjoining stools to my left and one of them, in ordering a Martini, said *"por favor."*

The other turned to the Martini man and asked, "You speak Spiggoty?"

"Naw. Oney a few words, like bonus dyas and like that."

"You frum the' States er er you frum Mexico?"

"I hail from L. A."

"Hell you say. I'm frum Glendale."

"Cheez. You in show business? I mean pictures?"

"Nawp. But I know a little about it and how it works. My wife's sister is substitute with the Corey sisters, you know, the trio, singers."

"How you mean substitute?"

"When one of them, one of the Coreys, get sick er hung over er something, then my wife's sister she steps in and takes 'er place. Whirr you live in L. A.?"

"Know where Liberace lives?"

"Yeh. General idea."

"I live in two blocks of his place."

"You know 'im? I mean personally?"

"Oh, sure. We speak."

"What kinda fella is he in real life, I mean, you know?"

"Not bad. Not as bad as he's painted."

"That's what I figgered. Guys like that take an awful lickin' frum th' newspapers."

"You can say that again."

"You said it."

So I got off the stool and went upstairs and read something in the paper that reminded me of that rough adventure with White Sombrero in the saloon at Pátzcuaro. A distiller in Greece has put out a brandy under the trade name of "Tipota," which means "nothing." It is to be served to those who say they want nothing.

March 23

TODAY we discovered a pertinent fact: that Mexican food should never be looked at before it is cooked and ready for the table. This became clear during a visit to the San Juan Market, one of the city's newer indoor markets. For one thing I wanted to look over the different kinds of sausages that are available; most of them turned out to be blood-red and none looked very appetizing. There seemed to be a preponderance of skinned rabbit heads wherever we looked in the market; even the booths for chickens held no aesthetic appeal, for the men and women in them were engaged in constant cutting and chopping and trimming and they seemed to take special pleasure in tossing and waving chicken guts back and forth in front of their customers.

In the last few years there has been a tremendous advance in food processing and retailing in Mexico City. The markets are being taken off the dirty pavements and moved into huge, modern buildings such as this one, and stringent rules have been put in force respecting the chemical treatment of vegetables. Moreover, Gringo-style supermarkets are being established all over the city and I'm told that the foodstuffs in these places are clean and free of trot-producing bacteria.

In the past many Americans living here have either done without green, uncooked vegetables, or they have subjected the vegetables to debilitating chemical baths which took much of the zip out of them. I thought that I saw an easy solution for them, and still wonder why they never tried it. I refer to home gardening. The reason Mexican vegetables have always been contaminated lies in the condition of the ground where they are grown and is traceable to lack of sewage facilities. Suppose the same conditions existed in the big truck gardens of the New York City area. It would not bother me too much, for I already grow green vegetables in a small garden and I am not so stupid as to contaminate the ground where those vegetables flourish. The Americans in Mexico City go in for big and complex gardens containing things to look at but nothing to eat. They could at least mark off one small corner for lettuce, and have all the salads they wanted. They could even put good soil in window boxes and produce enough lettuce to have a salad once or twice a week. For some reason they don't do it — at least I haven't been able to find any who ever thought of growing their own vegetables.

In San Juan market we saw, to be sure, mountains of beans — pinto beans and black beans and garbanzos and a half dozen other types, all piled into miniature Popocatépetls for the pleasure of the bean-eating Mexicans. Perhaps because of my Midwestern origin I'm an eater of beans. I was eating garbanzos, or chick peas, back in the years when most Americans never heard of them (many still don't know about them). I was raised on beans and I'm convinced that the Eagle Brand milk which nourished me in my beginning months was well laced with bean broth, or even bean paste. Because of my love for beans I have never had any use for the Greek philosopher, Pythagoras. The religion he invented was based on transmigration of the soul and the sinfulness of eating beans. I haven't been able to find out why he was against beans, and prohibited them to his followers, but I do know that he was an inconsistent man. He went around saying that he didn't believe in killing any living creature. Then one day he discovered that the square of the hypotenuse of a right-angled triangle equals the sum of the squares of the other two sides. He was so happy about it that he rushed out and sacrified a hundred oxen to the gods. What a hypocrite!

I can think of only two types of beans I would not enjoy eating. One is the Mexican jumping bean, which jumps because it has a moth larva lolloping around inside of it; and the other is an Alamo bean. Once when I was in the Alamo at San Antonio, I saw a dish containing the beans that were used during the siege — there was a drawing of beans to determine who would go for help, or some such thing, and the original dish of beans is still preserved. I don't think I would enjoy eating them, even if I were a Texan.

The standard way of serving beans in Mexico, of course, is *refrito,* and I for one have been mystified until lately over why they are called "refried" when the recipes clearly call for a single frying. It turns out that Mexicans have a special way of boiling their beans — when they begin to get tender, a spoonful of lard is tossed into the boiling water and this, theoretically, is the "first frying." Later, when the beans are mashed and fried, they become *refrito.*

As for the growing of beans, I suppose it is the same in Mexico as elsewhere, although the Indian races have had some singular ideas in the field of bean husbandry. I have a clipping which tells of the work of the Indian Bean Tester among the tribes of New York State, in modern times as well as ancient. "It was a method," the story goes, "of telling whether or not the ground was warm enough to plant beans. On the first warm day in spring when the robins were singing loud and lustily, a young brave would stalk to the center of the village or common and there pull off his breechclout and sit down. The women would gather around him in a curious circle, keeping watch for hours until he pulled his clout back on and walked away. If he didn't sneeze while all this was happening, they decided the ground was warm enough to plant beans."

The growing of chiles, or peppers, also has a special lore. Peppers should always be planted when the grower is in a towering rage, according to the folklorically-inclined. If the grower is unable to work himself into such a rage, then his peppers should be planted by a redheaded person. I find that as I grow older and continue reading the newspapers, I am the ideal person to plant peppers; I could, in fact, hire out as a pepper planter.

Few Gringo tourists care at all for tortillas, but we order them quite regularly and I like them so much that I didn't get into a pepper-planting rage when I heard about one Henri Chatillon, a fashion designer on the Reforma. Several years ago he started a new fad in hats, taking steamed tortillas, moulding them to the customer's head, and then covering them with shellac.

While on the subject of Mexican food, I must mention a dish I have heard about, called *embarrado,* which means mud; it is made of meat and chiles and looks a good deal like mud, but it is said to be very tasty. I'd order it if I found it on a menu, provided they didn't put any maguey worms in it, or sprinkle it with octopus ink.

Mention should be made, too, of the widespread use of flowers in Mexican cookery. The society of gourmets sometimes puts on a banquet in which almost all of the dishes have flowers cooked in them. Dating from Aztec times, the eating of certain flowers is supposed to be medicinal as well as gustatory. Acacia blossoms, covered with a light egg batter and fried until golden brown, will drive away the blues. A rose pie, in which the petals are mixed with sugar and lemon juice, is a cure for stomach trouble. And jelly made from the scarlet blossoms of the Jamaica tree will fix you up if your kidneys or liver are causing trouble.

Finally, a cooking tip from the Mexican *arte de cocina.* If you're cooking mushrooms and aren't quite sure about them, toss in a "tooth" of garlic. If they are poisonous, the garlic will turn black. *De nada.*

March 24

THE talk in the Bar Jardín is almost always lively and good. Today the topic was smuggling. Apparently there is a lot of it going on. Many tourists try to take "Aztec idols" back with them in spite of the law which forbids the removal of archeological specimens from the country. The nice thing about it is that almost all the "idols" smuggled out by the tourists are fakes; there are whole villages engaged in manufacturing them, and "seasoning" them by burying them in the ground for a few months.

Someone told about an American who had a heavy bumper for his Cadillac made out of solid gold and then plated with chrome. He drove the car to the border and he probably would have got by with it if it hadn't been for the ungruntled Mexican who designed the bumper for him. The workman got to brooding about the small amount of money he had been paid, and this led to an attack of spiritual reappraisal, and so he tipped the authorities. The smuggler was sent to jail, I hope.

We met an attractive young woman in a Mexican resort who had bought an Aztec idol, which was flattish and quite heavy. She knew exactly how she was going to smuggle the little man out of the country. She was going to put him in her girdle. I've often wondered how she came out, and for a while I tried to compose the lyrics for a song about a girl with an Aztec god in her girdle. Actually, I see little that's amusing in the thing. If the Mexican customs men found that forbidden idol in her girdle, then they would have been justified in examining the girdles of every woman leaving the country thereafter. This would, of course, fetch on hysterical protests, and howls for the Marines, and influence would be brought to bear, and international relations strained, and so on.

Most tourists think it is a slick sort of game to be played — these attempts to outwit the customs people. Not long ago a writer in Paris — a man who is almost a spokesman for all Americans living in the French capital — wrote a piece about the ginger-pep fun he had trying to smuggle some articles past the French customs officers. Oh, but he had a good time, and the laughs! And the piece he wrote was just priceless — funny as all get-out!

Attempts to cheat the customs, often on the part of prominent people, are reported in the newspapers with distressing regularity. An American bullfighter tries to smuggle a car into Europe; a Ping-pong champion steps off a plane from Europe with ten thousand dollars worth of Swiss watches hidden in a trick vest; a movie star is caught trying to smuggle expensive jewelry into the country.

As I said, it's nothing more than a little game, a sport, and if you can get away with it, then it becomes smart to brag about it to your friends. Yet I for one have no patience with these people — either the girl with the idol in her girdle, or the man with the Swiss watches in his vest. I used to grow furious because of the treatment I received from customs men when re-entering my own country. Being honest, I was violently indignant at the suspicious way in which they ripped through my belongings. But then I found out what was going on in the world, and I had to change my mind, and now I am firmly on the side of the customs men. It is because of the idiots who think it's cute to smuggle things that the rest of us have to put up with the delays and the searchings and the suspicions at the customs counter.

Dinner this evening at the home of Josephine Littlejohn, who is famous for the enormous house she occupies in San Angel, and for her soirées. Present were Paul Kennedy, the Oulahans and Bob Peck — faces that have become as familiar to us as the faces of our neighbors back home. At one point in the proceedings Nelle asked if someone could explain the difference between the Red Cross and the Green Cross, both of which operate in emergencies here. It is a frequent question asked by tourists and there is a standard answer: the Green Cross ambulances kill more pedestrians than the Red Cross ambulances.

Bob Peck told of going to a dinner party attended by members of the younger married set in high Mexican society. He was the only American present. The party was sedate and proper, no English was spoken, and everything was carried off in the style of the old Spanish aristocracy.

"It was the dullest affair I've been to in years," said Bob. "It was really horrible, until I mentioned you. I told them about how you were down here gathering material for a book, and that you were asking various people for opinions about Lázaro Cárdenas. From that moment on the party became a howling success. All the dignity went out of it, and they set to work on Cárdenas. They were actually screaming at one another. They were 100 per cent against Cárdenas, but each one wanted to outshout the others with his contention that he ought to be beheaded."

Everyone present seemed to know people of this type, the young aristocrats of Mexico. Someone said they have no nationalistic feeling at all, that they hold their country in contempt. They have no faith in any of the accomplishments of Mexicans. They really think that their native country is a farce before the world — simply because the Indians have been dragged up the social scale, given a semblance of education, and are now taking a hand in things.

March 25

AT MRS. LITTLEJOHN'S dinner last night the food was Mexican, at our request. Two girls cooked and served chicken with green *mole*. I asked Bob Peck (who lives at Mrs. Littlejohn's house) if he could get the recipe from the two girls, saying that I would like to include it in my book. He brought it downtown today and said he was up most of the night trying to wring it out of those two girls. They were thrilled to think that a Gringo wanted to take their *receta* all the way back to Nueva York, and they were eager to divulge their kitchen secrets. But, like all Mexican cooks and like all Spanish cookbooks, they have an airy disregard for precision. They cannot be pinned down as to quantities, such as teaspoonfuls or cups or pinches. A Mexican cookbook never orders you to do things; that wouldn't be polite. It just suggests, most gently, that it might be a good idea if you added a little so-and-so, provided you've got it. And that was the way with these girls and their *mole* sauce. They specified the use of five centavos worth of parsley, and half a handful of this or even more if you want it, a fistful of that tossed in later, and a few teeth of garlic but not too many, and a skillet half full of such-and-such. I am only able to say that the Littlejohn *mole* had sour cream and lettuce and parsley in it, plus baking soda, green chiles, green tomatoes, garlic, cloves, and ground green squash seeds. I said to Bob, "Just how in hell do you think I'm going to get any ground green squash seeds?" He replied, "Simple. Get yourself some green squash, remove the seeds and grind them."

Mole sauce is a big thing in Mexico and was invented by the nuns in a Puebla convent a long time ago. Tradition says that the spices and herbs that go into it must number exactly sixteen or it will not be good. The Puebla nuns, trying to cope with a surprise visit from the Archbishop, threw everything they could get their hands on into the pot — chiles, tomatoes, sesame seed, peanuts, pumpkin seeds, almonds, chocolate, black pepper, cloves, garlic, onion, raisins, and some other things, and thus was born *mole poblano*. Not long ago Don Vicente Mirando, a Mexican night-club owner, uttered a stirring tribute to the famous sauce. *Mole*, he declared, could be the instrument through which the world achieves lasting peace. "No man who eats *mole*," said Don Vicente, "could ever think of war and death." I say the same thing about beans.

If anyone should ever become interested in my opinion about books on the subject of Mexico, I am prepared to deliver a twenty-minute lecture on the subject. For the average traveler who enjoys reading about a country he plans to visit, I would recommend five books:

> *Timeless Mexico*, by Hudson Strode, the best up-to-date one-volume history of the country, the work of an intelligent man who writes so well that his book reads almost like a good novel.
> *Mexico Today*, by John A. Crow, an even more recent picture of the country written by a California professor who knows his business.
> *The Bernal Díaz Chronicles*, a new translation by

Albert Idell. This is the basic book about Cortez and the Conquest — the book from which all other writers, including Prescott, have drawn the bulk of their material. Also, it's fun to read.

Life in Mexico, by Mme. Calderón de la Barca. The number of times I've mentioned her should suffice to indicate how important I think her book is. Everyone else who knows anything about Mexico thinks so too.

Mexico Revisited, by Erna Fergusson. This accomplished lady has long had a close acquaintance with Mexico; just recently she got into her car and, driving alone, toured the country again. I never heard of Alma Reed until I read Miss Fergusson's book.

These books should be read before your trip to Mexico, if you have the time. Then, when you get home, sit down and read them all over again — it will seem as if you had never even opened them before. And after that, if you're interested in going further, you are ready for Charles Flandrau, and Anita Brenner, and that big, fat, fine historical volume, *Mexico and Its Heritage,* by Ernest Gruening.

I stopped in at the United Press today and found the Mexican employees whistling away, whipping their Yo-yos hither and yon, and doing their work at the same time. The most expert of the Yo-yo throwers demonstrated how well he has learned certain maneuvers, which he designated by name and then demonstrated. They are:

The Guillotine	— *La Guillotina.*
Around the World	— *Vuelta al Mundo.*
The Elevator	— *El Elevador.*
Rockabye Baby	— *Burmiendo al Niño.*
The Little Dog	— *El Perrito.*
Milking the Cow	— *Ordeñando la Vaca.*

As the young man went through each of these tricks, the maneuver that brought howls from his compatriots was the *Ordeñando la Vaca,* which is performed with two Yo-yos and involves up and down milking gestures.

There in the UP office I suddenly heard the sound of a fire engine and, looking out the window, saw the *bomberos* proceeding up the Reforma at a slow pace — on their way, perhaps, to a picnic or a fiesta. I remarked that this was the first fire engine I had seen in all the time I had been in Mexico. Someone told me that even in a city where skyrockets and other fireworks are common, there are very few fires. The reason is the city's altitude — there's not enough oxygen in the air to support a good fire; it is even difficult to get a blaze going in a fireplace and would be almost impossible if it were not for the kindling wood, which is usually loaded with resin.

March 26

I OVERHEARD one of the bellboys call one of the elevator operators a *"cabrón"* this morning and for a few moments I thought there was going to be a fight. This is a good example of how an innocent word can become a fighting word. *Cabrón* is the word meaning goat. It has come to mean, also, cuckold. No Mexican man would ever concede, even under horrible torture, that his wife was ever unfaithful to him, and so *cabrón* is just about the worst thing you can call him. I once used the word in polite company, not being aware of its awfulness, and almost got Article Thirty-threed.

Maxine introduced me today to an Englishman who has spent a lot of time in Spain as well as Mexico. He said that many of the bad things in Mexico are part of the nation's Spanish heritage. He ticked them off on his fingers: begging children; obscenity, especially among children; inability to give directions; a genius for fouling up ceremonies, whether civil or religious; red tape and pomposity among public officials. He said these things are common to both countries.

I have met an American woman, quite elderly, who drives an old car around the city with no regard whatever for the hazards and with no concern at all for the rules. She consistently travels the wrong way on one-way streets, parks in forbidden areas, sometimes even drives on the wrong side of the boulevards. Naturally she is constantly being stopped by policemen. She has a procedure for handling these cops and she told me it never fails. The moment an officer comes up to her, she says, "I am one hundred and one years old. Have an orange drop." She always carries several packages of orange drops, and she always hands one to a cop, and he is so startled by it and by her declaration of antiquity, that he always smiles and waves her on her illicit way. This is the cheapest *mordida* I've heard of in Mexico.

And another lady — I encountered her again today in the lobby of the Reforma. She is a handsome top-knotted blonde. She is constructed along Junoesque lines and her trademark is a blonde topknot the size of a watermelon, which makes it look as if she'd tip over easily. I have inquired about her and been told that she believes that she was the first wife of Prince Rainier. She contends that they were never legally divorced, and that the palace in Monaco is in her name. She spends much of her time in public places, and various American men strike up an acquaintance with her, with foul intent. But they achieve nothing, for she always backs them into corners and pleads with them to finance her claim against the Prince. Whenever I see her on the main trail, I try to find a short cut through the canyon.

March 27

THE days dwindle down, the time approaches for us to take our leave, and the clock seems to run faster than usual.

Charlie Bowers introduced me today to an American businessman and I had lunch with him and found him obsessed with an idea which he insisted on discussing with me. He said that cigarettes don't cause cancer. "I've reasoned it out," he said, "using common ordinary horse sense — process of elimination — all that sort of thing. Know what I think it is causes cancer? Little particles of tin. Every time you open a can you get 'em. The can opener's bound to shave off a few of these particles, they drop into the soup or tomatoes or beans, you eat 'em, they get into the blood stream, set up irritation. Bam! Cancer! The doctors don't know about this. I'm the only one knows about it, except now *you* know about it." I wasn't too thrilled at being the second man in the whole wide world to know about it. This man now told me that he was trying to figure the best way of capitalizing on his discovery, and he thought I might be able to advise him.

"I don't know which way to jump," he said. "The obvious thing to do would be to bleed the canning industry and if they wouldn't hold still for it, then I think I'd turn it over to the frozen foods people."

I told him I had no suggestions, that writers are notorious for having no business sense. At the same time a large question flicked across my mind. How do all those other authors manage to write such cheerful, optimistic books — crammed full of the goodness of people?

This evening the long-missing Pepe Romero showed up at the hotel, back at last from New York, fat and sassy and thoroughly happy, having sold almost all of the paintings out of his one-man show at the Hammer galleries. Pepe phoned upstairs to the Van Heflins and they came down and joined us for a drink. Later we all went over to Bill Shelburne's club for dinner, and I learned that Frances Heflin is a truly remarkable woman — she left *two* pairs of gloves at El Paseo last night, the pair she had been wearing and a new pair she had bought. The Heflins proved to be fine company; he's serious and intelligent and well-informed, while she's gay and giddy and unpredictable and inclined to speak her mind. Later we went to the Jacaranda night club because the Heflins had never seen the "dancing waters." When the show finally came on and the colored streams of water went into their ballet, swaying and swirling in time to the music, Van Heflin stared for a few moments and then exclaimed, "My God, this could replace actors!" We made it our big dissipation night and stayed out until three or four in the morning and wound up in our room with lots of good talk.

March 28

ON OUR way out of the hotel this morning we ran into Joe Nash, of the *News*. He knows we are always on the prowl for interesting stories and odd bits of information. So without being asked he stopped, chewed his lip, and then said, "No spaghetti sauce is any good without a little papaya juice stirred into it at the very last."

So we went on to one of Fred Davis's celebrated breakfasts. It is by way of being an accolade to have Fred Davis give a breakfast for you at his home. He is one of the real, important figures in the promotion of the popular arts in Mexico. His home is a museum, made up of room after room after room crowded with art objects. Present with us were Josephine Littlejohn and the two Mrs. Oulahans. During breakfast the senior Mrs. Oulahan told about how she's always had a mental block which prevents her from learning foreign languages. "People don't believe it," she said, "but every morning for two months, after I first got here, I came downstairs and said to the servant girls, 'Buenos aires.' I really thought that was what you were supposed to say."

Fred Davis came to Mexico from Illinois many years ago and to describe his collection would be to describe the whole history of art in Mexico from the Aztecs to Pepe Romero. Davis was very close to the Dwight Morrows, and designed and built their famous home in Cuernavaca. When Ambassador Morrow wanted to make a gift to the Mexican people, it was Fred Davis who proposed getting Diego Rivera to paint the murals in the Cortez palace.

I asked Mr. Davis if he knew Lindbergh when the flier came to Mexico and met, for the first time, his future wife.

"Indeed I did," he said, "and I might add that their courtship was rather unusual. They spent almost all their time sitting at opposite ends of a long table, each deeply engaged with a newspaper or a magazine. After about a week of this, their engagement was announced."

Back at the hotel Don Quixote hailed me, put his Yo-yo in his pocket, and said, "I told you is *Señorita* Dock, not *Señor* Dock. So, now is *Señorita* Dock gonna have leetle babies. I find out today." Apparently Don Quixote has now developed fresh interest in the duck for he was full of new information. He said that Pedro, the newsstand proprietor, and his wife, live in a small apartment. Pedro gets up early and goes to open the newsstand. Then his wife gets up and prepares breakfast, and the duck waddles around the kitchen watching the proceedings, giving forth gentle quacks of anticipation. The purpose of the little wagon is to haul the breakfast over to the newsstand, so Pedro can eat; at the same time the duck is given a tortilla. After his tortilla he proceeds down the street toward Woolworth's, where he has his puddle. The water for the puddle is provided by city employees who leave one of the faucets dripping all day long for Señor Duck.

"Is kept the water turned on," said Don Quixote, "so dock will go there, far away from the window of Cholly Bower, so when he makes noise, the dock, Cholly Bower will not hear."

I stopped in on Cholly Bower to talk duck. "I told you before," he said, "that I like ducks — with orange sauce. I still insist that newsstand ought to be on the other corner, and if they'll move it I promise you that I will appear in full dress in front of the hotel and make a public apology to the duck." I told him that I had learned how Señor Duck had been trained to do his frolicking some distance down the street, away from the hotel. "I can still hear him," said Charlie. "Every quack is like a bullet in my back."

This afternoon Fred Vosberg brought Hildegarde around and we had a pleasant session. She, too, has had breakfast with Fred Davis and he gave her a beautiful gold watch that belonged to either Maximilian or somebody in his court. Hildegarde has fallen in love with Mexico and like Denise Darcel is spending a lot of money on things. We've heard that Denise spent all the money she earned singing here — a real respectable sum — and sent for more, and spent that, and sent for more. Hildegarde is a bit more conservative. The trouble with women when they're abroad is that they spend all their money on senseless baubles and impractical native clothes. The trouble with men when they're abroad is that they spend all their money on women.

Dinner tonight at the Prescotts. Bob got out the Anglo-American Directory for 1956–1957 and showed me the biography of Fungo P. Nubb. Fungo P. Nubb describes himself as a "distance friction consultant" and that alone gives him a certain distinction, even if his name were not Fungo P. Nubb. His wife is listed as Filboida Telele Nubb. Their children are named Encarnacion Nubb, Filboid Nubb, Luz del Socorro Nubb, Fungo Nubb, Jr., Smedley Nubb and Pastora Nubb.

Even though I took pleasure from the euphonious loveliness of all the names, I was even more fascinated by Fungo P. Nubb's job as a distance friction consultant. Bob said that once when he was having a quarrel with his New York office, he thought of calling Mr. Nubb and asking him to iron out the distance friction. We talked tonight of calling him — his phone number was given. Bob said he had often thought of doing it, but always hesitated, fearing the whole thing would turn out to be a gag. "I'd much prefer," he said, "to go through the remainder of my life believing that there is a Fungo P. Nubb who is a distance friction consultant and who is married to a woman named Filboida."

The Prescotts don't like parties, a prejudice with which we are in full agreement. Bob is a collector of Bing Crosby records and has an elaborate hi-fi setup for playing them. So tonight after dinner we had Crosby for two hours, including several rare items. Among these was a recording of "Wrap Your Troubles in Dreams" in which Bing fluffed, and then continued singing, making up his own lyrics as he went along, fitting them perfectly to the music. I copied this part down, and these are the words he improvised: "Sang the wrong mel-o-dy, let's play it back and see, what it sounds like hey-hey, they cut out eight bars, the dirty bastards, and I didn't know which eight bars they were gonna cut, why don't somebody tell me what's goin' on around here, Holy Christ I'm goin' off my nut."

Mrs. Prescott told a story about how she was trying to teach a Mexican girl how to serve dinner — the proper placing of the cutlery and napkins, and so on. Mrs. Prescott spent two weeks drilling the girl and then gave a small dinner party. The poor girl did everything wrong, and spilled things, and Mrs. Prescott finally followed her into the kitchen and told her she was making one mistake after another. "I quit," said the girl. "But why?" asked Mrs. Prescott, who had been trying to be gentle. "I can't work for people who are so superstitious!" said the girl, and she did quit.

Outside the terrace doors we could hear occasional cackles and ani-mal screeches. The Prescotts said these noises have been bothering them for a long time, especially at night. Back of their place is a big house, a politico's "second house" — *la casa chica* — the place where he maintains his mistress. In this case the mistress is a former Indian servant who worked in his home and who had a lowly, rural origin. Now that she is set up in this fine house, she is indulging a whim; all her life she was accustomed to having domestic animals around her, and now she keeps them in the once-lovely garden of the big house — chickens, ducks, geese, a couple of pigs, and in her new-found prosperity she has added a dash of color — a peacock. This bird possesses a shrill, piercing cry that sounds like a death scream, and the people of the neighborhood are often startled out of their sleep by it. There is no such thing as a zoning restriction against these ani-mals and, even if there were, it would not operate in this case, for the girl's man is a big politico and big politicos never pay attention to rules.

For a brief time this evening I thought that maybe I had had enough of Mexico. The friendly American Prescotts with their children and their black cocker; the Crosby music; the animal sounds from the neighboring house, symbolic of cheating and dishonesty; the surrounding area where Rivera has his studio, where Trotsky lived, and King Carol, and where Madame Calderón came for visits — all this seemed a fitting place and a fitting atmosphere in which to wind it up and head back for the greening hills of North Westchester.

Half an hour later, riding down the broad and beautiful Reforma, I suddenly spoke: "Damn it, I don't want to go home yet!"

March 29

FIFTY years ago Charles Flandrau wrote of Mexican children: "They rarely cry, they rarely quarrel, and their capacity for amusing themselves with nothing is without limit. Had I the ordering of this strange, unhappy world, I think all children should be born Mexican and remain so until they are fifteen."

Twenty years later Stuart Chase observed that "Mexican children are without any exception the quietest and best-behaved children in the world."

During our first visit to Mexico I heard Nelle say: "A strange thing just occurred to me. We've been traveling around down here for a month and *never once have I heard a child crying.*"

We have been trying, during this trip, to find out why.* I think it is worth remark that Mexican children, in addition to being the best-behaved in the world, are also the most beautiful. Leslie Figueroa said in Taxco that the one book she most wants to do is a book made up solely of photographs of the faces of Mexican children. If you spend an hour in the plaza at Taxco, or in any other Mexican town, you will understand what she means.

* Most of the material in this section was written, in slightly different form, for the *Reader's Digest.*

Any consideration of children's behavior in Mexico must begin with the fact that the ancient custom of swaddling is practiced universally down here. Almost from the moment of birth a child is wrapped tightly so that he cannot move his arms and legs, and this continues up until the time he can walk. Babies born to American mothers in Mexico get the same treatment and if the parents object the nurses are likely to become sulky and even walk off the job. Most of the American mothers we talked to are convinced that swaddling is a good thing, that it develops a feeling of security in children. Mexican mothers say that if a child is not subjected to swaddling, "he'll turn out bad," and many American parents are willing to agree. An American newspaperman told me: "I've seen several cases where a baby, not wrapped, began to cry — and stopped crying the moment a *rebozo* was wrapped around him."

The American parents do have their troubles with the Mexican nursemaids. Even in 1958 many Mexicans believe the night air is freighted with all manner of miasmic poisons, and a child must always be protected against *los aires*. Hence the nurse covers a child's face with a blanket. An American who owns a hotel in Acapulco told me: "As soon as the sun goes down we have to perform a sort of sentry duty, keeping watch on the nurse. She puts a blanket over our baby's face, we rush in and take it off. We keep telling her the baby will suffocate — that a swaddled baby can't kick or pull the covers off — but she seems to think it would be better to suffocate than to be hit by *los aires*."

The "togetherness" that has become a big and important thing in the United States recently is an old, old idea in Mexico. From Chihuahua to Chiapas, there is likely no such thing as a baby-sitter. Wherever the parents go, the children go too. The mother and father go to the movies and the baby is with them, slung in Mama's *rebozo*, and in the darkened theater there is seldom a peep out of the child. They go to market with their parents, and they go to adult parties, and to fiestas — no matter what the hour of the day or night. I'm told that a Mexican child would bite off his own tongue before he would ever interrupt an adult conversation. *Me desmayo!* (I swoon!) When my own grandchildren are visiting us, not a shred of sustained, intelligent conversation is possible during all of the daylight hours.

It seems probable that some of the intensely close feeling a Mexican child has for his mother is traceable to the omnipresent *rebozo;* the infant is always carried about in that improvised hammock, he is always close to the warmth of his mother's body, and he remains close to her emotionally the rest of her life. Physical contact — the *abrazo* — is a big thing in Mexico, and there is always much embracing and kissing among members of a family.

The closeness of the Mexican family is evident in the fact that the sons rarely leave the parental home as long as they remain bachelors — they don't want to strike out on their own. And in many families, even after they are married they insist upon remaining in their father's domicile, being unwilling to undergo the separation. It is said that in many prominent Mexican families the grown children are offered the opportunity for extensive travel abroad, but that they turn it down simply because they cannot bear the thought of being away from their families.

Every Sunday Mexican parents do something with and for their children. With the poorer classes, it's a picnic in the park. With the wealthier, it's an opera or a concert and then dinner in a good restaurant. This is not just on occasional Sundays. It's *every* Sunday.

My own observation is that the Mexican father is much more affectionate and attentive toward his children than his counterpart in the United States. He is never too busy to give some time to his children. In Mexico City there is a prominent and wealthy industrialist who, one day each week, takes his five-year-old son to the office with him, and keeps the child there all day. It is not, he says, to instill in the boy a feeling for commerce; it is simply because he enjoys the child's presence.

A Mexican mother has an almost hysterical sympathy for a woman who is without children. Several years ago a New York woman of my acquaintance was wandering through Chapultepec Park on a Sunday, savoring the excitement, when she fell into conversation with a Mexican woman with a baby and an older child. The Mexican mother asked in Spanish where the American woman's children were. "I have no children," responded the American, whereupon the Mexican mother took her hand and began telling her how deeply sympathetic she felt. "There I was," said my friend, "the well-dressed American tourist, having everything, yet having nothing because I had no babies."

Mrs. Lorna Stafford told us what many others have observed — that the good deportment of Mexican children is best seen on trains and planes and in hotel lobbies, where they always sit quietly, never flinging their legs over the arms of chairs, never fidgeting and squirming, never racing up and down the aisles, and never whining for this and for that.

All the Indian races of Mexico have traditions of early training for their children in the field of general behavior. The Indians believe that if a child is disciplined early, it will not be necessary to discipline him later. If a child "turns out bad" it is a reflection on the parents, a cause for deep shame, and so the parents devote a lot of time and energy to preventing it.

The youngest children are taught certain basic things. They must not make noise just to be making noise. An old proverb is frequently quoted to them: *En boca cerrada no entran moscas* (If you keep your mouth shut the flies can't get in).

They are taught to work. Every child, no matter where his family stands in the social scale, has assigned duties and responsibilities. These usually include household tasks, which are performed ungrudgingly. In the Indian towns and villages where the native craftsmen operate, the child of, say, a pottery maker begins to learn to fashion pottery at the same time he begins to learn to talk. The Mexican children become self-reliant because they are given real responsibility at an early age. A common sight in Mexico is to see a herd of goats, sheep or cattle being led along a road or tended in a pasture by a couple of children no more than seven years old. In the United States we'd think twice before trusting children that young with such an important task. We'd think twice, and then we wouldn't do it.

The most common work assignment is that in which the older child looks after the younger. A typical sight in the plazas of Mexico is that of a father and mother and perhaps two children, a girl of, say, eight, and a boy of five. The little boy ranges too far afield from the family group. It is his sister's job to watch him, and herd him back into the family circle. Also, and this is most important, it is her job to see that he does not interfere with the peace and well-being of other people in the plaza. Mama and Papa never have to worry about the little boy because Sister performs her assignment with good-natured efficiency.

It is worth noting that the older children of Mexico are not permitted to shut the younger ones out of their games. This seems to be a big order — I've observed at home that older kids don't want any part of the younger ones (known as "brats") and even sometimes slug the brats if they try to horn in on the games. Yet it works otherwise in Mexico, and how they manage to bring it to pass is a matter beyond my understanding.

Another rather startling thing: sociologists, studying Mexican village life, say that children are *taught not to cry*. Again it is a matter of shame to the parents if they have a child who cries, and they devote much time to the task of convincing their youngest children that crying is almost sinful. The sociologists fail to note how some of these things, such as *not* crying, are taught, but I'm inclined to think that fear has a hand in it. In Tepoztlán, we were told that children are threatened with an evil spirit which lurks outside the houses and devours any children that it hears crying.

Finally, the children are taught to respect property. A Mexican child is seldom destructive of anybody's possessions, including his own. All children break things, of course, but a Mexican child is inclined to be very careful when he handles fragile objects.

There is physical discipline, to be sure, but it is not as severe as might be thought. The spanking of children is quite common, but not beating. The late Frances Toor, who spent twenty-five years roaming through Mexico collecting folk tales, wrote that "in all my travels and stays in Mexican villages I have never seen children ill-treated." In many areas they are ill-fed and ill-housed and made to work too hard, but so far as I could find out they are rarely flogged. In one town I heard of a child who had broken a valuable dish. The mother took a sharp fragment of the dish and scraped it over the child's arm almost to the point of drawing blood.

Shaming a child in public or in front of his friends is considered the most effective form of punishment among the Mexicans. In Tepoztlán a boy who has misbehaved is made to carry a bucket of corn through the streets to the mill, where he must stand in a line of women and girls waiting to have their corn ground into *nixtamal*. The boys of Tepoztlán, you may be sure, would much prefer a hard beating.

I have discussed the phenomenon of the Mexican child with a young New Jersey mother who is up on the latest doings of Spock, Gesel & Company. She is quite indignant about the whole thing. She is convinced that Mexican children are well-behaved out of fear; that they are intimidated into holding their emotions in leash all through childhood, so that when they become adults they are inclined to fiery explosions and wild and unpredictable misbehavior. She may be right, but I like what Stuart Chase wrote on the subject: "Mexican children never dominate anything. A ginger-whiskered Freudian might stalk among them scenting repressions, but I doubt if youngsters so exuberantly loved by their elders can suffer from this malady, while to the wayfarer their dignity and decorum is a source of never-failing delight."

It was certainly a source of never-failing delight to this wayfarer.

March 30

PEPE ROMERO had us to lunch today at his home, along with Howard Phillips, editor for many years of the magazine *Mexican Life*. Mr. Phillips has known every famous Mexican of modern times and once, when Pepe asked him to name the greatest of them all, the editor designated Orozco. His magazine is almost a one-man operation and he writes articles, short stories, essays and poems under a dozen or more pseudonyms. If you should read something in *Mexican Life* by Gerald Thorny, that is Howard Phillips. So is Guillermo Rivas, and Vance C. Dalton, Serge de Bourne, James Piggly Roasted, Maurice D. Silverspoon, Mayo de Wolf, Catarino Flannagan, Halifax Monroe Stairs, Henry H. Cackle and Stranahan Mustard.

There at Pepe's house, listening to Phillips talk about Dr. Atl and Alma Reed and Calles and D. H. Lawrence and Carleton Beals and Somerset Maugham and Diego Rivera and Felipe Carrillo Puerto, I performed the mental equivalent of kicking myself for not having cornered this man earlier. It often works this way — after three months we meet another person who knows everything there is to know about the country, and is able to talk eloquently on the subject, and now we have only a couple of hours with him when we could use a couple of weeks.

This evening we met Audrey Hepburn and Mel Ferrer at a press conference in our hotel. I wanted to see how a Mexican press conference compares with those back in New York. The Mexican reporters and movie critics who attended were quite dignified and genteel and soft-spoken, but the photographers were like jungle beasts. At home reporters, critics *and* photographers are like jungle beasts.

While we were sitting off to one side observing the party, Fred Vosberg told some tales of famous con men who have operated in Mexico City. The one I liked best was the man who had a project to paint the Panama Canal with luminous paint. He was organizing a huge corporation which would have the contract to supply the paint, and he had it all worked out in gallons, and his figures specified a fat profit for all investors. He had sucked some of the biggest men in Mexico into the deal before someone took the trouble to investigate.

This evening Charlie Bowers bowed to me in the lobby and saluted me with, *"Buenas noches,* Donald."

March 31

SEÑOR DUCK arrived at his puddle bright and early today, and it occurred to me that Señor Bowers is probably not going to get any relief until the bird dies. Don Quixote was present on the sidewalk and I asked him how old a duck ordinarily gets to be. "It all depends," he said, "on how hungry the peoples feel." We talked for a while and then I remembered that we had not yet gone to Guadalupe, and Don Quixote was free, so off we went.

Driving out to the shrine we passed a long stretch of wooded land and Dox Quixote pointed out the famous Mexican outdoor barbers (he calls them "barbs") who were stationed here and there among the tall trees. From a distance it looked as if these barbers used old straight-back kitchen chairs, and each had a cheap mirror hung on the trunk of a tree. "When you go to the outdoor barb," said Don Quixote, "you ask him what kind of service he gives, he says three kind. Haircot with view of mountans, haircot with view of the city, haircot with view of water. You say you want haircot with view of city, barb he turns the chair toward city; you want haircot with view of mountains, he turns chair toward the mountains; you say you want haircot with view of the water, he puts down bucket of water in front of the chair. In Mexico we have a yoke — if your friend has a haircot with stairsteps in back, we say, 'You been to outdoor barb.' Is very chip."

The Shrine of Guadalupe turned out to be a much bigger enterprise than I expected — it has the appearance of being almost as extensive as the Vatican. We spent an hour and a half roaming about among the crowds of pilgrims and watching the women walking on their knees across the vast concrete atrium — all the way from the main gate to the main altar. Most of the women were doing it the hard way — bare knees on the concrete — but a few were moneyed aristocrats and had servants with them, and these servants placed rugs or cushions in front of their mistresses; the servants were kept active snatching up the cushions from behind the mistress, and rushing forward and placing them in front of her again. In former times pilgrims by the thousands traveled on their knees from the center of Mexico City all the way out to the shrine, leaving a pathway of blood, but that is now forbidden. On this point, as on other points, Don Quixote was quite eloquent. As at Chapultepec, he envisioned the story of Guadalupe as a series of dialogues. He gave us the origin of the shrine as a dialogue between Juan Diego and the Virgin, and he explained the knee-walking business in a three-way dialogue between God, the Pope and the Archbishop of Mexico.

"God he saize to the Pope of Rome," said Don Quixote, "he saize to the Pope, 'Listen Pope. I no like the way all the peoples cut their knees in Mexico. Listen, you go get the Archbishop, I want to talk.' So the Pope of Rome got the Archbishop of Mexico, and God saize, 'Listen, Archbishop, I no like this knee business. You make the peoples go too far on the knees. You tell the peoples they don't walk any more from Mexico City, only from main gate. You tell them to walk on feet from Mexico City, walk on knees only from main gate. You understand?' And so the Archbishop he saize, 'Okay, we do.' And so, you see, now is much better."

We climbed up to the cemetery which is on the very hill where Juan Diego saw the Virgin. The graves and the little vaults are packed shoulder to shoulder in the limited ground, for, as Don Quixote said, everybody in Mexico would like to be buried here. We were wandering around when we came upon the grave of Santa Anna. I stood and meditated on the career of this weird character, and thought of the Santa Anna stories I like best.

Fighting the French at Veracruz, he was shot in the leg and it had to be amputated. At that time Santa Anna was such a great hero that the people considered even his severed leg to be immortal. It was pickled and given a guard of honor and escorted in a special carriage back to Mexico, where it was greeted by great crowds of cheering people, bands playing and cannon booming salutes. Then in an impressive ceremony the leg was buried under a splendid monument. Years later Santa Anna was defeated by the Texans (then known as Texians). He was now in disgrace and the populace was enraged against him. A mob tore down the monument, dug up the leg, paraded it through the streets and hurled it onto a manure pile.

In 1853 Santa Anna became Perpetual Dictator and Most Serene Highness of Mexico. He organized a glittering court and put on a big show of splendor. One day he saw a picture of the Czar of Russia's Imperial Guard — made up of Russians with long black beards. Santa Anna liked the look of them so well that he had his own Palace Guards — beardless Indians — fitted with false whiskers.

Another Santa Anna story is told by Professor Crow in *Mexico Today*:

In 1855 the general left Mexico with 100 trunks and 12 servants and spent several months of exile in the United States. While in this country he hired an American secretary, James Adams, a resident of New York. Adams noticed that the general was constantly chewing on something which he never swallowed. He was told that it was chicle, sap from a tree that grew in the jungles of Yucatán. A sudden idea hit Adams like a bombshell. He got together all the money he could beg or borrow, imported several bales of chicle, added a few popular flavors, and started the chewing gum business in the United States. It developed, as we all know, into a billion-dollar industry. Santa Anna had given chewing gum to the United States. It was perhaps the only worthy bequest of one of the greatest scoundrels of Latin-American history.

Driving back to the city I found out some things about Don Quixote himself. He is sixty-four years old, though he doesn't look much over fifty. He has nineteen children, ranging in age from seven months to forty-two years. He has been a guide for thirty-six years. He once had a small wooden carving, representing his own head, which he carried as a watch fob. When his fellow guides saw it, they said it looked exactly like Don Quixote as he appeared in the illustrations of a popular edition of Cervantes. And so the guides took to calling him Don Quixote.

He once worked in the United States as a pattern-maker in the auto industry. "Was in Chicago," he said, "and I was the best pattern-maker in the shop, but the boss he no like me because I am Mexican. He is the kind of man hates all Mexican. He was jealous against me and so he reported me to Washington and saize, I do not have my papers. And so Washington saize, Prove you are American. So I saize to this no-good boss, Listen, you big bom, I need no papers. I am American. I am Aztec Indian. I am more American than you, you big bom, and I am more American than this man in Washington. You got some big nerve, say I am no American. . . . But it did no good. They grab me and put me out of the country. I am not American. That is fonny."

April 1

TIME to go.

Charlie Bowers left with his family this morning for a month's vacation in Cuernavaca. He knew that I was leaving Mexico today, so I suppose he thought it would be safe now to go away himself. He hadn't got beyond University City before an exciting thing happened: *two* ducks appeared at the mudhole. I got one of the bellhops to go talk to Pedro and his wife and find out about the second duck. And the bellhop brought me glorious intelligence. I have been vindicated! I had it right all along — the duck we have been looking at for weeks is in reality *Señor* Duck. He is the Papa, and the new duck is the Mama, and the poop is that they are soon to become parents.

Carlos arrived at the hotel, but before we loaded up our bags, I had a small job to do. I got the vacation address of Señor Bowers and sent him a postal card — a picture of his own hotel, with the message, "X marks the spot where there are now *two* ducks. *Adiós!*"

At the airport we said our good-bys to Carlos. To me he said, "The magueys are going to miss you, you chip baster."

Well, not for long, I hope.

Epílogo

BACK home I cleared up the mountain of accumulated mail, wrote several magazine articles, and then settled down to the job of producing a book. It was painful work because almost every paragraph gave me a powerful urge to go back to Mexico. Then the painters arrived to do the house and I had an excuse. I put the hood over my typewriter and climbed aboard a plane and went back, intending to stay just a couple of weeks. I stayed six.

Carlos and I went to many of the places we had been before, but the most fun was in Veracruz. We enjoyed the *huachinango* and the marimba music at the *portales,* but there were other pleasures. We were in Veracruz while the World Series was being played. The people of Milwaukee are cold and indifferent toward baseball alongside the people of Veracruz. All business halted each day during the Spanish-language broadcasts of the Series games. Carlos and I listened in his car, driving southward along the Gulf to a little fishing village called Anton Lizardo, where we watched the men hauling in their nets while the story of the day's game came through the radio. I could only catch parts of it as it was broadcast from *"el corazón de Jonkee* Stadium." Carlos, ever the sports fan, often got so excited that he'd forget to tell me what was going on and then I'd yell at him, and he'd say, perhaps, "Cossy Stenjel is gone out to talk to the pitcher!" El Bravos de Meelwaukee y El Jonkees de Nueva York went at it day after day and we didn't miss an inning. Onk Bauer and

Ondy Poffko and Joe Co-yins and Eslaughter and Oddcock were frequently mentioned. Carlos was betting on the Jonkees and I had the Bravos. At one point when the Bravos were well ahead, Carlos said, *"De peores hoyos hemos salido,"* which he later translated, "From worse deeper holes we have come out"; it means the same as our, "I've seen a sicker horse than this get cured."

Carlos described a walk as "a fair base on account of bad balls." He announced excitedly that "They put out Espahn!" which meant that Warren Spahn had been yanked. He abused me and the Bravos constantly, sometimes giving me fake interpretations from the broadcasts, such as: "The High Commissioner of Baseball is now talking, they are having a big discussion, they say the Jonkees should pitch only with coconuts to the Bravos, then maybe the son of a bitch Bravos can hit something. I did not say this. Is the High Commissioner said it."

We traveled and drank and ate and swam and had a big time, and then once again I knew that the time had long since passed when I should be at home. I knew by now the feeling that inspired the lines written a long time ago by Anita Brenner: "For the dust of Mexico on a human heart corrodes, precipitates. But with the dust of Mexico upon it, that heart can find no rest in any other land."

I also knew what the late Josephus Daniels meant when he said: "I have been a lifelong resident of Mexico for two years."

And I stand with Charles Allen Smart in his resolve that he will observe an annual rite:

"At 11:00 P. M., on every September 15, no matter where I am, I am going to shout, 'Viva Mexico!' "

So am I.